Trees in Ancient Rome

Ancient Environments

Series Editors

Anna Collar, Esther Eidinow and Katharina Lorenz

The Ancient Environments series explores the worlds of living and non-living things, examining how they have shaped, and been shaped by, ancient human societies and cultures. Ranging across the Mediterranean from 3500 BCE to 750 CE, and grounded in case studies and relevant evidence, its volumes use interdisciplinary theories and methods to investigate ancient ecological experiences and illuminate the development and reception of environmental concepts. The series provides a deeper understanding of how and why, over time and place, people have understood and lived in their environments. Through this approach, we can reflect on our responses to contemporary ecological challenges.

Also available in the series

Mountain Dialogues from Antiquity to Modernity, edited by
Dawn Hollis and Jason König
Ovid's Metamorphoses and the Environmental Imagination, edited by
Francesca Martelli and Giulia Sissa
Seafaring and Mobility in the Late Antique Mediterranean, edited by
Antti Lampinen and Emilia Mataix Ferrándiz
The Spirited Horse: Equid–Human Relations in the Bronze Age Near East,
by Laerke Recht

Trees in Ancient Rome

Growing an Empire in the Late Republic and Early Principate

Andrew Fox

BLOOMSBURY ACADEMIC
LONDON • NEW YORK • OXFORD • NEW DELHI • SYDNEY

BLOOMSBURY ACADEMIC
Bloomsbury Publishing Plc
50 Bedford Square, London, WC1B 3DP, UK
1385 Broadway, New York, NY 10018, USA
29 Earlsfort Terrace, Dublin 2, Ireland

BLOOMSBURY, BLOOMSBURY ACADEMIC and the Diana logo are trademarks of
Bloomsbury Publishing Plc

First published in Great Britain 2023
Paperback edition published 2025

Copyright © Andrew Fox, 2023

Andrew Fox has asserted his right under the Copyright, Designs and Patents Act, 1988, to
be identified as Author of this work.

For legal purposes the Acknowledgements on p. ix constitute an extension
of this copyright page.

Cover image © Guido Cozzi/Atlantide Phototravel via Getty

All rights reserved. No part of this publication may be reproduced or transmitted
in any form or by any means, electronic or mechanical, including photocopying,
recording, or any information storage or retrieval system, without prior
permission in writing from the publishers.

Bloomsbury Publishing Plc does not have any control over, or responsibility for,
any third-party websites referred to or in this book. All internet addresses given in
this book were correct at the time of going to press. The author and publisher
regret any inconvenience caused if addresses have changed or sites have
ceased to exist, but can accept no responsibility for any such changes.

A catalogue record for this book is available from the British Library.

A catalog record for this book is available from the Library of Congress.

ISBN: HB: 978-1-3502-3780-3
PB: 978-1-3502-3784-1
ePDF: 978-1-3502-3781-0
eBook: 978-1-3502-3782-7

Series: Ancient Environments

Typeset by RefineCatch Limited, Bungay, Suffolk

To find out more about our authors and books visit www.bloomsbury.com
and sign up for our newsletters.

Contents

List of Illustrations	vi
List of Tables	viii
Acknowledgements	ix
Preface	xi
Introduction: Trees in Urban Spaces	1
1 Memory and Trees	33
2 Bringing Trees to Rome	53
3 Trees in the Triumph	69
4 Keeping Trees in the City	111
Conclusion: A New Leaf	129
Appendix: Categorized List of Contents for Books Twelve to Seventeen of Pliny's *Natural History*	131
Notes	145
Bibliography	173
Index of Trees	187
Index	189

Illustrations

1 An asynchronic overview of a selection of Rome's trees   29

2 Leaf types on Trajan's Column, as identified by Stoiculescu (1985, figs 4 and 5) and redrawn by author. Stoiculescu describes the resinous leaf types (A and B) as follows: 'Resinous species types included in the A and B species subgroup according to the crown and needle forms. Columnary crown: type 1 – long and pendent needles; type 2 – revolute, semilanceolate needles; type 3 – short and scaly needles; type 5 – needles grouped in pendent fascicles; type 6 – slightly revolute, lanceolate, big needles; type 7 – scaly and oblong needles; Pyramidal crown: type 10 (suggesting a primitive form of the actual pyramidal black poplar – Populus nigra L. cv. Italica – or the cypress – Cupressus sempervirens L.) Semipyramidal crown: type 8 – needles grouped in short fascicles; Rhomboidal crown: type 4 – long and scaly needles, catenary disposed; Ovate crown: type 9 – erect, fanned, exclusively disposed at the tree top.'   80

The leaf types of the deciduous trees (C – G) are listed thus: 'Foliaceous species types divided in five subgroups according to their form of leaves: C – pentapalmary lobate leaves (suggesting Acer genus), D – broadly ovate leaves, with 3–5 triangular lobes slowly decreasing to the top (suggesting Sorbus torminalis L.), E – unregularly obovate and pennate lobate leaves (suggesting Quercus genus), F – oblong leaves (suggesting Prunus genus), G – elliptic leaves (suggesting Fagus genus).'   80

3 Front view of the compital shrine, Forum Boarium, Rome. Photo taken by Andrew Fox (26 April 2016)   93

4	Detail of oak wreath on compital shrine, Forum Boarium, Rome. The stalks on the acorns suggest the *Quercus robur*, while the leaf maintains similarities to the *Quercus petraea*. Photo taken by Andrew Fox (26 April 2016)	93
5	A wreath of *Laurus nobilis*, on the head of a soldier directly below Titus on the northern internal frieze of the Arch of Titus (post 81 CE). The berries of the crown can be seen between the leaves. Photo taken by Andrew Fox (2 May 2016)	96
6	Wreath of *Laurus nobilis* around the base of Trajan's Column. A mixture of pointed and rounded berries can be seen. Photo taken by Andrew Fox (27 April 2016)	96
7	The fruit of the *Laurus nobilis*, Isola Sacra, Portus. Photo taken by Andrew Fox (12 May 2016)	97
8	Fragment of frieze with *Laurus nobilis* branches. Augustan Age (first century BCE–first century CE). Church of Santa Maria Antiqua, atrium (inv. no. 593994). By concession of the Ministry for Cultural Heritage and Activities and Tourism – Archaeological Park of the Colosseum	97
9	*Tropaea* on Trajan's Column, Scene LXXVIII. Source: Cichorius 1896: plate LVII	102
10	Attic red-figure *krater*, fifth century BCE, housed in the Louvre, Paris (G 496)	103
11	The Adonaea on the Marble Plan (Carettoni et al. 1960: Tav. 34). © Sovrintendenza Capitolina ai Beni Culturali	117
12	The Porticus Philippi on the Marble Plan (Carettoni et al. 1960: Tav. 29). © Sovrintendenza Capitolina ai Beni Culturali	120
13	Digital reconstruction of the Porticus Philippi. SketchUp model	121

Tables

1	Key to numbered trees in Figure 1	30
2	The ancient trees catalogued by Pliny the Elder in *Natural History* 16.234–40	41
3	Brief summary of the content of Books Twelve to Seventeen of Pliny's *Natural History*	64
4	The trees on the Arch of Trajan at Beneventum	81
5	The trees on the Great Trajanic Frieze	81

Acknowledgements

When I wrote the acknowledgements to my doctoral thesis, which this book loosely adapts, I began by saying that it had given me grey hairs. That was in 2018, and writing those acknowledgements at my dimly lit desk in the Humanities building at the University of Nottingham feels like a lifetime ago.

This project began as a five-minute presentation on the Ruminal fig tree in the first week of my Masters programme, prompted by Esther Eidinow, and carefully listened to by Sophie Kightley, who immediately enthused that I should 'write a book' about it. That one tree became a Masters dissertation and then a PhD thesis, supervised by Mark Bradley and Charles Watkins, who have both unfailingly supported this project from its infancy, and without whom this project would be something else entirely. Thanks are also due to Helen Lovatt and Diana Spencer, who examined the thesis and whose comments influenced the changes that were made for the book. I would also like to thank the series editors and reviewers for their helpful comments along the way, and Lily Mac Mahon at Bloomsbury for her support throughout.

Those changes were not without their challenges. They began during a postdoctoral fellowship funded by the then Midlands3Cities Doctoral Training Partnership (now Midlands4Cities), which was interrupted by the global pandemic. The writing groups that sprung up as a result of the pandemic kept me focused, and I am immensely grateful to Ellie Mackin Roberts, Kate Cook, Christine Plastow, Josh Nudell and Clare Vernon for their support along the way, on Slack, Zoom, Microsoft Teams, and every other platform that we could find. Similarly, the Columethods reading group has been an excellent reminder throughout of the reality of the trees that this book concerns itself with, and Vicky Austen's thoughts on gardens and garden planting have been especially stimulating.

Outside of the confines of academia, I have been supported by a superb group of friends, Rob Mead, Harriet Lander, Thomas Sims, Will Buck, Kieren

Johns and Jon Langston all providing valuable breaks from writing and, alongside the members of East London Hockey Club, putting up with the frequent monologuing about our wooded surroundings.

Finally, and most importantly, this book would never have been written without the unwavering support of my wife, Joanna. Constantly reminding me of what was important, sharing our home study with me during Covid, and putting up with me taking three hours to cook tea while tweaking an endnote.

I sat down to write the first pages of this book with my eldest daughter playing with building blocks on the rug next to me. I wrote the last pages holding my youngest.

Joanna, Corinna, Thalia, this is for you.

And, since you insisted, Corinna, also for the kitties.

Preface

While our intention in writing this preface was to provide a neutral introduction that could stand for the whole series, recent events are too dramatic and relevant to ignore. As we launch the series, and write this text, we are (hopefully) emerging from the ravages of the Covid-19 pandemic. Along with the climate crisis, this experience has increased awareness of human reliance and impact on the environments we occupy, dramatically emphasized human inability to control nature, and reinforced perceptions that the environment is the most pressing political and social issue of our time. It confirms our belief that the time is right to situate our current (abnormal?) relationship with nature within an examination of human interactions with the environment over the *longue durée* – a belief that has given rise to this series.

Ancient Environments sets out to explore (from a variety of perspectives) different constructions of the 'environment' and understandings of humankind's place within it, across and around the Mediterranean from 3500 BCE to 750 CE. By 'environment' we mean the worlds of living and non-living things in which human societies and cultures exist and with which they interact. The series focuses on the *co-construction* of humans and the natural world. It examines not only human-led interactions with the environment (e.g. the implications of trade or diet), but also those that foreground earth systems and specific environmental phenomena; it investigates both physical entities and events and ancient, imagined environments and alternate realities. The initial and primary focus of this series is the ancient world, but by explicitly exploring, evaluating and contextualizing past human societies and cultures in dialogue with their environments, it also aims to illuminate the development and reception of environmental ideas and concepts, and to provoke a deeper understanding of more long-term and widespread environmental dynamics.

The geographical remit of this series includes not only the cultures of the Mediterranean and Near East, but also those of southern Europe, North Africa including Egypt, northern Europe, the Balkans and the shores of the Black Sea.

We believe that encompassing this broader geographical extent supports a more dynamic, cross-disciplinary and comparative approach – enabling the series to transcend traditional boundaries in scholarship. Its temporal range is also far-reaching: it begins with the Neolithic (a dynamic date range, depending on location in the Near East/Europe) because it marks a distinct change in the ways in which human beings interacted with their environment. We have chosen *c.* 750 CE as our end date because it captures the broadest understanding of the end of Late Antiquity in the Central Mediterranean area, marking the rise of the Carolingians in the West, and the fall of the Ummayyad Caliphate in the East.

Our series coincides with, and is inspired by, a particular focus on 'the environmental turn' in studies of the ancient world, as well as across humanities more generally. This focus is currently provoking a reassessment of approaches that have tended to focus solely on people and their actions, prompting scholars to reflect instead (or alongside) on the key role of the environments in which their historical subjects lived, and which shaped and were shaped by them. By extending beyond the chronological and geographical boundaries that often define – and limit – understanding of the meaning of 'antiquity', we intend that this series should encourage and enable broader participation from within and beyond relevant academic disciplines. This series will, we hope, not only advance the investigation of ancient ecological experiences, but also stimulate reflection on responses to contemporary ecological challenges.

The editors would like to express heartfelt thanks to Alice Wright at Bloomsbury Press who first conceived of the idea and suggested it to Esther, and who has done so much to develop it, and to Georgina Leighton, in particular for her work in launching the series. We are extremely grateful to the members of the Series Board, who have provided such wonderful encouragement and support, and to our authors (current and future) who have entrusted their work to this 'home'. We have chosen the 'Mistress of Animals' or *Potnia Theron*, a figure found in Near Eastern, Minoan, Mycenean, Greek and Etruscan art over thousands of years, as the motif for the series.

Anna Collar
Esther Eidinow
Katharina Lorenz

Introduction

Trees in Urban Spaces

Rome's first monumental tree

Years before Rome's founding, two infant twins were washed up in the roots of a fig tree and suckled by a she-wolf in the tree's protective shade, at the edge of the swollen Tiber. They were discovered by Faustulus, and grew up to found Rome. The tree remained a fixture of the Lupercal, a remnant of the scene and a monument of the rescue, and was known as the *ficus Ruminalis*, or Ruminal fig tree. Centuries after the founding of Rome, the tree was moved, and Pliny tells us of its new location:

> A fig tree in the Forum itself, in the Comitium at Rome, is cared for like it is sacred, from the lightning-struck things buried there, and more still because of the memory of that tree under which the nurse to Romulus and Remus first protected the founders of the empire in the Lupercal. The tree has been called the Ruminal, since under it, the infants were found suckling the *rumis* of the wolf (which we now call the *mamma*) – a miracle depicted in bronze nearby, as if it had crossed the forum of its own accord while Navius took the omens. And it is not without some ill-omen that the tree withers, and is then, by the care of the priests, replanted.[1]

This account, from Pliny the Elder's *Natural History*, is among the last references to the tree that sheltered Rome's founders in Latin literature, and is our most detailed account of a tree which was used as a part of Rome's monumental cityscape throughout the city's lifetime. The tree of Rome is treated as a monument to the city's founding, and its surroundings bore a similar association: the Ogulnii brothers set up a statue of the she-wolf and the founders of the city at the Ruminal fig tree in 296 BCE.[2] The tree lives alongside the city, and its mortality is treated as a consequence of the city's ebbs and flows in fortune.

Even for this individual tree, its two iterations in the city were treated differently. Both trees died, on the slopes of the Palatine and in the heart of Rome's Augustan centre, and each death prompted a different response, indicating that each tree had a different relationship with its immediate surroundings. When the Ruminal fig stood on the Palatine, it had a finite lifetime, and the death of the monument is not noticeably ominous. Certainly, none of the extant sources that refer to this incarnation of the Ruminal, either literary or visual, show any concern for the tree's health. Dionysius of Halicarnassus, in his first description of the ancient site of the Lupercal, tells us that the area was heavily wooded, although he neglects to make any mention of a particularly famous tree at the site, which is cited as standing there by Varro, Livy and Ovid, either as a remnant of the original myth or as a memorial to it.[3] This omission could be as a result of his focus on the temple of Pan Lycaeum, and a desire not to dilute this space with an additional monument, which even to a Roman audience had a conflicted history, being both for Romulus and for Rumina, while at the same time being a cultural marker.[4]

To resolve this confusion, we can read the Greek historian's account of the exposure for guidance as to how the Lupercal grove appeared when Dionysius was writing. Here, the information is repeated, and it is clear that whatever trees were once at the Lupercal, they are long dead.[5] There is no reference to a famous tree having stood at the site, only to the grove, and Dionysius offers no indication that he is even aware of an individual monumental tree at the site. Other contemporary sources, however, indicate that the tree is dead. In the *Fasti*, Ovid, writing shortly after Dionysius, tells us that 'there was a tree. Traces do remain, and it is called Ruminal now, but was the Romulan fig tree'. Likewise, the mythographer Conon, who writes some time before 17 CE, tells us first of the fig tree in whose roots the twins were caught up, and by which they were saved. He then refers to a memorial fig tree set up in the Forum, in front of the Senate house, and enclosed in a fence.[6]

It is with these passages that Dionysius' omission of the Ruminal in its original context on the Palatine becomes plain: the Ruminal was, at the time of his writing, in a transitional period, between its long dead Palatine form and the memorial fig in the Forum, and the identity of this memorial was in something of a state of flux. The proof that Dionysius was aware of this fig tree can be found in his account of the deeds of Attus Navius, and the statue of the legendary augur, set up 'in front of the Senate house'.[7] This statue is further located as being 'near the sacred fig tree'. The placemarkers of the Senate house and the fig tree are required because the statue may have been removed from public display following damage the statue base suffered when Clodius' supporters burnt down the Curia Hostilia in 53 BCE.[8]

This nameless tree must surely be the Ruminal, since the only other fig definitely present in the Forum at this time was that of the fig, olive and vine group at the Lacus Curtius; the Silvanus fig outside the Temple of Saturn had long since been removed, and the very existence of the Navian fig is questionable.[9] What is clear from these accounts, and reconstructed in the Ruminal's proposed withered appearance on the fragmentary north-west relief of the Ara Pacis, is that the tree's vitality was unimportant in the communication of its message as being the marker of the original site of the twins' rescue by the she-wolf. The Palatine tree was allowed to die a natural death and its death was unobtrusively absorbed into the monument's life, until such a time that it became unrepresentative of the city's glory. This point of the memorial's lifetime can be placed to being in the early Imperial period, since the tree was known to be on the Palatine by both Livy and Ovid, but not by Conon and Dionysius.[10] At this point, the Ruminal was transferred to the Comitium, and the tree's identity was transferred to a new, living host, and death gained significance for this natural monument.[11]

The new tree, which continued to hold the title of the Ruminal fig, stood in the Comitium of the Roman Forum, in front of the Senate house, as both Dionysius and Conon relate. In the years to come, this tree would die, or would threaten to do so, and later authors picked up on this as being ominous, notably Pliny the Elder and Tacitus. Tacitus' account of the tree, referring to a withering in 58 CE, is the more specific of the two accounts, and deals with a partial rather than total death of the tree. Occurring at the end of Book Thirteen of the *Annals*, in the middle of Nero's reign, Tacitus tells us the following:

> In the same year, the Ruminal tree in the Comitium, which had sheltered the infants, Romulus and Remus eight hundred and thirty years before, by the death of its branches and the withering of its trunk was diminished to such an extent that it was taken as a prodigy, until it budded anew.[12]

Unlike the Augustan sources, which report the death of the Palatine tree as inconsequential to its status as a monumental tree, Tacitus reports that Neronian attitudes were markedly different, treating the death of the tree as a dire portent.[13] The Ruminal, in its position in the Comitium, stands at the beating heart of Rome's political and cultural life, surrounded by icons of Rome's noble and glorious past, including the Navius statue, the Lacus Curtius, not to mention the temples themselves, and yet here it is isolated, alone and abandoned. This serves only to highlight the utter desertion of the Roman moral compass in Nero's reign, with the heart of Rome withering away.

But why then does the fig tree renew itself? Why would Tacitus reverse the tree's ominous death? The answer lies in the rejuvenation itself. Tacitus has created the portent of a Rome that is rotten to the core, corrupting even the foundational tree, and then undercuts it with the tree's rejuvenation. It has been argued that the entire process of near-death and rejuvenation represents Rome's 'tragic resignation' to her fate.[14] But Tacitus' account of the omen is vague, and Pliny is similarly non-committal, referring to it as 'some ill-omen', suggesting some level of mutability in this natural monument's messaging.

Hunt reads Pliny's account as being evidence of 'the appropriation of the *ficus Navia* by the memorial associations of the *ficus Ruminalis*', which is in itself a death of the Navian fig.[15] This may not be entirely accurate, as has been laid out above, as there is no evidence that the Navian fig existed under that name until the eighth century, nor is it found in any account of the Attus Navius myth, while the statue of Attus Navius definitely stood next to a sacred fig tree, according to Dionysius, and is associated with it, as seen in Pliny's description of the tree.[16] It might be more beneficial to think of this transplantation not only as the birth of the monumental Ruminal, but also as laying the groundwork for the future Navian fig. The vulnerability of the Ruminal is evident as it is eventually subsumed by the Navian myth, which dominates the monumental space with the *puteal*. This myth, and the name of the Navian fig overpowers an identity which had remained consistent from the time of Pliny the Elder until Tacitus, potentially beginning with the Augustan account of Conon, who tells of a memorial fig tree in the Forum, relating it to the Lupercal fig, but not naming either.[17] The Ruminal's identity is one which is clearly mutable, shifting freely from the Palatine to the Forum midway through its lifetime as a memorial.[18] As such, the acquisition of new symbolism after the Navian monuments were removed – Festus makes no mention of the statue of Navius, which appears in every version of the Navian myth – is not unlikely, since this Ruminal in the Comitium was known to not be the original.[19]

The knowledge that the tree was not the original Ruminal is evident in Pliny's account, which refers to a complex and confused concern for the tree, thoroughly analysed by Hunt, and including the replanting of the Ruminal fig upon its death under the supervision of a priesthood.[20] It is unknown which priesthood this was, although it is easy to make the argument that it was an ancient cult of Rumina, such as the one which Varro alludes to in his comment regarding the placing of a fig tree (possibly the Ruminal?) at the shrine of Rumina.[21] Like the Silvanus fig, the Ruminal fig requires the attention of priests before being dealt with, and it is 'by their care' that a fresh tree is planted. The motivation behind the planting of the new tree may not have only been due to the portent. The Ruminal's new position at Rome's vibrant centre emphasized the vitality of the city. It was a place crowded with myriad monuments, with defunct ones being disposed of, as in the case of Attus Navius' statue. Even the Ruminal fig tree had to justify its continued existence in the crowded monumental space of the Roman Forum, and a dead tree would likely have been swiftly swept aside, without the lingering influence of whole groves, which became neighbourhood names.[22]

What is a tree, and what is a grove?

Crucial to understanding Roman relationships with trees is to understand what they meant by the terms used, and there are two terms which require definition: tree and grove. Modern understandings of 'tree' depend upon the structure of the plant, and a grove is a small cluster of trees. Roman definitions of both terms are not so simple, and require a degree of flexibility when seeing each term. When defining *arbor*, Lewis and Short simply suggest as the primary definition 'a tree'. Qualifications are then offered, of a tree type when *arbor* is paired with species term, 'to plant' in more generic phrases, or particular items for which *arbor* was used as a euphemism.[23] Roman understandings of what qualified a plant as a tree were slightly further extended than this simple definition suggests. Both Columella and Pliny the Elder suggest how we should understand the term. Pliny, in the *Natural History*, qualifies that he includes the vine as a tree on account of its size and its durability.[24] Meanwhile, Columella opens *On Trees* by telling his readers that there are two types of tree: those that grow of their own accord and produce timber, and those that grow through the care of humans and produce fruit.[25] In this, Columella is following Vergil's categories, established in the *Georgics*, and we can learn more about what Romans understood by the term *arbor*.[26] Later, Isidore of Seville also focuses on size, and applies a degree of progression in three terms related to plants or trees: a small plant is referred to as *herba*, a sapling as *arbusta*, and a tree as *arbor*.[27]

For these Romans, then, trees are large, have a long lifespan, and are either made of usable timber or are fruit-producing. This definition might lack finesse, or the specificity of modern definitions which rely on the structure of the tree, having a single trunk and branches spreading laterally to the ground, and on the tree also growing perennially. What it does offer, however, is an idea of how broad Roman definitions of trees are. Whether or not the tree is alive is not part of the definition, and this is reflected both in the focus on the produce, and in the flexibility of the term *arbor*, which is used euphemistically for things made of them, such as ships. A similar flexibility is found in species names, with *abies* (fir) commonly used as a substitute for ship, *buxus* (box) for flute, and so on, while cultural attitudes show that items made from trees retain the properties of the living trees themselves: Aeneas' ships remain trees from Cybele's grove in the *Aeneid*,[28] and the oak prow of the *Argo* retains the ability to make the same prophecies as the Dodonan oak whence it came.[29] More important than its present state is its provenance, and that the living tree either had lived, or perhaps was capable of living, a particularly long life. A dead tree, like Ovid's Ruminal fig on the Palatine, is still a tree, even if only vestiges remain.

Other terms in Roman literature that relate to trees are less simple. Trees were sometimes found grouped together in a *lucus* (grove), and this term has undergone rigorous etymological examination from Broise and Scheid and, more recently, Hunt. Both studies are particularly concerned with the Arval grove, a short distance from the city. Broise and Scheid suggest that *lucus* is etymologically linked to *lux* (light), and that to prune a *lucus* was to allow the *lucus* to fulfil its predestined etymological purpose.³⁰ However, as Dumézil acknowledges in his similar etymological discussion, *lucus* is used in Latin to refer to both a clearing and a wood, a difficulty which ancient authors also grappled with.³¹ Quintilian places *lucus* among his list of words derived from their opposite, as a place noted for being absent of light, and Servius also qualifies a *lucus* as a place 'which is not lit'.³² Isidore similarly comments that a *lucus* is a place of dense forest, characterized as having little light, before offering a similar clarification to that found in Servius' etymology, that they are lit by other means, bringing *lumen* rather than *lux* into the grove.³³ Hunt, following Quintilian's far earlier example, describes the ancient etymology from the absence of *lux* as 'absurd', but cautions against the 'light-centric' reading of *lucus* proposed by Broise and Scheid, given the artificiality of the light that ancient grammarians use to justify a positive association between light and the *lucus*.³⁴

The modern debate of etymology for *lucus* is similar to the confusion experienced by Romans, who struggled to define where a *lucus* began and where it ended. This begins in an ambiguous set of inscriptions from Spoleto and Trevi, dated to *c.* 240 BCE:

> Let no one violate this grove, nor take it away, nor carry off this grove's contents, nor enter/cut except on the day left for annual rite. On that day, what is done for the sake of the goddess' festival, may it be permitted to enter/cut without penalty … Whoever might violate it must give an appeasing sacrifice to Jupiter of an ox, should he violate it knowingly and with malice, let him give an offering of a cow and be fined 300 asses. The chief magistrate is responsible for the exaction of this fine and offering.

> Honce loucom nequ<i>s violatod neque exvehito neque exferto quod louci siet neque cedito nesei quo die res deina anua fiet eod die quod rei< >dinai ca[u]sa [f]iat sine dolo cedre [l]icetod seiqus … violasit Iove bovid piaclum datod seiquis scies violasit dolo malo Iovei bovid piaclum datod et a CCC moltai suntod eius piacli moltaique dicator [ei] exactio est [od].³⁵

The ambiguity of this passage, where a dialectal choice confuses the taboo action – it is either entering or attacking the grove – is replicated in a passage of Ovid's *Fasti*. Here, he advises a shepherd preparing for the festival of the Parilia to beg pardon in case he has transgressed on any sacred space with the following address:

'If I have grazed my flocks in a sacred place, or rested under a sacred tree,
And my flocks have taken food from graves in ignorance;
If I have entered a forbidden grove (*nemus . . . vetitum*),
Or the nymphs and half-goat god were put to flight from my eyes;
If my pruning knife has ransacked a grove (*lucus*) for a shady bough,
From which a basket was filled with leaves for a sick sheep,
Forgive my fault.'[36]

The nature of a fault against a sacred arboreal feature is multiple, and can either be resting against a tree, entering a *nemus*, or pruning a branch from a *lucus*. The difficulty of using trees as monuments, especially when their ideal state is an unviolated one, is apparent: there is no clear distinction between non-monumental and monumental nature. Ovid's shepherd, although familiar with the landscape, and practising the religious festivals of the city of Rome, is unaware of which trees are sacred. How the complex natural world around Rome is navigated was a challenge even to a Roman.[37]

And so, the question remains: what is a *lucus*? Is it a space devoid of light, or is it one that is lit by *lumen*? From both the Spoleto-Trevi inscriptions and Ovid's prayer, it seemed to have a defined edge, although Ovid suggests that the edge is unclear: how else could a shepherd have accidentally entered it? It seems obvious that the grove should include the trees; Ovid's shepherd may have lopped a shady bough off one, although this could have been part of the usual practice to introduce light into a *lucus*.[38] Other Romans indicate that trees were a part of groves, and they were not simply open spaces within a wooded area, such as Pliny's account of the elm in Juno's grove at Nocera, which describes an elm in a grove growing onto an altar.[39]

For Romans, a tree is a large wood thing used for the production of timber or fruit, and a grove is a loosely defined space that contains trees. Whether or not there is light continually present in this space is unclear, and would perhaps be dependent upon whether the space was in use at the time or not. There were boundaries to these spaces, understood by the ability to transgress them and suffer penalties for doing so. However, there is some degree of confusion as to where these boundaries are. They extend beyond the open space we might assume to be in the middle of a grove, used for altars like that found at Nocera. That there is confusion as to what qualifies as a grove in Roman understanding is unsurprising, since Romans themselves were confused, evident from their conflicting etymologies and catch-all prayers to cover any potential offences. Natural features, including trees and groves, are live and ambiguous issues in the ancient world, and understandings of what these natural features are may vary subtly but substantially according to each individual.

Trees in scholarship

This book crosses a number of areas within modern scholarship that address the natural world, and draws upon some key influences from non-classical scholarship to build an approach to the trees of the Roman world that explores their role as landmarks in the city. Previous engagement with the natural world, and the arboreal elements within it, has comprised focused discussions of utility, religion, landscape and gardens, and war and empire. These discussions are supplemented by studies of trees in post-medieval England, and this book will draw on a cross-disciplinary methodology to approach the social and cultural functions of trees. To do this effectively, I will assess earlier scholarship engaging with trees, starting with the theme of utility – a defining feature of trees in the Roman world.

Utility

In the highly influential *Environmental Problems of the Greek and Roman World* (rev. edn 2014), Hughes takes the approach that the modern Western world inherited an 'impoverished environment' and attempted to flourish in it.[40] While Hughes' thrust is to discuss a negative human impact on the environment in the ancient world, he does not blame urban industrial progress for deforestation in the Roman period, preferring to focus exclusively on the impact of agricultural advancement on the environment.[41] This assertion follows one made by Meiggs, in *Trees and Timber in the Ancient Mediterranean World* (1982), that 'where plains were restricted it was natural for agriculture to move into the hills'. To illustrate this point, Meiggs directs his readers to a passage of Lucretius, which states much the same thing.[42] However, Meiggs takes a more pragmatic approach than Hughes, and examines the total cost that agriculture is likely to have had in ancient deforestation, coming to the conclusion that it would be minimal. By placing the discussion of deforestation within a monograph on the timber trade, he invites us to consider a potential other cause of deforestation: the utility of trees, and their timber.

Meiggs approaches the trees of the ancient world as a commodity. They were exploited for their timber, and this forms the basis of his monograph. He takes on a number of disparate topics, from a number of regions and eras, building upon his own broad experience of the ancient world.[43] The breadth of Meiggs' experience and evidence is clear from the first chapter, which provides a survey of how widely dispersed the source material is, and of potential conflicts that arise, particularly when dealing with multiple languages, and authors who may not have been experts in the fields they wrote about. Since the trees are examined as a resource and their social and cultural value is rarely exploited, their financial value is taken as more important. This provides a useful basis for the appreciation of trees in the Roman world, displaying to a reader the number of uses to which a tree could be put, and reminding any reader that the writers of the ancient world will have been aware of the benefits of particular types of timber. However, Meiggs is careful to remind his readers of other associations, and in his chapter on farms, parks and gardens, he presents the use of a garden that is most relevant to his practical focus: its potential for income, before turning to discuss more luxurious, less practical gardens, which came to be used as leisure spaces with formulaic, impractical designs. Here, he draws on a variety of evidence to assess that the pine tree Vergil identifies as being fairest in the garden is the *Pinus pinea* L., and it is only through the combination of approaches and the consultation of multiple sources that Meiggs is able to make this judgement, based not on the practical but on the aesthetic value of the tree and its role in poetry.[44]

In a more recent chapter about raw materials in the Roman economy, Wilson briefly addresses timber, and distances the economic value and the utility of trees from their religious associations with the example of the *dendrophoroi*, or 'tree-carriers', who formed *collegia* and were listed alongside the other trades, such as shippers and woodworkers.[45] The *dendrophoroi* were lumberjacks, and Wilson notes that they were primarily involved in shipbuilding rather than other forms of the timber trade; he uses the absence of any *collegia* in Mauretania, the source of wood used for furniture, as proof of this. The exploitation of raw materials is, for Wilson, evidence of a well-established awareness of the value in natural resources, and of an economic system driven not just by availability, but also an awareness of transport, as the majority of the *collegia* are situated in coastal regions. Typically studies of the utility of trees are focused either on a specific application, a specific wood, or a specific region, even in Meiggs' chapters (see his 'Cedars of Lebanon' chapter). This is often to the exclusion of other aspects of the tree, and their role in the cultural practices of the time, such as religious activities.

Religion

Prior to Meiggs' monograph, trees had primarily been considered in a religious capacity, with scholarship focused on the motif of a sacred tree in Roman culture, and the mysticism of the grove. In the mid-nineteenth century, Barlow wrote that 'most nations, if not all, would appear ... to have had a sacred tree'.[46] This statement follows a section specifically concerned with sacred trees, which has addressed the ash (focusing on Yggdrasil, the Viking world tree), the oak (Druids and Germans), mistletoe (the Golden branch borne by Aeneas to the underworld) and the Christmas tree, and then proceeds to discuss groves as an entity. The section then moves to bushes, and to sacred trees in the eastern world, particularly in the *Nackas* of Zoroaster, in an attempt to validate Barlow's earlier statement that sacred trees are near universal in their coverage.

The perceived universality of sacred trees has led to a jumble of elements, roughly joined together in an attempt at harmony with little apparent link between them, and this is evident in Tylor's typically swift discussion, which in five pages moves from demons inhabiting trees in Africa, to the Dodonan oak, to tree nymphs, before finishing with peasant folklore in Europe surrounding fairies in trees.[47] Through providing these comparative case studies, Barlow and Tylor helped shape the growth of arboreal scholarship in the early twentieth century. Their framing of the trees (especially in Tylor's case) as being animated by a divine power was particularly influential, and placed trees in the animistic tradition, which 'invested trees with that mystic or sacred character whereby they were regarded with a superstitious fear which found expression in sundry acts of sacrifice and worship'.[48]

At the start of the twentieth century, Baddeley claimed that it was 'ordinary knowledge' that the worship of trees was a form of early religion, and compared the Roman relationship with the oak tree to that of the Khonds, a tribal community in India, with the 'cotton-tree'.[49] The influence of this comparativist tradition, which had attempted to establish a foundation for religion, is keenly felt in Baddeley's article on Rome's sacred trees. However, it is in the word *numen* (a word which Lewis and Short define as 'divine majesty',[50] among several other meanings, and means a number of different things to an equally large number of ancient and modern authors) that early writers on Roman religion found the strongest evidence for an animistic tradition. Rose and Wagenvoort both identify *numen* as being central to Roman religion, and both do so by comparing it to the Melanesians, the inhabitants of a group of islands to the northeast of Australia.[51] Baddeley, perhaps influenced by the same tradition, points to hamadryads, a variety of woodland spirit that inhabit trees in mythology and exist for the lifetime of the tree, as evidence of the *numen* within the tree, and proclaims that tree worship is 'unsurprising'.[52]

Numen as a word appears in two passages which are commonly cited by early scholars of Roman religion:

> There was a grove beneath the Aventine, oaks draped in black shadow,
> Where you may cry 'There is a *numen* there!'[53]

> These trees were temples of *numen*, and even now simple country-folk dedicate a pre-eminent tree to a god with ancient rites. We adore the statues of shining gold and ebony no more than we do the grove in its silence. Varieties of trees are kept permanently dedicated to their own *numen*, for Jove the oak, Apollo the laurel, Minerva the olive, Venus the myrtle, Hercules the poplar. We even believe that Silvanus and the fauns, and the various goddesses and their *numina* are given to the woods by the heavens.[54]

These two passages shape the early response to trees and their place in the ancient world, and are found quoted as examples of early animism throughout nineteenth- and early twentieth-century studies.[55] It was in these approaches to Roman religion, and religion more generally, that the idea of the Roman sacred tree became a fundamental part of early scholarship, and this led to confusion in approaching trees which did not conform to the rules, as in the case of the Ruminal fig. Bailey relegates this tree to a cursory addition at the end of a paragraph, following the (significantly less well attested) Capitoline oak, around which the *spolia opima* were dedicated to the deity Jupiter Feretrius, for whom there was a temple on the Capitoline hill. This tree, Bailey claims 'was also no doubt a sacred tree, but there is no trace of any worship of it or its indwelling spirit'.[56]

This confusion, which is derived from a conflict within strictly regimented rules by comparativists, is a result of a lack of nuance in understanding trees in the Roman world, sacred and otherwise, and the continued association of trees with spirits, or *numen*, by the nineteenth- and early twentieth-century scholars may have encouraged the decline of considerations of the Roman sacred tree, which is brushed aside by scholarship in the following century.[57] It certainly seems that way to Hunt, who produced the first major work exclusively on trees in the Roman world in the past twenty years.[58] Early in her monograph, Hunt quotes Ferguson's full discussion, which she calls 'unthinking' and 'dismissive':

> Trees were sacred: Pliny the elder has a long section on the subject. There was a sacred fig tree on the Palatine. Augustus put a palm shoot among his household gods; the emperors had a grove of laurels at Veii, plucking a branch to carry in triumph and replanting it; the Flavians had their own oak. Groves were especially sacred; witness Vergil or Ovid or Lucan.
>
> In this grove on this hill with its leafy summit
> Some god lives, though I do not know who it is.[59]

From the outset of *Reviving Roman Religion* (2016), Hunt makes clear that her aim is to provide nuance to the issue of the sacred tree in the Roman world, and to draw the sacred tree out of a pigeonholed view of something obscure from a distant and unusual past. This is made apparent by the immediate answer she gives to the question 'What is a sacred tree?' Hunt warns that the answer she is going to give will only offer a 'loose definition which has little to do with the sacred tree in the popular imagination'. Instead, she directs us to the complex meaning of 'sacred' in the English language, and challenges legalistic models of the Latin *sacer* on the same basis, arguing that the word is likely to have had multiple connotations. In doing this, she disputes the 'one-size-fits-all model of Roman sacrality' which offers a 'broad-brushstroke approach' to sacred trees in Rome, and proposes that a sacred tree should be understood as a tree with some religious capital, though not necessarily consecrated, and certainly not every tree.⁶⁰ *Numen* is treated cautiously, partially following Warde-Fowler's observation in the early twentieth century that the term is so important it requires careful definition.⁶¹ Hunt confronts this immediately, and proposes that any translation of *numen* is fundamentally impossible, and it is easier to determine what modern scholars mean by their usage of the term.⁶² The difficulty of understanding this word when applied to trees is compounded by the verb *colo*, used to indicate both practical and religious care. This word, which Hunt discusses in relation to actions made toward the Ruminal fig, is deemed to be capable of dual meanings, and in the passage Hunt discusses is used to indicate both physical and religious concern.⁶³

Hunt's nuanced understanding of the sacred tree, influenced by a wide range of evidence like Meiggs' earlier approach, indicates a seismic shift from a wholesale approach in earlier examinations of trees in religious settings.⁶⁴ Contrary to these approaches, trees should be dealt with on a case-by-case basis, explored and examined in relation to their individual presentation in the source material as opposed to being treated as a homogenous group, a nuance which will be applied here; contrary to Ferguson's understanding, not all trees were sacred, and the trees examined in this study include both those which are clearly sacred and those which are clearly not.

Landscape and gardens

Both 'landscape' and 'garden' are loaded terms in classical scholarship, and definitions of both are complex and wide-ranging. Austen convincingly argues that gardens cannot be solely spatially defined, and that they have the ability to transcend the boundaries placed on them in the physical world.⁶⁵ Even confined to what Romans might physically experience, there is a distinction between different types of garden, most clearly between the *hortus*, traditionally treated as a small-scale space primarily for growing vegetables and directed by human need and labour, and the plural *Horti*, used for grand parks and estates in and around the city.⁶⁶ As a term, landscape is harder to define, largely because it might appear to lack consistent hard boundaries, being such a vast descriptor. Spencer encourages us to think outside the physical limitations of framing and boundaries, and to consider landscape as both a cultural and a personal phenomenon. A landscape is an area parcelled out from its surroundings, and ceases to be raw space, instead becoming a place, imbued with meaning for the parceller, and thus able to be discussed as a site within a broader 'fabric of visual meaning'.[67] This definition does not define the landscape as necessarily fixed, nor one with an objective meaning. It remains subjective to the individual observer, and this is an element of landscape studies that carry through to trees which, as Hunt has already noted and has already been discussed above, under 'Religion', do not cope well with a broad-brushstroke approach. Both landscape and garden, then, are highly flexible terms within ancient interactions with the world around them, and both can be used for highly individualized responses.

A challenge in discussing trees is placing them in the natural landscapes and cityscapes in which they sit. Studies of landscape offer a bigger picture of trees in the ancient world than the focused studies of Hunt and Meiggs, on religion and utility respectively: Meiggs' rapid pacing across the Mediterranean belies the scale of his topic, and Hunt sometimes overlooks issues such as lifespan (the fig tree, no matter Pliny's evidence, is not extremely short-lived, and can survive in the right climate for hundreds of years).[68] The link between landscapes and religion is well founded, and the role of the city of Rome in Roman religion is examined by Beard, North and Price.[69] They direct attention to a speech made by Camillus in Livy's *Ab urbe condita*, also highlighted by Edwards, in *Writing Rome*.[70] In this speech, which reminds Romans of their ties to Rome and convinces a beleaguered people to remain in the place, rather than move to Veii, Camillus draws upon the significance of the site of Rome, and compares the location to the days of the year, permanently fixed.[71]

Religion and memory are often intrinsically linked in the Roman world, and many religious rites have precedents in myth. An example of this can be found in Edwards' discussion of the hut of Romulus, which was cared for and maintained by priests, and may have been a venue for religious activities.[72] This, like the Ruminal fig, combined sacredness with a memory of a rustic Rome, and its humble beginnings with a thatched hut that once housed Romulus and Remus themselves.

Outside of the mythologized landscape of Rome, a popular landscape in scholarship is the manufactured one of Pompey's Porticus, constructed in the late Republic, possibly from the spoils of his Pontic wars, and certainly to house them. This landscape is treated alongside the *Horti Sallustiani* by Spencer in *Roman Landscape* (2010), and there is a degree of equity between the two, despite their clear differences in both form and function.[73] Reconstructions and archaeological investigations can help understand landscapes such as that created in the Porticus, and Spencer employs the reconstruction from Gleason's assessment of the relationship between the architecture and the garden to identify a grove that was simultaneously wild and yet cultivated, or 'harmoniously natural and highly urban and artificial'.[74] This nature, which Spencer presents as having been manipulated alongside the architecture for Pompey's 'self-promotional agenda', is reflected in Statius' description of Pollius Felix's country estate, and the unison between the rural and the urban may suggest a Pompeian nod to Rome's rural beginnings. In her comparison of the Porticus Pompeiana to the garden, Spencer highlights both *topopoesie* (topopoetics: the reading of a place through poetry) and *rus in urbe*, both common features of Latin poetry at the time. The phrase *rus in urbe* is found in Martial's *Epigrams* and it is compared by Watson and Watson to other passages in Martial's *corpus*, and other contemporary literature.[75] They propose that 'the Romans ... preferred villas where the amenities associated with city living were combined with an artificially created rural ambience', and this attitude is found elsewhere in garden scholarship. Throughout Spencer's examination of the landscape in the Roman world, landscape is presented as a vehicle for communication, and the creation of a rural space inside a villa served as a private expression of imperialism and territorial control.

Von Stackelberg's examination of gardens in *The Roman Garden: Space, Sense, and Society* (2009) places the garden on a level with the landscape, like Spencer's approach to the controlled garden-esque space in the Porticus Pompeiana. The garden is treated as 'a vehicle of cultural communication', and it is easy to see how the same term can be used to describe as politically active a space as the Porticus. In her examination of the politically communicative gardens, such as the one in Pompey's complex, Von Stackelberg focuses the garden on the owner, and differentiates the *hortus* from the other public arenas used for politics such as the Forum. In this way, the garden should be treated as separate from the landscape, as a less confused and more controlled place to communicate to the people. This use of the garden as a location for controlled encounters came into its own in the early imperial period, and Augustus capitalized on the garden complexes of his predecessors to create public spaces in which he could control these encounters and direct them to a more favourable outcome.[76]

A garden had another function in the Principate, identified by Von Stackelberg in her discussion of Pollius Felix's estate, as described by Statius:

> Nature has favoured these places, in others she has ceded, conquered by her worshipper (*victa colenti*), and she is softened (*mansuevit*) into unfamiliar, docile ways. Here, there was a mountain, where now you see plains; and here was alight with sun, where now you enter a building; where now you see groves on slopes, there was not even earth: the owner has tamed it (*domuit possessor*), and the ground rejoices as he shapes the rocks and expels them, following his lead. Now, look to the cliffs, submitting to the yoke (*iugum discentia*), the buildings as they grow, and the mountain, ordered to retreat. Now, let the hand of Methymna's prophet, the lyre of Thebes, and the glory of the Getic plectrum embolden you: and may you move rocks too, and may lofty forests follow you[77]

She notes the militaristic language of subjugation and dominance in the passage, and applies this to the political climate that Statius and Pollius Felix were operating in under Domitian. It was a challenging time for personal expression of power, and involvement in public life was fraught with danger. The villa estate, for Von Stackelberg, had become a means by which an individual could experience absolute control over a territory and not have to run the risks associated with holding public office.[78] In this regard, the *hortus* of a villa estate was the equivalent of the villa's empire, controlled by its owner, much like the eastern gardens discussed by Totelin (2012), while the *Horti* of Rome reflected its own growing empire, and, in the case of the Porticus Pompeiana, were cluttered with monuments acquired through conquest.[79]

During the growth of Rome's empire, the city became a cosmopolis, a world city which incorporated elements of its territories, and this is shown in the literary output of the early Principate. McEwan, in a discussion of Vitruvius which heavily influenced later approaches to the *De architectura*, observes that 'the *corpus* of *architectura* was, reciprocally, shaped by the body of Empire', and we have already seen above that Livy's *Ab urbe condita* roots the reader and the Romans in Rome, emphasizing its importance and centrality in a growing world.⁸⁰ There has been a large amount of scholarship produced on the establishment of the cosmopolis, most notably *Rome the Cosmopolis* (Edwards and Woolf 2003), and this was followed by studies of the mechanism by which a large number of goods were imported: the triumphal procession. From Östenberg's *Staging the World: Spoils, Captives, and Representations in the Roman Triumphal Procession* (2009) to Beard's *The Roman Triumph* (2007), these discussions of one of the Roman processes of introducing foreign goods to Rome examine the changing political landscape, and how the city is used as a performative space.

War and empire

Trees are examined as a triumphal import in Östenberg's monograph, and Leach views the creation of an artificial cosmos within the city's walls as 'an exaggerated assertion of man's power to control nature and tame the wilderness by his art'.⁸¹ Östenberg examines trees in her chapter focused on captives, and she is quick to identify the comparable role trees play to spoils more traditionally regarded as captives: prisoners, hostages and animals. The trees are, according to Pliny, 'led' in triumph, and Östenberg notes that the language used is identical to the language used for other captives, as opposed to representations.⁸² This, she argues, leads to the conclusion that Pliny 'equates the population of trees with that of human beings', with particular reference to the balsam, which is described as 'paying tribute alongside its race'.⁸³

A consequence of the equivalency that Östenberg identifies between trees in the triumphal procession and the captives they are displayed alongside and the comparativist, animistic approach to trees discussed above, under 'Religion', is that they are viewed with some caution in a military context. Of particular interest is a well-known grove outside of Massilia, felled by Caesar in 49 BCE to make room and supplies for his camp, and described in Lucan's *Civil War*.⁸⁴ Among the earliest of the studies of the grove is Phillips' (1968), which assesses the historicity of the incident. After he quickly ascertains that the incident is fictitious, and probably invented by Lucan, he takes it as an *inventio*, designed to further characterize the figure of Caesar in Lucan's poetry.⁸⁵ To do this, Phillips places the felling of the grove, considered sacred by the local population, alongside other famous fellings in literature, and promptly reads the passage with an animistic slant. This is in line with Lucan's own narrative, which places emphasis on the issue of violation and sacrality, although Lucan is undoubtedly employing a hyperbole which does not need to dominate discussions of the passage, and Phillips ends his article with an indication of the point of Lucan's invention: to further highlight that 'the divine gives way to Caesar with disheartening regularity'.[86] For Phillips, the trees of Lucan's epic are freely available communicative media, and the landscape of war is a useful canvas for developing literary themes.[87]

The use of trees, or landscape in general, in descriptions of warfare is not unique to Lucan, nor is it unique to literal descriptions of warfare, as in the grove examined by Phillips. Statius' martial description of Pollius Felix's country estate and the military language used can be linked to Greek precedents, and the use of farming can be read as a noble form of warfare.[88] This approach was common, and the garden has been treated as a war zone between the unsanitized wild elements and the contained rural space. However, Edwards suggests that we should be tentative in applying a strict distinction between rural and urban activities and spaces, and reminds us of the paradox of Romulus – that he was both the first king of Rome and remembered in the city, but was himself a rustic king who never lived in a city.[89] This muddying of the waters underlines the complexity of discussing trees and landscapes in ancient Rome, and the natural dialogue between the areas of scholarship that have been examined above.[90]

Post-classical trees and monumentality

Outside of the ancient world, we find that this dialogue already exists, and is particularly evident in Watkins' *Trees, Woods, and Forests* (2016). From the outset, Watkins outlines the 'rich, intricate and multi-layered' relationship between humankind and trees, and he reflects this in the content of his monograph, which covers a range of topics, from woodland management in the ancient world to representations of trees in artwork.[91] The underlying element of these (ostensibly disparate) topics is that multi-layered relationship, which is built on and influenced by the relationship humans have historically had with trees in a variety of spheres.⁹² Watkins approaches trees within the framework of this relationship, and emphasizes their permanence as stable objects by which 'we can match our individual lives and the lives of nations and civilisations'.⁹³ Watkins' approach to trees as fixed features of a landscape, providing stability and continuity in the lifespan of humans, is a useful one, and helps us to place ourselves in the context of ancient Rome, as opposed to looking back at the trees of the ancient city as long dead and obviously transitory features of the city, unlike the statues which have survived in a tangible form. To those Romans who met in the shade of the trees around them, they would have seemed as permanent as the modern elm trees which Watkins uses to highlight the effect of a tree's death.

In the case of an arboreal death, particularly in the instance of a familiar tree, Watkins sees an acute sense of regret and loss, and the large-scale removal of woodlands creates a community-wide reaction (he uses the group Save England's Forests as an example).⁹⁴ It is in these threats that the high regard that trees are held can be best seen, and Whyte explores this in the specific context of a boundary elm threatened with removal in post-medieval Norfolk (2013). Here, Whyte explicitly sets herself apart from the trend to focus on the practical aspect of trees in her field, and declares her intent to study the role of this tree and trees more broadly in identity construction.⁹⁵ To do this, she aims to move past the 'ideational landscapes of elite writers' and focus on 'the social and symbolic meanings of trees in everyday vernacular contexts'. While this is easier to do in periods more recent than ancient Rome, it is a reminder that trees are, on the whole, a publicly accessible feature and repository of memory. While the trees of sacred sites, such as those examined by Hunt (2016), and those in tightly controlled spaces, such as the *horti* analysed by Von Stackelberg (2009), may have had limited public access, the majority of the trees of Rome were publicly accessible, from the Ruminal fig on the Palatine and in the Forum to the groves that remained in Rome from Evander's wooded landscape. Whyte continues to remind us that the trees of her period were appreciated by people regardless of class difference, whether or not they were preserved, a quality also applied to the trees of Rome.

The trees that Whyte uses in her article are, she notes, identified by their contemporaries as 'surviving from the ancient past, carr[ying] meaning in the present and the past'.⁹⁶ This, combined with the borrowed title of Whyte's article (taken from Bradley's monograph, *An Archaeology of Natural Places* (2000)), begins to suggest a monumental approach to trees. Whyte applies Bradley's methodology to her article, arguing that, despite the difference in time period – Bradley is concerned with prehistory – Bradley's methodology is nevertheless useful. Bradley argues that the term 'monument' cannot be properly applied to a natural feature, since a key aspect of 'monument', for him, is that it is constructed by human labour, and is just as easily deconstructed.⁹⁷ In spite of this methodological approach, both Whyte and Bradley continue to explore natural features in monumental terms, and Bradley proposes that the similarity with artificial monuments is because natural features acquire 'a significance in the minds of people in the past'. This is expanded upon by Whyte, who adds that while people 'experienced and gave meaning to material objects, monuments, and entire landscapes', it is the creation of monuments within those landscapes that inscribes memory onto it. Whyte does distance herself from Bradley's methodology, and points out the difference between trees and natural places as a whole, which are the focus of Bradley's book, in an attempt to reclassify trees as having the potential for monumentality. The first key point she identifies is that trees are not a permanent feature of the place, unlike geographical features, and that their 'ongoing preservation was to a large extent the result of human decision making, and their destruction the cause of tension and conflict within local societies', much like a monument. Again, similar to a monument, the tree 'structured the spatial order of everyday landscapes by providing tangible reference points, places to meet, and landmarks to denote jurisdictional boundaries and spaces'.⁹⁸

In the ancient world, what defines a monument is equally fluid, and scholarship has focused on artificial monuments, from small statues to colossal temples.⁹⁹ Thomas, in *Monumentality and the Roman Empire* (2007), qualifies monumentality as reflecting the attitudes of society, while also presuming a relationship with the individual. The duality of this 'interactive relationship', Thomas suggests, is a result of the monument's position on the ground and the ideals formed by the imagination in response to it.¹⁰⁰ Thomas goes on to explore monumentality in natural landscapes, and proposes that the Acropolis is only monumental due to the buildings placed upon it, which compete with their surroundings. As a result, he qualifies his earlier definition of monumentality by adding that it is 'an agent of commemoration, of sacred human memory, and of the relationship of man with the gods'.[101] It should not be forgotten that Thomas is specifically discussing architecture here, and that human involvement is required; he often refers to 'monumental architecture', as opposed to 'monuments'. Meyers, who is writing on the experience of monumentality, emphasizes the connection between memory and monuments in the ancient sources, and acknowledges that the usage of the term *monumentum* in Latin literature sometimes reflects this.[102] She ventures briefly beyond the realm of buildings, and proposes that the ancient *monumentum* may not be a specific structure, but could be a space, with the only absolute necessity being that it has strict boundaries.[103] By Bradley's approach, a tree cannot be a monument, since it is not constructed by human labour. However, when the lack of a clear definition in the ancient world is considered, alongside the unique place a tree holds, as expressed by Whyte, a tree that communicates some aspect of human memory, either to a religious past or to a mytho-historic one, and even a grove, can be a natural monument.

Whyte proposes that trees function as a meeting place in post-medieval England, a part of the spatial structuring within the landscape. Similarly, Zanker argues that statues were used as a meeting place in the ancient world, which is seconded by Edwards.[104] Edwards focuses her chapter in *Rome the Cosmopolis* (2003) on the import of foreign statues into Rome in the first and second centuries CE, and the corresponding rise of luxury found in the literature of the period.[105] When discussing spoils, she places them within the narrative of conquest, in the triumphal procession, as they are used to demonstrate the extent of the empire and to represent the conquered in Rome.[106] Like statues, which Pliny treats as similar to trees, trees were also displayed in the triumphal procession and were used to represent the extent of the empire, although they too did not have to rely upon the formula of the triumph to be incorporated into the city.[107] These trees, all considered foreign, proved to be challenging to Roman ideas of identity, made more challenging, as Edwards argues, because it is difficult in the process of imports to determine when a piece of foreign *spolia* becomes Roman.[108] As foreign natural monuments in the city, these trees contributed to the growing cosmopolis that was Rome, and in some instances memorialized, or perhaps monumentalized, conquest.[109]

The nature of the evidence

An overriding feature of recent works on trees and nature in Rome is the willingness to work with as wide a range of evidence as is available. This book will be no different. Trees and the landscape more generally are parts of the ancient world that are universally received, unlike elite literature and private artwork. They are ever-present background pieces in literature about the city, and stood next to statues and temples in public places. There was no fundamental distinction between the tree in the Roman Forum and the one grown in a garden, and the monumental and memorial trees of Rome's public spaces were experienced by all members of society equally. To understand the role of trees in the city as fully as possible, this book will pull in evidence from literature, visual and material culture, and archaeological plans of the ancient city. A result of this lack of ancient distinction is that there are trees held in high regard across the city, written about, carved into stone, planted in positions of prominence, and preserved in a wide variety of different ways. To cover all of these trees in one monograph would not be feasible, and this book takes a case study approach, similar to that of Meiggs' *Trees and Timber in the Ancient Mediterranean World*, which faced a similar challenge.

Also similarly to Meiggs' approach, our evidence comes from a wide variety of sources, and it is only through the combination of these sources that a complete picture can be seen. Meiggs uses the expected agricultural manuals of Columella, Cato and Varro, alongside Pliny's *Natural History* and Theophrastus' *History of Plants*, but combines these with records of timber purchases from Eleusis, Delphi, Delos and Epidauros.[110] One detailed example of timber use is found in a tablet that details the structure of the arsenal of the Piraeus in Athens, examined by Dinsmoor, and translated in full by Meiggs.[111] This combination of evidence, however, does not tend to draw on Latin poets, and Meiggs directs his readers to a number of passages from Vergil and Horace to elucidate their lack of accuracy in the presentation of arboreal landscapes.[112]

The most famous of these is the opening of Vergil's *Eclogues*, where the poet describes a shepherd underneath a *fagus*, or beech tree.[113] This is a well-known intertextual echo of Theocritus' *Idyll* 12, in which a traveller hurries to a φηγός, or oak tree.[114] Vergil, for Meiggs' purpose, is too whimsical in his identification of the tree under which Tityrus rests as a beech, and is 'more interested in the sound than the substance; he certainly did not believe that *fagus* was an oak'.[115] Meiggs advises caution in extrapolating practical information from the poets, although he does indicate that 'useful information' regarding trees is present in the majority of Greek and Latin sources – an observation proposed by later scholarship on the utility of wood.[116]

Challenges are posed by relying on the poets for understanding the city beyond the issue of transliteration and poetic licence identified by Meiggs. The city is often the backdrop for events depicted in poetry, and while the testimony of poets such as Propertius and Martial can tell us how a handful of elite Romans saw these buildings, the poems rarely focus on the buildings themselves, more on their uses and the emotions they conjure. The literary evidence, then, is sporadic, and only a handful of continuous examinations of trees exist, typically agricultural manuals such as Columella's *On Trees* and portions of Varro's *On Rural Things*. As a result, our literary evidence is largely in snapshots and small segments, and rarely offers a coherent narrative approach to elite interactions with trees. In order to build up a complete picture of Romans' relationships with the trees in their city, more evidence is needed, but this is also not without its challenges.

Visual and material evidence offer a similar challenge in that these items of evidence can only provide momentary depictions. Explorations and examinations of how these monuments work in the space rely on archaeological evidence, typically through planting pits or sometimes circumstantial evidence of planting such as pots. In rare instances, root cavities, pollen samples, or even wood can be found, but since trees are archaeologically fugitive, the bulk of evidence that trees were present in ancient spaces is through a compilation of different types of material to establish the likely presence of trees.[117] This combination approach allows for us to make the most informed conclusions that we can about where trees were, and how Romans interacted with the trees around them.

A beguiling challenge, when engaging with trees in the ancient world, is to seek out their modern equivalents. This is traditionally done by trying to match the trees written about with their Linnaean names, or by close analysis of leaf types in sculpture and coinage. A well-known example of this is Silphion (= *silphium*), a plant Pliny the Elder identified as extinct by the reign of Nero, when the last branch was found.[118] Over the years, a number of attempts have been made to identify Silphion, which appears depicted on a number of coins and is identified as being an effective abortifacient as well as a pleasant spice. These attempts are not restricted to the discipline of ancient history, and the most recent effort, by pharmacist Mahmut Miski, has captured public imagination and was the focus of a *National Geographic* article on the topic.[119] Miski prioritizes the culinary attributes of Silphion over the abortifacient and contraceptive ones, which had previously led to a different identification.[120] While the conclusions have been that this plant is of the *Ferula* genus, identifications beyond that have varied, and useful discussion of the plant have been lost to attempts to pick it out from among the weeds. There is little benefit to knowing the precise subgenus of a plant in the ancient world, especially when speaking conceptually, and fruitful conversation can happen without that focus.

A focus on the precise identification of plants also disguises a concern within ancient evidence and with ancient authors: how confidently and consistently could they identify which plants they were writing about? To even broadly equate each of the terms used for oak with a specific subgenus is difficult without additional information (such as visual depictions), and even in those instances identifications must be made tentatively and specifically: Pliny's *aesculus* may not be the same as Vergil's or Columella's. An example of good practice in this can be found in Stoiculescu's leaf analysis of Trajan's Column (see Figure 2). Resinous trees, bar one type, are identified solely as being resinous, while deciduous trees are identified by their genus, not subgenus. The most specific resinous identification, of either *Populus nigra* L. or *Cupressus sempervirens* L., is tentative and has little impact on the argument; the article focuses on the Dacian forest, and the two trees of this type appear on the Roman side of the Danube. Following this example, this book will not engage in attempts to identify trees beyond the genus or the original Latin term where there is no benefit in doing so for the argument.

There are times when a benefit can be found for identification outside of argument: to clarify modern confusion. The best example of this is in the ancient *laurus*. This tree is confidently identified as the *Laurus nobilis* L., the bay tree, or the laurel, outside of the United Kingdom. In the United Kingdom, however, there is confusion on account of modern naming convention, which identifies a different plant – the *Prunus laurocerasus* L. – as the laurel. This plant is very different from the *Laurus nobilis*. It does not smell, it absolutely should not be used in cooking, and has no special relationship with Apollo or the Pythian oracle. It shares a leaf type with the *Laurus nobilis*, is also evergreen, and has similar-shaped fruits of a different colour. Despite my reluctance to push modern identifications on trees, Romans were conscious of the variations between the trees around them.

An arboreal cosmopolis

Trees in Roman literature and art are rarely a homogenous block of greenery in the city. Authors take care to identify species types, and visual evidence such as coins and statuary differentiate between the varied species. This has been established in studies of the Ara Pacis and of Trajan's Column, and the literary focus on different trees is evident from the wide variety of terms that Romans used to identify trees and their variant species.[121] A survey of the available literary evidence for Roman engagement with trees demonstrates that engagement was not restricted to one of the four areas which have typified previous scholarship on trees, and that each Latin author used trees in a number of ways, revealing a complex relationship in the source material. While previous tree-focused scholarship has explored either the practical or religious applications of trees in the Roman world, there is a large corpus of literary evidence for the social role of trees in the ancient world, and it is this aspect of ancient interactions with trees that this book will primarily explore. It should not be a surprise to regular readers of Latin literature in the imperial period that the most prolific individual author on trees is Pliny the Elder, nor that trees are typically treated as a resource as opposed to being treated as an end in themselves. What may be less expected is the Roman occupation with the oak, which is the most common tree represented in literature, especially using the term *quercus* as opposed to any of its variant terms, such as *aesculus*, *ilex*, or *robur*.[122] Some caution must be applied when identifying specific subspecies of tree from the ancient evidence, since the different terms for oak are not used consistently across the various authors, and there are sometimes transliteration errors, as with *fagus*/φηγός, the one meaning beech in Latin, and the other oak in Greek.

In the compilation of all available evidence on a given tree, we can find interactions that illuminate perhaps unusual choices, as in the case of the Trojan Horse. The horse, Vergil tells us, is made of *abies*.[123] This wood is commonly used for ships in Vergil's poetry, and three of Vergil's twelve references to ships are *abies*.[124] However, when Cybele is discussing the fate of the Trojan ships with Zeus, she tells the god that they are made of the *pinus*, *picea* and *acer*, taken from her own wood.[125] In Greek literature, we find that *abies* was considered a fine material for ship building, particularly warships, in Theophrastus' *History of Plants*.[126] Vergil's comment that the wooden horse is made of fir, then, could be taken to be an indication that the horse was composed of the old warships no longer needed to transport dead Greeks home from Troy. The construction of the horse is consistent across Latin poetry, and Propertius refers to the wood used as *abiegnus*, a variant of the more common *abies*.[127] Taken further, when Vergil uses the same type of wood to refer to Trojan ships, as at 5.663 and 8.91, it could be read as a deliberate use, and this would indicate a circularity, as the vessel that carries the Greeks in to destroy Troy is made of the same material as the vessels that save Troy and bear its warriors to Italy.[128] This holistic approach to the ancient evidence demonstrates that the complexity of a post-medieval relationship with trees, as explored by Whyte (2013), is evident in the ancient relationship, and there was no universal approach to trees as expected by the early comparativist, animistic religious scholars. As Hunt explained in her analysis of what makes a tree sacred, each tree has to be approached without a broad brushstroke, and this book will also take an individualized approach.

When examining Rome's trees, the first question asked has to be about the diversity of Rome's arboreal population, and whether this diversity was reflected in how it was presented at the time. The variety of tree terms indicate that there was an awareness of different species, though there is not always consistency in the application of the specific terms with regard to sub-genus. Archaeological evidence further suggests that the timber of Rome was diverse, and not sourced exclusively from the Tiber valley, as Strabo suggests.[129]

This diverse population of trees proliferated the ancient cityscape, and appeared throughout the public spaces of Rome. These trees, some of which are mapped in a synchronic overview of Rome in Figure 1, vary in form, from groves to monumental individual trees to avenues of trees. The monumental trees are found clustered on the left-hand side of the Tiber and in the metropolitan centre of the city, while the gardens and groves are found on the city's outskirts, possibly as a result of space being a high-value commodity in the city's crowded centre. Unlike the gardens, which are spread around Rome, the monumental trees follow the city's typical centres, from the Palatine and the Capitoline to the Forum Romanum, according to the city's expansion. The draining of the marshy landscape of early Rome would have helped the growth of trees in the valleys between the city's hills. While most maps of ancient Rome, such as Lanciani's *Forma Urbis Romae* (1893–1901), focus on the monumental architecture of the city (which appear here as anonymous grey blocks), Carandini's recent *The Atlas of Ancient Rome* (2017) frequently concerns itself with the trees in the city plan, as well as the green spaces more generally, providing a guide to the city's *Horti* as one of the earliest maps (Vol. II, tab. II). The map included here is not intended to be exhaustive; there were likely trees that have not been identified in our ancient sources or been excavated in the ancient city. These may be incidental promenade trees, like the pines and the planes that line Rome's roads today, or groves like those on the Caelian hill, which was once called the Mons Querquetulanus (Hill of Oaks), or they could be trees that were only important in the immediate vicinity; Martial's reference to a pear tree at his apartment building is the only reference to that pear tree, and few apartment buildings were fortunate enough to be immortalized in elegy. Other trees, such as the grove of the Vestals in the Forum and their Capillata tree, are simply in too congested a space to be shown on the map. Even without these trees included, and only focusing on the monumental or named trees and groves, this map demonstrates how widespread trees identified in the cityscape were.

Figure 1 An asynchronic overview of a selection of Rome's trees.

These trees are a mix of those that existed from the foundation of the city and those that were introduced at a later date, and it is this journey of trees to Rome that this book focuses on, through a series of case studies, offering snapshots into Rome's varied relationships with trees across their route to a permanent position in the city. Chapter 1 will explore the memory of these

Table 1 Key to numbered trees in Figure 1

Number on Map	Tree, Grove, or Horti	Number on Map	Tree, Grove, or Horti
1	Vatican Oak	15	Lotus and cypress at the Vulcanal
2	Horti Luculliani, and possible cherry trees	16	Ruminal fig in the Comitium
3	Horti Sallustiani	17	Possible site of the Navian fig
4	Evergreen trees at the Mausoleum of Augustus	18	Fig, olive, vine group at the Lacus Curtius
5	Box hedging and bay trees at the Porticus Vipsania	19	Horti Maecenatis
6	*Ad Pirum* (Martial's Apartment)	20	Aesculetum
7	Plane trees in the Porticus of Pompey	21	Oak tree at the Temple of Jupiter Feretrius
8	Dacian trees in Trajan's Forum	22	Fig tree outside the Temple of Saturn
9	Lotus of Lucina	23	Ruminal fig and grove at the Lupercal
10	Horti Agrippae	24	Twin bay trees outside of Augustus' House
11	Unknown trees in the Porticus Philippi	25	Cornel from Romulus' Spear
12	Laurels at the Temple of Venus Genetrix	26	Grove of the Camenae at the Porta Capena
13	Inter Duos Lucos (groves between which Romulus established Rome)	27	Horti Caesaris
14	Tarpeian Grove	28	Arval Grove, five miles southwest of Rome on the Via Campana

trees in Rome, their echoes within the cityscape, and the importance of provenance. It will take two groves, the Julio-Claudian laurel grove at the Villa of Livia on the Via Flaminia and the Grove of the Camenae at the Porta Capena, and explore how these two groves can be used to communicate different messages. Throughout this chapter, the presentation of the multivalent role of the tree around the city of Rome and its potential as a site of collective memory will demonstrate that, unlike the fluidity of a river and other natural features, a tree is anticipated to be a fixed feature of a landscape. Chapter 2 will begin the journey of a foreign tree being introduced to the city, through Pliny the Elder's *Natural History*. This chapter will examine the struggle between utility and luxury that dominates the *Natural History*, and how Pliny's structure of the *Natural History* directs his readers to consider his accumulation of knowledge as an act of conquest in itself, and an exertion of power over the natural world. Chapter 3 will continue this examination of conquest over the natural world and explore the role of trees in the triumphal procession, as crowns, trophies and spoils. It will explore how trees are used to communicate control and conquest, and focus on one of the means by which foreign trees were physically introduced to the ancient city. Chapter 4 will describe the final stage of a tree's journey into the city and assess how and why green spaces were incorporated into the monumental cityscape. It will take three buildings and investigate how trees were planted in them, and how the trees planted were determined by the use of the space, or influenced the use of the space themselves. The book will then close with a case study of the Mausoleum of Augustus and the trees planted there, ultimately answering the central question of the book: what was the impact of trees in the Roman city?

1

Memory and Trees

Rome's primeval landscape was heavily wooded, or at least Vergil imagines it to have been, and the echoes of Rome's arboreal citizens are carried through into the early imperial city plan. In the sole trees that form depleted reminders of the groves that once covered the cityscape, and the neighbourhoods named after the groves demolished for their creation, Rome's cultural memory is built around these remembrances. These trees are often loaned importance by their provenance, whether by age or because they were planted by a notable individual. Sometimes, both of these provenances come into play, and trees such as the cornel cherry tree at the top of the Steps of Cacus on the Palatine gain additional prominence.

This tree, grown from a spear improbably thrown by Romulus as he stood on the Aventine, is reported by Plutarch as having lasted until some moment in the reign of Caligula, when it was damaged by building work and died.[1] Until that point, it had been a focal point of the neighbourhood, and had been cared for by any visitors to the spot, who would call upon anyone they met to help preserve the life of this cornel cherry tree. Without the provenance of Romulus' spear, its geographical location at the top of a major route up to the Palatine hill, and its longevity, this tree would likely have been cleared for building work on the hill, as so many other trees were. Even after its death, the memory of the spear tree was preserved; Plutarch recalls it decades later, and the echoes of Rome's past cityscape resonate through accounts of Rome in the early Principate.

This chapter will examine these echoes, beginning with Vergil's well-known account of the landscape of proto-Rome in the *Aeneid* and the neighbourhood names from around the city, several of which contain echoes of a landscape that would otherwise have been forgotten. The chapter will then explore the question of provenance, and examine trees held to be important to the city and to Romans more generally as a result of their provenance, before moving to two case studies. The first of these considers the use of a grove in communicating the power of a dynasty, the Julio-Claudian laurel grove at the Villa of Livia, while the second focuses on the Grove of the Camenae outside the Porta Capena, whose messaging has been overwritten by the evolving city. It will explore how the past trees of Rome (real and imagined) influence the present cityscape, and how trees were used across generations to communicate legacy, and how vulnerable that cultural memory is in public settings.

Echoes of trees: Evander's Rome

In the *Aeneid*, Evander shows Aeneas a proto-version of Rome, the centre of which is shaded by a 'huge grove', and Vergil directs the reader to consider this wooded city alongside its contemporary:

> From here, he shows Aeneas a huge grove where brave Romulus established the asylum, and under an icy cliff, the Lupercal, named for Lycaen Pan (in the Arcadian style). And he also shows the grove of the Argiletum. He calls the place to bear witness, and narrates the death of Argus, his guest. From here too, he leads Aeneas to the Tarpeian seat and the Capitoline, now gold, but then wooded, and covered with cruel brambles. Then as now, the dire religion of the place shook the countryfolk to their core. Then as now, they trembled at the woods and the rocks. 'In this grove,' he says, 'on this hill with its leafy crown, a god lives, though we do not know which one; the Arcadians believe they have seen Jupiter himself, when he shakes his darkening aegis with his right hand and summons the storm. Further, in these two towns, with their broken-down walls, you will see the remnants and the monuments of the men of old. Janus, the father, built that one, Saturn the other. One was called Janiculum, and the other Saturnia.' As they spoke, they came to the house of humble Evander, and they saw cows all around, lowing in the Roman forum, and in the beautiful Carinae.[2]

In Vergil's tour of *ur*-Rome (and Evander's tour of pre-Rome),[3] Vergil woods four sites that would be known to an audience in Augustan Rome: Romulus' asylum, the Argiletum, the Tarpeian Rock, and the entire Capitoline. The Lupercal, which is shaded by an 'icy cliff' and not linked to the 'huge grove' at the heart of the city, is the only site which would have been wooded in Rome's recent history, with the Ruminal fig tree reported there as recently as in Livy's *Ab urbe condita* and in Ovid's *Fasti*.[4]

The wooded areas of Evander's settlement are echoed in Augustan Rome's cityscape. The Argiletum, named for the slaughter (*letum*) of Argus as opposed to using the suffix -*etum* to denote a grove, was a major thoroughfare into the Roman Forum, and the grove's name was preserved in the street's. The echoes of the woods imagined in Vergil's description of Rome are not always as obvious. The thick brambles that cover the Tarpeian rock serve as a prelude to the location's future, and the landscape is repeated in Propertius' contemporary description of Tarpeia's death: it is 'thorn-covered', and when she comes down from the Capitoline hill her arms are torn by brambles.[5] While these depictions are of a fictionalized landscape, they serve to indicate an approach in Augustan poetry whereby Rome's cityscape echoes an idyllic pastoral scene.

The 'huge grove' at the centre of Evander's *ur*-Rome, however, is more concretely found in Rome's contemporary city than the vague emotive echoes of a thorny Capitoline. The Asylum, established by Romulus at the founding of the city of Rome, is situated between two groves, or *inter duos lucos*, a phrase that recurs in descriptions of Rome's urban plan.[6] Whether the two groves were considered to be a feature of the landscape at the time of the Asylum's establishment is unclear: Livy uses them as a location identifier ('In the place which is fenced off these days, between the two groves as you go up the hill, Romulus opened the asylum');[7] while Dionysius names the contemporary as opposed to the historic site ('[the place] which is now called in the language of the Romans "the space between the two groves"'), before indicating that the name describes the mytho-historic location.[8] There is an obvious issue in taking Vergil's account too literally, and we have to remind ourselves that it is not a historical account: Evander's Rome is not the original Rome, but a reflection of the Augustan one. That an area with an arboreal toponym like *inter duos lucos* is shown as one large grove in the *Aeneid* does not indicate that it actually was a large grove at the time. In the absence of any additional evidence, it only serves to demonstrate that Vergil is reading the contemporary toponym back into Rome's *ur*-landscape. This is apparent throughout the passage, especially in the description of the Capitoline hill's grove, where Evander fancies that the Arcadians have seen Jupiter; it is surely no coincidence that Vergil's characters have seen the god in a place where multiple temples now stand to him.

However, the additional evidence, which comes from a range of sources, suggests that this is a popular reading, and it has been suggested that Vergil's choice to present Evander's Rome as wooded is part of an overall Augustan effort to turn back the clock on Rome.[9] This description forms part of an overall trend to present a harmonious Rome, in touch with its pastoral past and its current monumentalization. This trend is evident elsewhere, and has already been discussed in the context of the movement of the Ruminal fig tree in the Augustan period. Additionally, the link created between the past of Rome and its present, here by the echoes of Rome's early landscape in Augustan toponyms, helps Romans understand their contemporary city, and the links to the ancient storied monuments lend credibility to Augustan Rome.[10]

Echoes of trees: Neighbourhood names

Outside of the *Aeneid*, we can find echoes of Roman trees throughout the city. This is noted by Varro, who identifies four distinct places named after trees, and also in Pliny's *Natural History*:

> On the Aventine there is the Lauretum, so named because it is where King Tatius was buried, who was killed by the Laurentes, or perhaps from the laurel wood, because there was one cut down there and a *vicus* was built there: just like between the Sacred Way and the Macellum is the Corneta, from the cherry trees (*cornus*) which gave their name to the place after they were cut away; or the Aesculetum, from oak (*aesculus*); or Fagutal, from beech (*fagus*), where we also get Jupiter Fagutalis because his shrine is there.[11]
>
> Certainly, Rome was distinguished by the types of its woods, Jupiter Fagutal is named even now after where there was a grove of beech trees (*fagus*), the Porta Querquetulana, the Viminal hill (where people get osiers (*vimen*)), and all the Luci, some even named after two types of trees. As dictator, and when the plebeians had seceded to the Janiculum, Quintus Hortensius passed the law in the Aesculetum that an order of the plebs should be binding on all citizens.[12]

Between them, Varro and Pliny identify several different places in Rome which draw etymologies from trees: the Lauretum and Corneta in Varro's *On the Latin Language*; the Porta Querquetulana and Viminal hill in Pliny's *Natural History* (which Varro elsewhere relates to willow groves, or *vimineta*);[13] and the Fagutal and Aesculetum in both.[14] Pliny also mentions 'all the Luci', referring to areas of Rome named after other groves and trees not included in the list. These lists are not complete, and in the fifth book of Varro's *On the Latin Language* alone, we find more tree places. First, Varro suggests that the Esquiline hill is named after *aesculus*, on account of oak trees planted there by Servius Tullius. He prefers this etymology to the alternative, from *excubiae*, or watchtowers, on account of the Esquiline being a heavily wooded area in his time, home of the Fagutal, and close to the Lares Querquetulani (from *quercus*), the Lucus Mefitis and the temple of Juno Lucina.[15] Varro indicates that the Germalus is named after the brothers Romulus and Remus (*germani*), and has been so named because of the proximity of the Ruminal fig tree, using the tree as a location identifier for the site of the twins' rescue.[16] Later, Varro makes reference to a myrtle grove which had stood at the centre of the Circus Maximus, and an etymology from a myrtle grove (*myrtetum*) that stood Ad Murciae, the contemporary name for the site.[17] Varro tells us that a 'vestige' of this grove was retained at the shrine of Venus Myrtea, which is also known as the Murcia.[18] This small shrine was found 'under the Aventine' and abutted the Circus Maximus.[19] There are other sites not referred to in Varro's or Pliny's tree toponyms, including an alternative name for the Caelian hill: the Mons Querquetulanus, per an antiquarian tradition.[20] These various names, scattered across the ancient city of Rome, remind us of a time before it was a crowded urban jungle, and both monumentalize and lend permanence to Rome's early arboreal layout.

This arboreal city plan is not limited to Rome's larger places, to hills and whole neighbourhoods, and can be found on a much more intimate level, for example in Martial's apartment block, which he names Ad Pirum.[21] As in the example of Ad Gallinas Albas, the name of Livia's villa derived from the omen of the white hens, the usage of *pirus*, or pear tree, strongly suggests that there was a pear tree that grew in or nearby Martial's apartment building. Like the broader place names, such as the *vicus aesculeti*, the usage of *pirus* in the name of Martial's property is evidence that a tree is being used as a geographical identifier, fully embedded in the fabric of Roman life, and Martial uses it here without any requirement to, without any attached symbolism, and without any context to qualify his reference, as we saw in Pliny's reference to the *aesculetum*. This reference from Martial offers an indication of the role of trees in urban planning. They are, evidently, found in residential areas as well as the well-documented urban centres. These residential trees are not famous or important trees – Martial's *pirus* is the only attested pear tree in Rome – but they proliferate in the city, as trees do today, and could be found on street corners throughout Rome, even in less affluent areas such as the Vicus Aesculeti.

The method of navigating the city through the use of historic groves, or vestiges of groves that once stood in a site, through a remembered city rather than an actual one, is common in Varro's tour of Rome, and gives voice to an unspoken dialogue between the wooded cityscape of the past and the monumentalized city of Varro's and Pliny's present.[22] Those trees that do remain, such as the myrtle tree at the shrine of Venus Myrtea, the Lucus Mefitis, or the Ruminal fig, do so because they have been successfully limited to the boundaries established by the city growing around them, evident in Conon's description of the physical boundary placed around the Ruminal, and in Varro's discussion of temples later in *On the Latin Language*.[23] That nature which can accept the limitations imposed upon it can thrive in the monumental cityscape, and will be welcomed within it.

Memory and provenance

Varro's tour of Rome travels through a city which exists only in echoes, and both his and Pliny's lists of tree toponyms allude to a factor which determines the echoes that persist in the city's memory: provenance.

The *aesculetum* is preserved in the Vicus Aesculeti, but is noted by Pliny as being the site of a famous Plebeian political victory, and the Esquiline's oak trees were planted by Servius Tullius. The roots of a place resonate through to its present iteration and influence its standing in cultural memory. Where these roots involve a famous planter or event, we find a firmer anchor than one of loss; there were countless trees that will have been removed for the site of Rome, and only a small fragment are preserved in tree toponyms. The link between the site of Rome and cultural memory is a well-established one in discussions of the ancient city. For Freud, Rome existed simultaneously with itself, and nothing that was within the city was ever destroyed:

> Let us, by a flight of the imagination, suppose that Rome is not a human habitation but a physical entity with a similarly long and copious past – an entity, that is to say, in which nothing that has come into existence will have passed away and all the earlier phases of development exist alongside the later ones.[24]

Edwards has described Freud's Rome as 'time made visible', and explains that this is close to the ancient understanding of the city, where Evander's Rome can coexist with the golden Capitoline he shows to Aeneas.[25] This site is multilayered in the Roman imagination, and the contemporary and archaic sites of Rome coexist in the poem. For Larmour and Spencer, this remembered city is evidence of Rome functioning as a continual site of reception, adapting at key moments in the city's history.[26] This cultural memory is not one that was restricted to text, as we saw in the last section; while Evander's Rome in the *Aeneid* is a good example of two sites coexisting simultaneously on the same spot, Rome's past was also echoed in the city layout, in building and neighbourhood names, and Dupont explores the importance of places in Roman consciences:

> Roman memory, lacking any anchorage in the inspired works of ancient poets, was rooted in the sacred ground of the city. To walk around Rome was to travel through its memory, past Romulus' cabin, Cacus' rock and Egeria's wood. What had happened in these places in former times was not precisely known: there were plenty of stories about them but they differed enormously from one version to the next. What mattered was that these places were sacred, the reasons were less important.[27]

Later, Dupont uses the tree group at the Lacus Curtius, a fig, an olive, and a vine, to give an example of her approach. The Lacus Curtius was a problematic area for any coherent origin, with three separate myths associated with it. However, there was one consistent element, and that is the tree group.[28] For Dupont, it does not matter whether Curtius himself was a Roman or a Sabine, hero or enemy respectively. Instead, she points to the one thing that was known with certainty, and reminds her readers that 'it was essential that each year without fail this and every other sacred site received its due of offerings and prayers'.[29] Bypassing the problematic leap to sacrality – there is no evidence that the Lacus Curtius group was treated as sacred, or of any ritual activity focused on it – we find that the nostalgic association of the site, itself a *lieu de mémoire* by Nora's definition, is more important than the literary accounts of its origin.

In discussing Rome's trees, the idea of memory, and of a city connected with its remembered past as intrinsically as Rome was (and is), is crucial. The landscape changes and alters, is built upon, burnt and restructured in the flashpoints that demand the city become a reception of itself, and there are casualties in this process. By the early Principate, Rome was no longer the wooded land that Aeneas, who never saw Rome, was shown around by Evander, nor were groves like the *aesculetum* on the Campus Martius still present. However, the memories of these groves are preserved in the fabric of the city.

For some trees and groves, like the Lacus Curtius group, the Ruminal fig tree and Romulus' spear, their origin is what gives the trees importance in the city of Rome, while others like the *aesculetum* and Egeria's wood (which will be examined later in this chapter) are remembered for the events that occurred within them. These trees, and the others dotted throughout and echoed in Rome's cityscape, are notable for their age, preserved reminders of a distant past, markers of the city's durability, and this is evident in a passage of Pliny the Elder's *Natural History*, where he discusses the ancient trees of Rome.

Pliny and Rome's ancient trees

Towards the close of his arboreal books in the *Natural History*, Pliny includes an account of the exceptionally old trees of Rome, commenting on the city's place in its surroundings and its role in the landscape's history. To qualify for this catalogue, a tree was required by Pliny to be within the city's boundaries and over 500 years old. Immediately before this list, which is comprised of only four trees, Pliny introduces the theme of 'The age of trees' with a significantly younger olive tree, important for its provenance, since it was planted by Scipio Africanus. The close association of this tree with those in Rome, both in terms of the structure of the *Natural History* and its provenance, encourages it to be read as an equal to the trees within the city boundaries, and as such it will be included here. Pliny's discussion of ancient trees is briefer than we might expect from a usually thorough natural historian and comes within a larger section on the extraordinary trees in the Empire, concluding with Greek trees.[30] The trees included in the Roman section are each notable for a particular characteristic, whether it is age, situation, or provenance (see Table 2).

This account of historical trees is accompanied by an admission of ignorance within the *Natural History*: that there are probably trees in the distant areas of the world, or in the impassable forests which have reached immense ages, and are unknown to Pliny and to mankind as a whole.[31] He treats Rome's ancient trees with great respect, observing their age in relation to the city, and includes a variety of species, which he has made an account of in both his foreign and his native sections earlier in the *Natural History*. Here, he seeks to offer a series

Table 2 The ancient trees catalogued by Pliny the Elder in *Natural History* 16.234–40

Species	Place (Number on map: see Figure 1)	Point of Origin	Time of Origin	Notable Feature	Time of Death
Olive	Scipio's villa at Liternum (with a myrtle of conspicuous size)	Planted by Scipio	Possibly planted while in retirement, between 185 and 183 BCE		Unknown
Lotus (Nettle?)	Precinct of Lucina (11)	Unknown	Unknown, prior to 374 BCE		Unknown
Unknown (*Capillata*)	Unknown	Unknown	Older than the lotus in the precinct of Lucina		Unknown
Lotus (Nettle?)	Volcanal (17)	Dedicated by Romulus from spoils of victory.	753 BCE		Unknown
Cypress	Volcanal (17)	Possibly as above?	753 BCE		54–68 CE

of factual observations with regard to the ancient trees that are found around Rome.

The four trees within Rome are preceded by the olive tree planted by Scipio Africanus, at his estate in Liturnum, on the Campanian coast, at the mouth of the Volturnus river. This tree appears to have been individually unimportant excluding its provenance and age, and is instead part of a larger group, which includes a myrtle tree, noticeable for its (presumably large) size, a cave and a guardian *draco*.[32] The myrtle tree may have been of a similar age and provenance to the olive tree; certainly Pliny's use of *item* implies this. However, the tree most commonly associated with the estate is the olive, since the olive grove on the estate had been restored by Aegialus, the owner when Seneca the Younger sojourned there in the first century CE and wrote to Lucilius.[33] Given the size of this restoration, its depiction in a letter that rails on the topic of luxury, praising Scipio's rejection of it, and its location at the villa of a famous Roman, we can assume that Pliny was aware of Aegialus' continuation of Scipio's garden keeping.

Henderson has offered some indication of a potential second point of importance for this olive tree beyond its provenance in his analysis of Seneca's letter, which quotes an excerpt from Vergil's *Georgics*.[34] The passage in question claims the 'tree which rears itself from dropped seeds grows late, giving shade to later generations'.[35] This quote, which follows Seneca's observation that 'there is none among us [old men] who is not planting an olive grove for their successor', is linked by Henderson as a comment not only on trees in general, but also with a focus on the olive tree at Scipio's estate, later identified by Pliny.[36] This tree was known by Pliny to be particularly durable, and he points to several famous old olive trees in the sections that follow this one, which address trees across the known world. But if the olive as a *genus* was considered to be 'proverbial for the lag between planting and harvesting that makes it a gift for posterity' by Pliny, as Henderson understands Seneca to have believed earlier, then Pliny's inclusion of it here is emblematic of Scipio's concern for the future, both as a part of a grove and as a tree in its own right.[37]

The focus of Pliny's account of Scipio's olive and myrtle trees, complete with the cave and the *draco* that guards Scipio's shade, should be read as the olive tree. The myrtle is subordinated to the olive in the account, appearing afterwards, and reliant upon the verb *durant* from the preceding clause. The olive, meanwhile, is dated by its planting by Scipio, in a move which both Seneca's Vergil and Seneca himself identify as being a dedication to future generations. This approach is similar to Pliny's framing of his account of old trees being preserved by 'human memory', which, if read in conjunction with Seneca's letter and the attitudes of Aegialus, is a transplantation of ideas, and as part of the 'altruistic legacy' identified by Henderson as central to Seneca's account of tree planting.[38]

There is no evidence that Pliny, who lists his sources for his books alongside the contents, ever read this letter by Seneca or Vergil's *Georgics* in the compilation of this book, since these two authors are not named in his list of authorities for Book Sixteen.[39] However, this list is noticeably short, particularly for a book which considers the various natures of forest trees and approaches historical traditions. Unlike the previous book, Book Fifteen, which lists sixty-six individual authorities and deals with fruit-bearing trees, Book Sixteen only has twenty-two listed authorities. Some of the deficit could be accounted for by Locher's assessment of Pliny's contents, laid out in Book One of the *Natural History*. These contents identify, in a formulaic fashion, the 'Total: x facts, investigations, and observations' in each book of the *Natural History*.[40] Locher suggests that these three – *res*, *historiae* and *observationes* – can be identified as three distinct categories for the contents of each book. *Res* suggests 'undocumented factual information without further additions', *historiae* 'historical reminiscence' and *observationes* indicates Pliny's personal experiences.[41] It is unclear where oral histories and human memory fit within this, and this is sure to have been a key aspect in the composition of some sections of the *Natural History*. Pliny also does not indicate what proportion of the facts presented are from each category. However, even if one of these categories was more likely to contain fewer authorities for Pliny to cite than the others, it is still a substantial lapse for the book's bibliography. For Pliny, a man for whom plagiarism amounted to theft and 'the sign of a barren mind', and for whom the sharing of cited information was his foremost duty, this is an unusual omission of evidence.[42] This attitude, which has been explored by Lao in a chapter regarding the treatment of knowledge by Pliny as a thing with financial worth, leaves his lack of authorities for Book Sixteen all the more puzzling.[43]

This curiosity, however, can be somewhat assuaged when we look at the body of Pliny's text in the discussion of Rome's ancient trees. As Hunt has noted, the natural historian is reluctant to cite his sources when discussing the ages of trees, resorting to anonymous citations and impersonal verbs.[44] As a result, we can understand that the crucial aspect of Pliny's understanding of the age of trees is not official source material, but is instead the *memoria humana* which has preserved the stories of the trees' extraordinary ages.

It is important, then, that the trees Pliny refers to in Rome itself are all linked to a story or superstition, or to an artificial location. These are hubs of cultural memory, or *lieux de mémoire*.[45] The lotus tree, for example, formed part of a grove that gave the goddess Lucina her name and is dated to 379 AUC (375 BCE), which is marked out by Pliny as a year in which no magistrates were elected. Similarly, there is the older, religious centre of the Capillata, to which the Vestals' offering of hair is carried.[46] Other trees in Rome include another lotus, found in the Volcanal, whose roots extend below the Forum of Caesar, and is the only tree with a cited authority, Masurius, who dates the tree to be 'of equal age to the city', and now stands alone, following the collapse of the cypress tree next to it, at the end of Nero's reign.[47] One other tree, identified by Pliny as still living in his time in the suburban areas of Rome rather than the city proper in his contents list, stands on the Vatican hill dated to be 'older than the city' by the Etruscan-lettered tablet at its base, which indicated that 'the tree was already deemed venerable then'.[48] As emphasized by the dating of the lotus of Lucina, Pliny dates all these trees (except the hairy lotus) against the city, creating what Hunt has identified as an 'arboreal version of the *ab urbe condita* dating system'.[49] Through establishing this arboreal calendar, Pliny establishes the coexistence and the integration of both city and nature, although not going so far as to suggest a symbiotic relationship, which would have provided an awkward transition into the following book, which focuses on the care of trees and the means through which man might control and exploit the nature around him.

Pliny does establish the historically interconnected world of man and nature with the omen of the cypress tree which 'at the end of Nero's reign, collapsed and was neglected'.[50] He argues that the 'particular association of the cypress tree with Vespasian can be properly understood' if the two omens are read together, and he points to the lotus tree that stood next to the Volcanal cypress. The spread of this tree's roots, McCulloch states, represents the 'course of Roman history from the founding of the city up to the close of Nero's principate, when the cypress tree fell down and was left neglected', and the resurgence of the cypress on Vespasian's estate symbolizes a re-founding of Rome under the new Emperor.[51] However, Tacitus neglects to mention the Volcanal cypress in his account of the close of Nero's reign and prioritizes the *ficus Ruminalis* in the Forum and its withering.[52] The twin omens, of Tacitus' fig tree in the Forum and Pliny's cypress in the Volcanal, could be read together as Roman nature rejecting Roman rule. This disconnect between nature and man in Nero's reign is made even more apparent from Pliny's final word of the account of Rome's trees: *neglecta*.

The cypress tree, old as the city, lies neglected and it is on this note that Pliny chooses to end his account of Rome's old trees, moving to old trees outside of the city. Having advocated the integration of trees with the city, emphasizing their coexistence by dating them against each other and linking them to religions at the heart of Roman society with the Vestals, he closes his account with a natural world that is isolated from the city but still reflecting it, continuing its link to human memory. The catalogue has a symmetry to it, again augmented by Seneca's letter and his description of Scipio Africanus' bath house. Scipio was, unlike Nero, a paragon of the Stoic rejection of luxury, and his bath house is extremely modest, rejecting the fashions which Seneca deemed overly luxurious.[53] Through comparing the beginning and end of Pliny's catalogue of trees, we can see that the trees addressed are representative of the men who control them. The olives, planted by Scipio, secure a harvest for future generations, fulfilling their duty both to act as vessels of a memory passed from human to human, and to provide food. Meanwhile, the cypress, which has stood for the duration of the city, harmoniously growing alongside it, collapses toward the end of the luxurious reign of Nero, having been neglected by the master of the city. In this catalogue of Rome's oldest trees, then, Pliny provides us with a synopsized view of Rome's changing relationship with trees, from the ideal of his *exemplum* Scipio to the hero's antithesis, Nero.

A dynastic grove

If individual trees like Scipio's olive can act as repositories of memory and can outlast the life of the planter, then the longer lifespan of a grove might be expected to represent a memory for a longer period of time. The Julio-Claudian laurel grove at Ad Gallinas Albas, Livia's villa outside of Rome, lasted the duration of the dynasty, from 39 or 38 BCE to 68 CE, when Suetonius and Cassius Dio tell us it withered.[54] This grove had survived throughout this dynasty until its fall, and its provenance was a key factor in its preservation: it was grown from a laurel branch clutched in the beak of a reprieved hen, fallen from the talons of an eagle into Livia's lap. The hen was saved by Livia and the branch planted, from which a flock flourished and a grove was grown respectively.[55] These laurels provided subsequent triumphal branches for the Julio-Claudian dynasty, and withered to the root towards the end of Nero's (abruptly coppiced) life.

A number of possible locations have been mooted for the laurel grove of the Caesars within the Ad Gallinas Albas villa, which contains a garden terrace, a small internal garden, a central courtyard space, and the well-known subterranean garden room.[56] The most likely location for the laurel grove is the garden terrace, a 74m × 74m space bounded with double-aisled porticoes on three of its four sides. On the fourth southeast-facing side, there is now a steep drop overlooking the Via Flaminia towards the city of Rome, and it is in part because of the dominance of its environs that this is the most commonly proposed location.[57] Although farming activity in the area has disrupted the ancient levels, a number of fragmented pots for planting (*ollae perforatae*) and molluscs indicate that the garden terrace was populated with a large number of pots.[58] Since laurel trees grow well in pots, it could be easily surmised that these pots held the laurels of the Julio-Claudian laurel grove, if we assume that the laurel grove was indeed on the garden terrace, as has been regularly argued.[59]

The laurel grove of the Caesars maintained consistency throughout the dynasty, and its relevance was sustained through the imperial practice of taking branches of the first tree and using them for triumphal crowns and for the laurel branch carried by the emperor in a triumphal procession.[60] After this, accounts diverge. According to Suetonius, the branch was then propagated at Ad Gallinas Albas, and the new tree added to the grove. He goes on to explain that every time an emperor was approaching death, the tree they had grown withered too.[61] In Pliny's account, the branch was planted in an undisclosed location, and the laurel woods (he uses *silvae*) that grow from them still exist in his time, named after the emperor who planted the first tree. He reports that the original grove has thrived since it was first planted, and does not include the withering of the original laurel grove at Ad Gallinas Albas in his version.[62] In both accounts, the continuity of the groves is maintained, and the provenance of both the original and any subsequent plantings is paramount. Like Scipio's olive, the provenance of the tree is important, although the laurel grove also comes with added features, which make it more notable than its provenance alone. By containing the grove within a private residence and making triumphal ornaments exclusively from this grove, the Julio-Claudians geographically annexed the imperial claim to the triumphal procession.[63] This physical manifestation of the political dominance of Augustus' family would have been further exemplified by the position of the grove on a hill, if we are to take the identification of the garden terrace as an accurate location.

It has been suggested that the positioning of the grove on a hill resembles a sanctuary-like topography, and echoes another Augustan grove, also in pots, on the hill at Nikopolis, overlooking Actium.[64] This hill functioned as a sacred site, on which a dwelling-place of Apollo was set up in honour of the spot on which Octavian pitched his tent the night before the battle of Actium. Inside this dwelling-place, terracotta planting pots were found.[65] There is no evidence to link the hill of the Ad Gallinas Albas *lauretum* to Apollo, and the assertion that the *lauretum* was to be associated with the Julio-Claudians is more plausible. Augustus made several attempts to co-opt the laurel as 'his' plant, and the placement of the laurel grove at the villa of Livia, a central hub of the Julio-Claudian power base, would have done exactly that, demonstrating the continued renewal and resurgence of the dynasty.[66] Through its dominant position on the Via Flaminia, then, both spectating on and being spectated by the passers-by on a major route into and out of Rome, the Julio-Claudian *lauretum* acts to present the deep association between triumph and Julio-Claudians through the integration of the laurel into the Julio-Claudian house as well as its household. When combined with the isolation of the trees from the people passing below, tantalizingly out of reach atop a hill and in a private dwelling, the trees represent the exclusive rights to the triumphal procession of the Julio-Claudian dynasty.

The laurels in the *lauretum* are not the only dynastic trees, nor the only tree which portended the future of either individuals or dynasties in the first century of the Principate. An oak prophesied the future of Vespasian and his two siblings, growing out branches to mimic the lives of the three individuals on the occasion of each of their births: a small branch which died quickly for Vespasian's short-lived older sister; a vigorous second branch to represent the life of Vespasian's generally successful brother; and a tree-like branch to stand for Vespasian himself.[67] Unlike the Julio-Claudian *lauretum*, there is no archaeological evidence for this tree, and no confusion around whom this oak tree is sacred to, as Suetonius directly informs his readers that it was sacred to Mars. This is in itself unexpected, since the oak tree is more commonly associated with Jupiter in the Roman world, and Mars has no known tree associated with him. An individual tree is a suitable totem for the much shorter Flavian dynasty, which only passed from father to son to brother. Meanwhile, the longer lifespan of the grove, combined with the inaccessibility and control able to be exerted by its position in a private villa, allow for this communication of power to be maintained consistently across multiple generations.

A corrupted grove

Not all groves were as fortunate as the one at Ad Gallinas Albas, protected by its position in a private villa, and groves in public spaces were considerably more vulnerable, even when protected by a valuable provenance, rooted in Rome's early history. An example of this can be found just outside of Rome, at the Camenae grove near the Porta Capena, the fragility of which is discussed by Juvenal in the first century CE. In an effort to prevent damage to groves, especially to sacred ones, some protections were put in place through Italian law, although this was again not without its own challenges, which have already been discussed above. These ranged from a lack of clarity on the nature of violations, to apparent confusion as to where a grove's boundaries lay, and while the topos of an unviolated woodland is common in depictions of trees and groves in Latin literature, whether or not a grove had been violated was ambiguous. However, the consequences of violating a grove could be severe, as an extreme law found in Festus' epitome of Flaccus' dictionary demonstrates: 'A pre-eminent grove (*capitalis lucus*), where, if anyone violates it, it is cleansed by the head of the violator.'[68] When considering this brutal law, Dowden relates it to the reality of 'civilised lawgiving', in which such a drastic measure as Festus offers here is replaced by a more reasonable fine, as found in the Spoleto and Trevi inscriptions.[69] Hunt, meanwhile, cautions against the establishment of a universal law based on these two different laws, reminding us that the *capitalis lucus* is not just any grove, it is an unusual one.[70] However, like the groves Ovid's shepherd must simply hope they have not violated, the *capitalis lucus* lacks a clear definition in ancient sources, and the shepherd must simply hope that they have escaped this more severe punishment and still pray for forgiveness for any inadvertent violation. While the law deals with explicit physical actions, there were other ways a grove could be changed, and could evolve in response to the changing times.

The Camenae grove

A little distance outside of Rome, we find a public grove which has, on the face of it, a similar historic provenance and religious status as the Julio-Claudian laurel grove. On the Appian Way, just past the Porta Capena, there lay the grove of the Camenae, an alternative name for the Muses in Roman literature, or perhaps for local goddesses of the springs within the grove.[71] This grove, according to both Livy (who is the source for the dedication to the Camenae) and Juvenal, was the fabled meeting point of the king Numa with the nymph Egeria.[72]

This provenance is not a firm one, and it is apparent from Livy's account that he regards this story more as a cunning artifice than an actual occurrence, relating that Numa 'pretended' to meet with Egeria in order to gain the authority that would allow him to instil the fear of the gods into his people.[73] This scepticism is continued throughout Livy's description of the meetings between Numa and Egeria: he later describes Numa making trips to the grove 'as if to meet the goddess'.[74] This scepticism surrounding the grove's provenance may help explain why it had been entirely overtaken by the time that Juvenal and his friend Umbricius visit it, as Umbricius leaves Rome at the close of the first century CE:

> Here, where Numa met his mistress, Egeria, by moonlight,
> Now the grove, the sacred spring and the temples are leased

To the Jews, with their hay-lined baskets and their furniture;
For every tree has been ordered to pay its rent to the people.
The Camenae have been ejected, and the wood now begs for scraps.[75]

This sacred grove, a *nemus* for the Camenae, but a *silva* without them, has been altered from its religious status, and is now somewhat divorced from its provenance. In looking at the grove, we see a formerly religious space, one of the oldest in Rome, dating back at least to the second king, but now isolated from the city, and forced to pay rent (*mercedem*). It is unclear why the rent is due, or if it is required for the continuation of the grove's lifespan, although Courtney theorizes that Juvenal is suggesting that the trees are having to beg for money from the Jews, like the Roman paupers such as Umbricius.[76] That they are begging (*mendicat*) is obvious, and the implication is that a formerly noble Roman grove has been polluted by the foreign influence, which serves not only to isolate it from Rome, but also to isolate Rome within its surroundings. This latter point is evident through Umbricius' diatribe, which forms the bulk of the poem: he is leaving Rome because it is no longer the Rome he recognizes, and the grove's isolation from the gods serves to demonstrate its isolating influence on Rome.

However, the grove's provenance is not entirely overridden, the sacred springs have been retained, the temples still stand, and most importantly, Juvenal still knows the grove for its provenance, and the valley bears Egeria's name (3.17). Juvenal is even aware of the shady nature of this provenance, with a gentle nod to the fakery of the caves, and the artificiality of the marble covering the native tufa (3.17–20). The grove remains as it was originally – a place of deception and trickery, where a veneer is applied to make activities seem more palatable to the immediate audience. As the grove evolves in Juvenal's poetry, it retains elements of its past, but is influenced by its inhabitants and their interactions with and within the space. And this is the crux of Juvenal's distaste throughout the poem, that Rome has changed as a whole, and to the problem of provenance lending publicly accessible spaces credibility.

The grove of the Camenae has evolved since it was commemorated as Egeria's and Numa's meeting place, and this highlights the challenge of maintaining the integrity of an ill-defined, publicly accessible space. Unlike the Julio-Claudian laurel grove, able to be static in a private venue, the Camenae grove is subject to the constant development of Rome, and it is this development that prompts its evolution from the site of meetings that probably never happened but were nevertheless formative in Rome's early myth-history to the Jewish market that so upsets Juvenal and Umbricius.

***

Rome's cityscape in the late Republic and early Principate was inextricably intertwined with its arboreal past. From idealized forest landscapes in Vergil's *Aeneid* and the neighbourhood names of demolished groves, to the monumental trees and groves that still stood in Pliny's city, the early landscape of the ancient city was not forgotten, and was in fact preserved. In some cases, this preservation was a result of establishing hard boundaries around a tree, as in the case of Romulus' spear, enclosed by a fence, and in other instances trees could be privatized, like the Julio-Claudian laurel grove.

Most of Rome's arboreal cityscape did not exist in stasis, and grew and changed with the times. As new laurel groves were planted by triumphing emperors, Rome's monumental trees and groves grew in number, and they changed as the city did. The evolution of the Camenae grove is a gradual one, a journey of seven hundred years, in response to the gradual abandonment of the grove as a shrine and the growth of Rome's Jewish population, and by Juvenal's time the arboreal landscape around the Porta Capena has shifted. Changes were not always slow, and those changes that had laws made against them were typically much more sudden and much more violent, speaking to the physical vulnerability of a grove to an axe. While the changes were often unclear, demonstrated by Ovid's advice to the shepherd, when one of Rome's trees fell it could be shown as symptomatic of the city's condition at the time. When the Julio-Claudian laurel grove died, it echoed the death of the dynasty, and the cypress tree that fell in Nero's reign reflected the disharmony between the city of Rome and the site of Rome under his rule. Rome's arboreal landscape, then, reflected both Rome's past and its present, carrying memories of the city's history through to its current population, and reacting to the changes in the city as it grew around it and as new trees were introduced.

2

Bringing Trees to Rome

Pliny's *Natural History*, written in the latter half of the first century CE, catalogues and collates all the known trees of the world across six books (Books Twelve to Seventeen). Through this catalogue, which is not one compiled without bias, some of Pliny's focuses become apparent: the need to explore and evaluate the use and abuse of nature as a resource, the exertion of power and control over the natural world, and Pliny's desire to preserve his idea of Romanness – rejecting foreign imports as totems of *luxuria*. These cultural influences are evidenced throughout the *Natural History*, a work of such extensive scope that it combines the symbolic and cultural value of trees with their practical application. This has not always translated to modern approaches to Latin literature, which treat most texts as approaching one aspect or another: Columella's *On Trees* and *On Rural Things* are considered practical handbooks, while Vergil's *Georgics* are regarded as dealing with the symbolic aspects of trees.[1]

From the destruction of citrus trees in Mauretania for tables to the plane tree's shade, luxury and overexploitation of natural resources are balanced against the utility of an object, and the provenance of a luxurious tree such as the plane is not forgotten. Meanwhile, at the outer edges of Roman territories, non-Roman trees that cannot be naturalized to the city thrive, and Pliny must contend with this within his own understanding of Roman supremacy over nature. The *Natural History* itself is an exertion of control over nature, an attempt to direct the disparate resources into a coherent structure. Throughout his account of the known arboreal world of Rome's territories and beyond, Pliny wrestles with conflicts. Utility battles against luxury, with trade standing on the sideline, and the opposition of Roman and non-Roman is evident in the structure of the books. These conflicts affect how trees are introduced to

Romans and how they are then used in the city, and this chapter will examine how they play out in the arboreal books.

Utility and luxury in Pliny's *Natural History*

Through the exploitation and control of a landscape, a society can exploit the utility of nature, and this is a common trope of the *Natural History*, which places utility in direct contest with luxury, as in a discussion on fragrances in Book Twenty-One: 'These days, nature and luxury are matched together and are at war with each other.'[2] In Books Twelve to Sixteen alone, Pliny employs the categories *usus*, *utari* and *utilitas* 103 times, and thus directs his readers towards his way of viewing the natural world – as a resource. The first indication we have of his preference for utility, and what *utilitas* entails, is in the prefatory letter, which accompanied the *Natural History* and dedicated the books to their recipient, Titus. Here, Pliny relates that he favours those who perform in spite of difficulties and aim to give *utilitas* over those who succumb to giving pleasure (*iuvandi*). To aid Titus in discerning his meaning, Pliny uses an example, that of Livy, who began a now lost volume of *Ab urbe condita* with an admission that he had achieved everything he had desired, and was now writing primarily to sustain his own mind.[3] While this was perhaps not the intent of Livy when he stated that he intended his readers to find *exempla* in his histories, Pliny takes the historian's remarks to indicate that he was writing for the good of the Roman people, and to further their glory.[4] As a result, the focus on utility throughout the *Natural History* can be identified as a focus on social utility rather than a strictly practical utility, as De Oliveira has done.[5] This moves emphasis towards elements such as commercial value and historical provenance, the latter of which we have already seen is prevalent in Roman understandings of the trees around them.

Toward the end of the arboreal books, Pliny qualifies the utilities of trees, and gives them an order of importance:

> For there are some entirely wild trees, and some more assimilated to city life (*urbaniores*), since it is customary to distinguish them by these names: the latter, which benefit humans by fruit or some other gift, and shade, may not inappropriately be called urbane (*urbanae*).[6]

As well as linking utility with the city, Pliny identifies that the utilities of trees are as follows:

> (i) to feed humans (a basic function of trees, and their original purpose across Roman literature, from the acorns in Lucretius' *De rerum natura* to the oak trees dripping honey in Ovid's *Metamorphoses*);[7]

> (ii) to provide some other gift, an example of which would be timber, which Pliny details at the start of the arboreal books to be used for the construction of ships, buildings, and statues;[8]

> and (iii) to offer shade, which is the least noteworthy utility and must be found alongside another. It is, however, still counted by the author in spite of his opinions regarding the plane, which was 'imported only for shade'.[9]

By conducting a series of case studies around these three utilities, the moral challenges faced when introducing, growing and using trees in Pliny's philosophy will become apparent. In particular, we will examine how Pliny balances social utility with luxury, and the circumstances in which luxury can be given room to manoeuvre.

The fruit of the vine

The primary utility of trees in benefiting mankind is to provide fruit, and this is the topic of two books of the *Natural History*. The first tree to be included in this account of fruit-bearing trees is the vine. As the sole focus for the fourteenth book of the *Natural History*, the vine offers a contained yet expansive insight into Pliny's approach to the utility of a tree, and it is a tree that Pliny presents as facing its own struggle with luxury (it can grow excessively, leading to its own destruction).[10] Despite this struggle, or perhaps because of man's cultivation and care in helping the vine overcome the dangers of luxury, Pliny identifies it as a champion for Italian supremacy, especially in the scent it produces when it blossoms, which surpasses all the 'good things' in the world.[11] Scent is a secondary utility in Pliny's classification system, and Pliny moves to the fruits produced by the vine, the varieties of the vine, their wines, history, and alternatives for the remainder of Book Fourteen.

The typical second purpose of a tree, timber, is also explored in Pliny's treatment of the vine in the earlier part of Book Fourteen. Vine timber, Pliny tells us, lasts without decay for 'many ages', and has historically been used for a number of long-lasting items, from a statue of Jupiter to columns and staircases, all made of single pieces of vine wood. As has already been mentioned, this timber is the longest surviving of all, although Pliny goes on to clarify that these timbers are 'from the woods' (*ex silvestribus*), and moves his discussion away from the wild vine to the cultivated one.[12] This is a deliberate choice from Pliny, who has directed his readers at the start of the fourteenth book to agriculture and the cultivated vine as opposed to the timber of the uncultivated vine.

The cultivated vine is the primary focus of Book Fourteen, and it is the cultivated vine that is most at risk from luxury and the destructive excessive growth that Pliny describes in Book Seventeen. Here, Pliny explains that the cultivated vine requires the care of man to keep it from over-reaching as it luxuriates destructively. In this example, the vine tree prioritizes its growth over the production of fruit, and in doing so causes its own demise. As Wallace-Hadrill has noted, this luxury is markedly different from that of trees in blossom, which cause no harm to themselves or others by blossoming, and the vine needs controlling by human hand, much like the corn which is excessively fertile, causing the head to collapse under its own weight.[13] It is apparent in these examples that there is a limit to acceptable utility in a plant in Pliny's *Natural History*, and it is when that limit is transgressed that man must intervene, and rein nature in.

Agriculture is the rein that Pliny suggests, and the opening of Book Fourteen points to a decline in early studies of agriculture and a rise in the cultivation of greed.[14] In the same section of Book Seventeen that he criticizes the luxuriating vine, he provides a detailed account of how to care for it, and the limits that ought to be placed upon the plant, while the corn is to be left available to be grazed on by flocks, as a remedy to its excessive growth. By framing his argument for agriculture in the context of fruit trees, and of a tree that is (unusually for the *Natural History*) beneficial in both cultivated and uncultivated varieties, Pliny is making the case for directed agriculture, and for the efficient exploitation of key aspects of a crop's utility, in this instance the grape grown from the vine.

The timber of the citrus

In ranking timber, Pliny prioritizes longevity, historical importance, quantity of timber produced, and financial value. He counts the vine's timber as valuable from its history. Pliny links its identification as a tree in 'the early days' (*apud priscos*) to its use in a series of ancient items: a statue of Jupiter at Piombino, a bowl at Marseilles, the pillars of the temple of Juno at Metapontum and finally a staircase in the temple of Diana at Ephesus, which ascends to the roof.[15] Despite its brief appearance in Pliny's book on the vine, timber remains a key element of judging a tree's worth throughout the *Natural History*, and Pliny dedicates a portion of Book Sixteen to trees whose wood is valued.[16] This section, which follows a discourse on the benefits of a tree's pitch and resin, prioritizes timber in every tree that has not until this point been discussed.[17]

Historical importance and quantity of timber are both key factors in the first tree of Pliny's account of the timber trees: the ash. This tree is identified by Pliny as being the 'most productive of all', and has had attention brought to it by Homer, in its use for the spear of Achilles.[18] Immediately following these remarks, and apparently as an aside, Pliny advises caution to buyers of cedar timber: the ash grown on Ida in the Troad can appear to be cedar when stripped of bark.[19] Without the further context of the *Natural History*, this comment comes without warning, and might surprise a cursory reader, as Pliny anticipates most to be.[20] However, as we explore the *Natural History* further, Pliny's financial concern becomes more apparent, and it is especially evident in his accounting of the cost of citrus wood.

Wallace-Hadrill argues that it was Pliny's contention that 'the further you have to go for it, whether underwater, underground, or to the far east, and the more it costs, the less natural it can be'.[21] This observation, which comes within a comparison of nature and luxury, the one identified by its simplicity and cheapness, the other by its complexity and dearness, suggests that Pliny's rejection of luxury would have caused some issues with the wider cultural tradition in which he wrote, where trade and the import of foreign goods had become of paramount importance to the Roman ruling class.[22] Symptomatic of the growing importance of trade was Pliny's scrupulous account keeping of the amount spent by aristocrats over the past century on wooden tables. These tables, made of citrus wood, were a status symbol, and were owned by a number of famous, wealthy, or famous and wealthy Romans in the late Republic and early Imperial period. The tree, which had been known to Homer as an aromatic wood burnt on Calypso's fire,[23] is north African in origin, and was also known to Theophrastus, implying that it had been valued as an import for centuries before Pliny wrote the *Natural History*, and before the Roman aristocracy took it on as a status symbol.[24] The timber was prized for its decorative and structural qualities, both of which are described in intricate detail by Pliny.[25] This description does not focus on the greedy overexploitation of the landscape, which led to the obliteration of Mauretania's supply, and is more concerned by the nature of the timber, although this too could have been a sticking point for Pliny, who chastized the vine for similarly over-luxuriating towards its own destruction.

Cato was the first Roman to rail against citrus wood, denouncing it as being Carthaginian, a powerful invective from the senator, as reported by Festus.[26] Varro comments in a similar vein, preferring the simplicity of an old villa to the new one he describes at Reate, which is bedecked in citrus and gold, alongside a number of other equally luxurious features, which he views as being counter to the original design of the villa as a simple farmstead.[27]

By the time of Pliny's writing, after the tree had been used in a triumphal procession by Caesar,[28] citrus wood tables had become popular in Rome, and the tree became synonymous with over-indulgence for the natural historian.[29] Pliny begins his diatribe against the citrus wood table with an observation and a comparison between the jewels of women and the citrus tables of men. This comment is not one of Pliny's own devising, but is instead anecdotal, taken from the sayings of the time: 'table-madness, which women use as a retort against men on behalf of their pearls.'[30] From this point, Pliny enters into a list of well-known citrus tables, opening with Cicero's table, worth half a million sesterces, a fact which Pliny viewed as being all the more remarkable because the orator was known to struggle to keep up with the aristocracy.[31] What follows is an impressive account of the tables in the empire, with the amounts spent on them or their worth at the time. Pliny highlights the largest table he knows of, Ptolemy's, which was formed of two semi-circles joined together almost seamlessly, and was four and a half feet in diameter and three inches thick, but spends far more time discussing the tables of Tiberius and his freedman, Nonius.[32] Nonius' table, at almost four foot wide and one foot deep, is larger in volume than Ptolemy's, and made from one solid sheet of citrus wood. Meanwhile, Tiberius' table, while impressively large, is not solid citrus, having been covered by a veneer of the wood. Pliny derides the practice of veneering wood later in the *Natural History*, but explicitly targets the practice of veneering wood with tortoiseshell designed to appear like wood. His open disdain for such fashion statements, when the only goal is to increase expense at the cost of maintaining the table's original fabric is typical of his rejection of luxury, which revolves around an embrace of all things natural.[33]

Veneering was to become more common in Pliny's time, and the vast tables of the early first century CE and before had become a thing of the past: the Mauretanian citrus, the best variety of citrus timber, had been exhausted.[34] It is on this note that he finishes his accounting of the fabulously expensive tables in the Roman Empire.[35] Just as the cypress tree collapsed in Rome after the city's overindulgence, so too does the supply of citrus timber, which is not quickly restored: Meiggs estimates that to reach a diameter of four feet, necessary for Nonius' table, required a growth of approximately 200 years.[36] The extent to which this will have impacted the country of Mauretania, the home of this citrus and modern-day Morocco, is only evident in the accounts of authors such as Lucan, who reveals that the timber is the only source of wealth to the Mauretanian people.[37] Like the vine that piqued Wallace-Hadrill's interest in the excess of natural things, so too has the citrus over-reached itself, and tempted Romans to, as Lucan tells us, 'seek dishes and tables from the end of the earth.'[38] And even the absolute Stoic, Seneca, was known to have succumbed to this temptation, having furnished his house with hundreds of luxurious tables.[39]

Pliny's account of the table madness that had gripped Rome's aristocracy includes instructions on how to detect quality in the tables' manufacture, and the price that one could have expected to pay for the genuine product. This concern for authenticity, and desire for buyers to be purchasing the real thing instead of a counterfeit, is mirrored in the advice Pliny gave on the stripped timber of the ash tree and its similarity to cedar in appearance. In this instance, Pliny appears to have prioritized the purchasing of the tables over the moral degradation, and the gluttony of luxury that it will inevitably bring.

However, it is not simply a case of trade (*commercium*) outweighing *luxuria*, nor is Pliny dismissing the luxury of the tables with a passing witty remark about 'table madness', although this statement does do something to trivialize the issue of luxurious imports to Rome in particular. The overexploitation of the citrus trees does obviously upset Pliny, but he appears more enamoured by the tables, as evidenced by his lengthy account of their desirable qualities.[40] The tables are also a hallmark of a luxurious life, and there are only a few things that suggest such a life in a more apparent manner than the citrus tree, according to Pliny, who, after his table discourse, turns to the tree itself, although he remains distracted by the tables, closing his description of the citrus tree with a statement as to their novelty.[41] Lao, in her essay on Pliny's understanding of luxury, points to the creation of an 'exchange economy' in the *Natural History*, and Pliny's quasi-account-keeping of both his sources and his descriptions of luxurious items.[42] She advises her readers to treat Pliny's text as an inventory of the world, cataloguing nature according to the worth of each individual item within it, and she attempts to move away from a purely imperialistic approach to reading the *Natural History*. Flagging previous explorations of the place of *luxuria* in Pliny's philosophy, which is typically characterized by Pliny's negative interactions with it, Lao highlights the joint roles of *commercium* and *luxuria* in Pliny's inventory of the natural world.[43] She presents the knowledge that he has collated in the books of the inventory as a luxury in itself, and draws on Pliny's own presentation of it, couched in the language of commerce, which is used to discuss luxury in equal measure.[44] Lao's understanding from this is that Pliny's view of commerce and luxury is one of balance, that the benefit of the former can offset the detriment of the latter, and he demonstrates this in his financial accounting of foreign and luxurious produce at the going market rate.[45] While Lao directs us to the lengthy account keeping in Book Twelve, highlighting the continual detail regarding price, with minimal focus on other aspects of the foreign trees, she could have easily directed her readers to the scrupulous accounts of the citrus wood tables and the prices which had historically been paid for them.[46]

Beagon looks to Seneca for an answer to the conflict between *commercium* and *luxuria* within Pliny's writing, and reminds us that *commercium* is an essential part of Roman Stoicism, a system of ethics to which Pliny loosely subscribes. Seneca tells us that *commercium* is crucial to the establishment of the one-world state that Stoicism imagines, and Beagon extends this to explore the use of trade as a 'prime means of promoting more general communications'.[47]

By communications, Beagon means *commercium* in the most general sense, ranging from the business of trade to the business of war, and as with *luxuria*, Pliny could not, and does not, offer a wholesale condemnation, instead singling out some forms of *luxuria* as his focus. In this, the citrus tables present a number of dilemmas for Pliny: they are a luxurious item, although the term *luxuria* is never applied to them, but benefit the Roman Empire through trade, while being unavoidably foreign in origin. Further to this, they represent the overindulgence of mankind in their natural surroundings, having so completely deforested the area that even after Pliny's discerning description of the key qualities to look for in a citrus wood table, he places those made of a single trunk on an equal footing with those made of multiple trunks.[48] As a result, he cannot treat this item, the hallmark of a luxurious life, as harshly as he treats the tortoiseshell veneer that was so popular in Nero's reign. It is, after all, natural, and is nature being utilized to benefit man through the trade opportunities and financial benefits it represents, and which is Pliny's chosen focus as he runs through the historic owners of such tables.

Commercial concerns resonate throughout the trees and timber sections of the *Natural History*, and Pliny's tone remains similar, inventorying the world for prospective buyers. He advises, for example, to coat timber in cedar oil, 'lest it suffer maggots or decay'.[49] Later, he tells of historic lengths of timber, such as the largest ever to be seen in Rome which was used in the construction of Nero's amphitheatre of 59 CE, and exhibited by Tiberius on the bridge for the *naumachia*:

> It is believed that the largest tree to be seen in Rome to this day was that which Tiberius displayed as a marvel on the bridge at that same *naumachia* mentioned earlier (at 16.190), having brought it back with all the other timber, and it remained until Nero's amphitheatre. It was a timber of larch 120 feet long, and two feet thick. From this, the scarcely believable height of the tree could be understood, by measuring from base to top.[50]

There is no discussion of luxury in this example, and the incredible lengths of timber themselves draw no criticism from Pliny in this section. Instead, he is focused on the extraordinary nature of the trees that produced such timbers, and nature's ability to produce such a large tree. Unlike in his despair at the deforested citrus, there is no appreciation of the limited supply of such trees required to produce these timbers in the moment, and awe takes over.

The shade of the plane

Pliny opens the arboreal books of the *Natural History* with the plane tree, after a section on the utilities of trees, and an anecdote of the first Gallic invasion of Italy (a Gaul named Helico had taken some figs, grapes, oil and wine back home with him, and wanting more of them is a perfectly reasonable reason for war, according to Pliny). In direct contrast to the two chief utilities that Pliny identifies (food and timber), the plane is presented as imported solely for the sake of shade.[51] He invites the surprise of his readers, and tells them it is justified, before offering a potted history of the plane's journey to Italy, which came via Sicily as decorative trees, first to provide shade over the tomb of Diomedes on the island of San Nicola in the Ionian Sea and then to Sicily either for general planting or to shade the palace of Dionysius I of Syracuse in the early fourth century BCE. From here, the plane spread across Europe, and Pliny notes that it has travelled as far as Belgium, and that the tribes there must pay rent for their shade.

Shade is a third-level utility in Pliny's classification of utilities laid out at the start of this section, and needs to be included with another utility to be counted as one. The plane is only found used for something other than shade in two places in the *Natural History*. The oil from its berry is used for lamps,[52] while it has a range of medicinal properties in its seed pods, leaves, bark and flowers.[53] These limited utilities are not enough to warrant its rapid spread across the Italian peninsula, and Pliny refrains from any praise of the plane in these passages – the berry's oil is only used for lamps in scarcity – and the plane remains a tree primarily known for its shade.[54]

When Pliny deals with a plane tree that provides an excessive amount of shade, his invective against luxury returns full force. The Gortynian plane tree is an evergreen deciduous plane tree (possibly the *Platanus orientalis var. cretican* L.), and the first one is counted among Pliny's famous plane trees at the start of Book Twelve.[55] It has an aetiology myth attached to it, which Pliny derides as being inauthentic (since a tree of the same species is on Cyprus), and was the subject of propagation as a 'novelty'. After it was discovered that these propagated trees were also evergreen, the tree was taken up outside of Crete, and was imported to Italy during the reign of Claudius by an anonymous Thessalian eunuch who had moved from being a freedman of Marcellus Aeserminus' household to one of the emperor's freedmen. This is a move that

Pliny ascribes to a desire for power above all else, and is a subject of criticism for him. His true focus, though, is on the intentional breeding of an evergreen plane tree, since 'there is nothing better about [the plane] than it shading from the sun in the summer and letting it in in winter'. The evergreen trees, he tells us, are 'monsters' (*portenta*) that still exist in Italy alongside those he seems to prefer, which Italy 'has conceived for itself'. In this new variety of plane tree (it was introduced during Pliny's lifetime), even the tertiary utility that Pliny tells us the tree was imported for has been removed, and the tree has become an aesthetic import, and one without any of the commercial benefit, an underpinning feature of social utility, that was found in the citrus tables.

A fundamental aspect of the contest between luxury and utility in the *Natural History*, especially in the natural world, is balancing the two. De Oliveira directs us to consider utility not only in practical terms, but in social terms as well. As a result, practical utility is balanced with commercial and cultural benefit, in the trade value of a tree and its timber, and the historical significance of the tree. For the vine, all three aspects of social utility – practical utility, commercial value and cultural benefit – come together in Pliny's *Natural History*. The citrus and the plane are more problematic imports, and show some of the moral challenges of introducing trees to Roman and Italian society within Pliny's philosophy. Pliny values woods with a historic utility, from the statues, pillars and staircases from the vine's timber, to the specific yet mythological utility of the ash, as Achilles' spear. By historicizing these timbers, he confers value onto them, a value which is lost in the Gortynian plane's counterfeit aetiology. This historical value can also be seen in the extraordinary lengths of timber, and in the vast citrus tables, which echo the trees which made them. For the citrus tables, however, commercial benefit is king, and the moral challenge of balancing utility and luxury in an import is made significantly easier by the immense value of the final product.

The structure of Pliny's *Natural History*

Contest and conquest is a running theme of the *Natural History*, most apparent in the continued balancing act of utility and luxury. A push for control over the natural world is evident in the structure of the *Natural History*, alongside a desire to introduce the foreign world to Rome. Murphy has proposed that the *Natural History* seeks to define things by opposition and contrast,[56] and one of the central oppositions in the *Natural History* is between Roman and non-Roman, with Roman power being the uniting force behind the world. The praise of Roman power as this uniting force is a theme in the arboreal books, particularly in Pliny's invective against luxury at the opening of Book Fourteen.[57] This leads to the *Natural History* having an imperialist and triumphalist tone, which has featured in a number of modern commentaries on Pliny's wide-ranging work.[58] However, Pliny's writing has also been criticized for its disparate nature and apparent lack of structure, as well as the frequent digressions (although Pliny does advise Titus in his prefatory letter that there will be no digressions).[59]

Pliny includes a list of contents for the six books devoted to the role of trees in the ancient world, as he does for the other thirty books of the *Natural History*. This contents list, translated in Appendix One and labelled according to the categories of Trees, Fruit/Other Produce, Historical References, and General/Other, is commonly presented as the 'first book', and was intended by Pliny to save his patron (the future emperor Titus) time. To do this, Pliny identifies the major topic of each book, which is then divided into sub-topics, to prevent Titus from having to read the entirety of the *Natural History*.[60] The six arboreal books, Books Twelve to Seventeen, are commonly listed as plant books alongside the more floral Books Eighteen and Nineteen, and even when the books are distilled into their simplest topics (see Table 3), there is evidence

Table 3 Brief summary of the content of Books Twelve to Seventeen of Pliny's *Natural History*

Book Twelve	Overview of trees; Indian and Far-Eastern trees.
Book Thirteen	Near-Eastern and African trees and their products (perfumes and papyrus); Greek trees.
Book Fourteen	Vines and wines.
Book Fifteen	Fruit-bearing trees, focusing on the olive, the myrtle and the laurel.
Book Sixteen	The oak; pitch; timber; life cycles of different trees; the age of trees.
Book Seventeen	Cultivation of trees.

of digression: on perfumes and papyrus, and the whole book on vines and wines. The extent of the digressions in the arboreal books is apparent in the list of contents, and Pliny's overall digressive nature might make the *Natural History* more comparable to Herodotus' *Histories*.[61]

In these six books, the digressions provide information that would otherwise be out of place in the *Natural History* and they move the books along their journey from the extremities of known territories to Roman cultivation of trees. This is most apparent in Pliny's digression at the opening of Book Sixteen, where he acknowledges that his next topic, following fruit-bearing trees, should rightly be 'acorn bearing trees', but that he feels he should first comment on those regions that have no trees.[62] Then, passing over the places he has already mentioned (in his digression on the happiness of Arabians in Book Twelve), he directs his readers to two tribes, the Greater and Lesser Chauci, who can be found in Germany. The oak, which he was about to discuss (and does, after his discourse on the Chauci), is associated with Germany, and he lists a number of German forests to open his account of the tree.[63] It is in the choice of tribes as opposed to the topic that the geographic structure of the *Natural History* can be found. Pliny brings the narrative from India to Rome's cultivated trees, the narrative following Pliny's own circuitous road map to the centre of the empire. In Book Seventeen, Pliny's digressions are minimal, and he only has one aside: a brief comment on grafting.[64] This book also marks a change in topic, from the nature of trees to the cultivation of them, and a transition into the following, non-arboreal books.

On a larger level, however, there appears to be a broader theme to the arboreal books, which is explored in other portions of the *Natural History*: imperialism, or triumphalism as Carey argues for.[65] Carey also states that, through cataloguing the world, Pliny has incorporated conquest into the work, and that cataloguing itself is an act of conquest.[66] Elsewhere, Naas, while exploring paradoxes in the *Natural History*, points to the contradiction inherent within viewing the *Natural History* as a vehicle for imperialism via the conquest of knowledge, and reminds her readers that Pliny blames the decline of knowledge on imperialism.[67] She continues to explore the theme of imperialism, amidst a number of other paradoxes related to the pursuit of knowledge and imperialism, and establishes Pliny's complex relationship with empire, both as a force for good, in the expansion of knowledge through expansion of territories, and as a prompt for laziness in times of peace. However, in terms of triumphalism, Pliny's attitude is clear: the display of knowledge accumulated through conquest is not only necessary, but also praiseworthy.

Knowledge is also framed as expansionism, and the world Pliny displays to us is a Roman one, catalogued and explained using Latin bureaucratic frameworks of *colonia*, *municipia*, and so on.[68] This knowledge is limited by the extent of Roman exploration up until this point, and the act of surveying the world is not, in and of itself, an act of conquest; Murphy points to the tradition of a general surveying the land before conquering and ruling it, but goes on to argue that the two are inextricably linked.[69] Therefore, when Pliny opens with a survey of the known world, he could be seen as preparing his readers (or marshalling his troops, to continue Murphy's military comparison) for the conquest of the known world, bringing it under Roman control. This control still does not automatically translate to conquest. Instead, it is an extension of power, and an advert for the exertion of Roman power, marking it as the centre of the world, to which all knowledge is gathered; Sri Lanka, or Taprobane, is considered part of a separate world until Pliny reveals what he has learnt about it following the visit of emissaries in Claudius' reign.[70] In the arboreal books, Pliny's survey similarly makes Rome the centre, and he addresses trees from the outside in, highlighting the first times the trees were brought to Rome, either as timber or as the tree itself.

An example of this is the citron, which Pliny acknowledges cannot be grown anywhere except in Media and Persia, shortly before making a similar admission about the ebony.[71] His knowledge of the citron's rejection of other lands, which remains uncited, is based on practical experience: 'various nations' have tried and failed to grow it in their lands, attracted by its medicinal qualities. However, they have found that it cannot be grown anywhere other than its home country, where no other tree is as 'highly praised'. Implicit within this exposition is a Roman attempt to grow the citron, as is again implied with the ebony, which Vergil relates cannot be grown in Rome.[72] This treatment of foreign trees which cannot necessarily be naturalized begins early in the arboreal books, and after the first tree, the plane, which is preceded by a brief secondary introduction to notify readers that we are now going to be dealing with the 'exotic trees' which have not been naturalized to Rome, and these other trees will be explored among the fruit trees.[73] Through the separation of fruit-producing trees according to geographical boundaries, Pliny establishes a definition of what is arboreally Roman by first defining what is not – a typical tactic of the *Natural History*, which frequently seeks to define 'Romanness' by opposition to that which is not – and does so from the opening of the arboreal survey.[74]

At the opening of Book Twelve, Pliny presents a list of associations between trees and the divine, linking trees to Roman deities, and identifying all woodlands as being under the care of woodland spirits.[75] By placing the arboreal world in a Roman setting, Pliny highlights from the opening of the arboreal books that the world he is observing is, to its very foundation, Rome-centric, and this complements his approaches elsewhere, explored by Carey in the creation of a Roman totality.[76] Before the discussion of the Roman deities, Pliny identified the origins and early uses of trees, exploring the 'gift' that they offer to mankind:

> For a long time, the benefits of the earth were hidden, and trees and woods were believed to be the greatest gift offered to mankind. From these, they first derived food, used their leaves to soften their caves, the bark for clothing.[77]

This gift, which is universally offered, is Pliny's motivation for placing the discussion of trees before mined materials, since they were discovered later, and he is mapping the evolution of mankind's exploitation and control of the resources available to them.[78] It is in Rome's control of trees, particularly naturalized fruit-bearing trees, that the pinnacle of arboreal exploitation is found, and the movement from the exotic trees to the fruit-bearing ones could be read as a journey toward Pliny's idea of civilization's pinnacle, which centres on Rome. In Pliny's worldview, the world and nature exist as an exploitable resource, and the level of exploitation can be seen as a measure of a culture's level of civilization, where there exists a tipping point into excess and luxury.[79]

***

Social utility competes with luxury for trade's association in the *Natural History*, and Romanness defines itself by being not not-Roman. No conflict in Pliny's writing is simple, and each conflict brings new forces to bear. Where trade can benefit Rome's import of a luxurious product more than its luxury can damage the importer's morality, Pliny supports this as an aspect of social utility, and where a tree is unable to be naturalized to Rome, the tree can be treated as a foreign object of interest. In some cases, a simple utility can be applied to trees, of timber or fruit, and Pliny treats these trees as generally unproblematic: the vine, for example, has a clear benefit to Romans, and mankind more generally. In other cases, trees like the plane provide a luxurious utility and no commercial benefit, and Pliny must reckon with how this ranks in his worldview. Throughout his examination of the natural world, Pliny is introducing foreign trees to his audience, and his cultivation book begins to suggest how these trees can be incorporated into the Italian arboreal landscape. These trees are presented as foreign objects of interest, and the method by which some, like the ebony and the citrus, were imported and physically shown to the Roman people in the triumphal procession echoes Pliny's approach.

3

Trees in the Triumph

Roman rulers are defined by their surroundings, and horticultural symbolism is manipulated to communicate messages in a range of examples from Roman history. The first Roman leader to be associated with nature through their horticultural practices is Tarquinius Superbus, whose garden maintenance is presented by Livy as a metaphor for his governance. In Livy's account, the last Roman king is presented with a report of the Gabii by a messenger from his son, Sextus. Superbus, in place of a verbal answer, strolls into his *hortus* and swipes the heads off the tallest poppies in the garden with his stick. The nonplussed messenger relays this to Sextus, who takes appropriate action, and executes or exiles the chief men of Gabii in order to gain sole control of the state before it was transferred to the Roman king.[1] That Tarquinius Superbus both had a *hortus* and tended to it himself (albeit in a rather brutal fashion) should come as little surprise, and is typical of the Roman kings, who Pliny tells us all tended gardens, as well as referring to this tale twice in the *Natural History*, calling the message 'savage and bloodthirsty' – a characteristic of the reign of Rome's last king, while not being a usual Roman trait.[2] To associate a ruler with their cultivated surroundings is not exclusively Roman, and Totelin explores comparable Eastern examples, such as Attalus III and Mithridates VI Eupator.

These rulers, termed by Totelin as 'botanizing rulers', are taken as precedents for the Roman use of a leader's interaction with nature as a metaphor for their rule. Attalus III, the final king of the Attalid dynasty, who reigned in the first half of the second century BCE, is the tender of a garden which was dominated by plants that were not easily kept in order, and his garden became overgrown as his country disintegrated.[3] Meanwhile, Mithridates' garden was characterized by its poisonous plants, and these are read as indicative of the deficiencies in the character of the gardener. While both of these examples deal with smaller plants – Attalus' garden in particular is characterized as being full of *gramina* by Justinus,[4] and dismissed as frivolous by Plutarch[5] – the planting of Cyrus the Younger, recorded by Xenophon of Athens, is of trees, and the garden metaphor is, in this instance, far more positive.[6] The trees here are ordered, and the king (who planted the trees himself, and enthuses as to their regularity) is a reputable ruler of his kingdom, which is similarly ordered and controlled. The act of gardening is also held to be comparable to that of war, and this may indicate a fourth-century BCE precedent for the attitude found in Pollius Felix's garden, recorded by Statius:

> Nature has favoured these places, in others she has ceded, conquered by her worshipper (*victa colenti*), and she is softened (*mansuevit*) into unfamiliar, docile ways. Here, there was a mountain, where now you see plains; and here was alight with sun, where now you enter a building; where now you see groves on slopes, there was not even earth: the owner has tamed it (*domuit possessor*), and the ground rejoices as he shapes the rocks and expels them, following his lead. Now, look to the cliffs, submitting to the yoke (*iugum discentia*), the buildings as they grow, and the mountain, ordered to retreat. Now, let the hand of Methymna's prophet, the lyre of Thebes, and the glory of the Getic plectrum embolden you: and may you move rocks too, and may lofty forests follow you.[7]

The comparison also presents the reflection of war and peace, in which the Roman practice of agriculture is the practice of peacetime. The use of the garden as a metaphor for the governance of Eastern rulers and for the early Roman kings' control of their kingdoms has led to an assertion by Totelin that the metaphor is Eastern in origin, taking her lead from the Eastern 'botanizing rulers' catalogued by Stronach.[8]

However, herbage acting as a metaphor for country can be found in one of Rome's oldest traditions, which Pliny ties to Germany: the *corona graminea*. This crown, also known as the *corona obsidionalis*, is reckoned by Pliny to be the oldest of the crowns awarded in Rome. It was given to one man who saved either an army or a city from total disaster and was constructed of the grass from the site of the victory.[9] Pliny relates this to an ancient practice, which was still German tradition. This involved the handing over of a location's *flora* as a sign of total surrender, representative of giving up your burial place and your homeland.[10] While this is, like Attalus' garden, distant from trees, it suggests a relationship between the landscape's *flora* and the territory. This relationship, particularly the role the vegetation plays in representing the country, is carried over into Roman usage of trees and plants in the triumph.

The triumphal procession, one of the best-known military practices in Rome's history, is replete with vegetal imagery like the triumphal architecture erected by Trajan, and this chapter will examine three instances of such imagery in the procession, beginning with the import of trees as *spolia*. This practice, which began in the Republic, possibly a result of the rivalry between Pompey and Lucullus, was continued to at least the Jewish triumph of Vespasian and Titus over a century later, and this chapter will examine the mechanics of this display, asking which trees were displayed and how they were imported, before a case study of a potential triumphal import. It will then explore two other uses of trees in the triumphal procession: in crowns and in *tropaea*. Here, trees are harnessed in their parts, not as the totality, and their communicative properties are manipulated to suit specific purposes. Three crowns will be focused on: the grass crown, civic crown and triumphal crown – three crowns where the foliage used was selected with specific care, and which can be examined in both literary and material evidence. The *tropaea* and the *spolia opima* involve trees as vessels for the armour of defeated enemies, either as a monument to the point at which an army was put to flight, or as a result of commander-to-commander combat in the case of the *spolia opima*. Through an examination of these three symbols of victory in the Roman world – exhibited spoils, crowns and *tropaea* – this chapter will discuss the exploitation of arboreal symbolism in the Roman world, and how this was translated from the brief triumphal procession to have a more lasting legacy after the celebrations had concluded and begun to fade from public memory.

Triumphal imports

In 74 BCE, Lucullus brought the cherry to Rome from Pontus, and may have planted his *spolia* in his *Horti* on the Pincian.[11] Perhaps in response to this, Pompey displayed the ebony in his Pontic triumph of 61 BCE.[12] This display kickstarted a tradition, according to Pliny the Elder, which included the import of the balsam by Vespasian and Titus.¹³ This tradition, to 'lead trees in the triumph', has precedent in the Egyptian Ptolemaeia, and an account of this festival is preserved in the second-century CE *Deipnosophistai* of Athenaeus which presents Kallixeinos' second-century BCE original.¹⁴ In this account, the extent of Ptolemy II Philadelphus' empire is displayed, and among the objects shown are two thousand ebony logs, presented by Ethiopian gift bearers. This world-display bears striking similarities to Pompey's 61 BCE triumph, which extended beyond the region he had conquered, and brought items from across the eastern reaches of Rome's control and beyond. This section will first address the attested imports of trees in literature, and how trees might have been transported across the breadth of Rome's territories for the triumphal procession. It will then move to a case study of a potential triumphal import, one without any literary attestation, but with a wealth of material and archaeological evidence to suggest it. Through employing the skills deployed in this case study, we may be able to identify future arboreal triumphal imports in the city of Rome.

Which trees were displayed?

There are two triumphal imports found in our literary sources: the ebony already mentioned, shown by Pompey in 61 BCE, and the balsam, shown by Vespasian and Titus in their Jewish triumph of 71 CE. Wood is additionally referred to in two other triumphal processions, both Julius Caesar's, in his Pontic and Gallic triumphs of 46 CE, and can be read in a similar fashion to the confirmed live arboreal imports.

The ebony,¹⁵ imported by Pompey, is one example of a live arboreal import, and ancient authors are aware that Pompey will have had to go beyond Pontus to find the ebony: Solinus, in the early third century CE, identifies Pompey's display as an import from India, while Vergil claims that it 'only grows in India'.¹⁶ This latter point is disputed by Pliny, who cites Herodotus' claim that the Ethiopians were forced to pay a tribute of a hundred ebony logs to the Kings of Persia.¹⁷ Although both Greek and Latin appear to use ἔβενος and *ebenus* (and *hebenus*) to denote trees and wood of a variety of genuses, ebony is one of the less common woods attested to in Latin literature. Meiggs has suggested that its absence indicates that it was not a popular furniture wood, and that citrus wood (as we have seen in Pliny's *Natural History*) was the luxury furniture wood of choice.[18] This dearth of references to ebony indicates its rarity: this was not a tree that had been seen before, at least by the majority of Romans. This would make the tree an ideal import for Pompey in his bid to one-up Lucullus' cherry.

Prior to Pompey's triumph over Mithridates, Lucullus had returned from the same region, with his *spolia* already prepared for a presumed triumph. This triumph did occur, three years later, but was not remembered as the traditional procession.[19] Instead, Plutarch tells us that Lucullus created a static triumph, laying out the armour on the Circus Flaminius, before leading a procession of the remainder of his spoils into the city.[20] However, the delay to this procession had led to one item of *spolia* being impossible to display: the cherry tree.[21] Whether or not Lucullus intended to display this tree in his presumed triumphal procession is unknown, but he is credited with having brought it back from his Pontic wars in 74 BCE by Pliny.[22] There is, of course, some gap between the dates here, and a suggestion that Lucullus never intended to exhibit the tree, merely collecting it for the *Horti* he would later construct, is feasible. However, the fact remains that Lucullus returned from the Mithridatic Wars with a novel tree, never before seen in Rome, and Pompey reacted in kind.

Since the ebony displayed by Pompey was identified by both Solinus and Vergil as being Indian,[23] it was evidently associated with the Roman Empire's extreme eastern borders, and with the furthest extent of Alexander the Great's march across Asia. This has proven to be a sticking point for Totelin, who categorically (and correctly) states that the ebony 'is not a Pontic tree'.[24] Kuttner, meanwhile, credits Pompey with displaying 'the Asian landscape' in a more complete form than that desired by Totelin, and this leads to the question of how important the correlation between tree and territory is.[25] The ebony, with its Eastern associations, is a sensible import for Pompey, and suggested a further conquest than he had achieved, as well as containing Alexandrian implications.[26]

The ebony presented a new challenge for Pompey, the import of which followed the type set by Lucullus. Lucullus' naturalization of the cherry was easy, and the tree had spread to Britain within 120 years of Lucullus importing it.²⁷ Meanwhile, the ebony proved far trickier to grow in Rome, and no surviving farming manual mentions the tree.²⁸ Therefore, if Pompey wished to have a natural monument from his triumph, he would need an alternative, with similar characteristics and symbolic ties to the region, to house alongside his other spoils. Pompey housed these spoils in a theatre complex that commemorated his triumph, and the Porticus in this complex was known for its shade,²⁹ a characteristic shared with the ebony tree, as identified by Pliny and Lucan.³⁰

The tree that Pompey planted in his Porticus to create this shade was the plane tree, and the evidence for these trees in his theatre complex is both literary and archaeological, with one of the best-known pieces coming in Propertius' *Elegies*:

> I understand Pompey's porticus is worthless,
> With its shady columns, its noble Attalid drapes,
> And the plane trees, rising evenly in a thick row.³¹

Meanwhile, archaeological evidence can be found in the Marble Plan, which has rows of drilled holes, potentially representations of trees,³² and soundings beneath the Teatro Argentina have discovered remains of trees in an avenue formation.³³

It is a commonly accepted conclusion that the Porticus of Pompey was intended to celebrate his Pontic triumph, leading from Martial's description of it as Pompey's 'gifts' (*dona*), as well as the amount of time and funds required to construct it.³⁴ As a result, it is reasonable to suggest that the trees planted in the portico were intended to be the same as those carried in the triumphal procession, and are likely to have survived the intervening centuries between their import following the triumphal procession and Martial's recollection of a 'double grove' (*nemus duplex*).³⁵ As a result, the continued legacy of Pompey's eastern victories, and of his Pontic triumph especially, will have outlasted the other spoils, and influenced interactions within the space for years to come.

Only one other tree is attested in literature as being a triumphal import, and we have significantly less evidence for its location. In the *Natural History*, Pliny tells us that the tradition begun by Pompey was continued in the Flavian Jewish triumph of 71 CE, and the balsam was introduced to Rome.³⁶ While the pursuit of identifying the variety of tree beyond its genus has rarely been attempted so far, it is important here, given Pliny's description:

> This type of tree was displayed in the city by the emperors Vespasian and Titus, and it is a remarkable fact that, since Pompey the Great, we have led trees in triumph. The balsam is now enslaved, and pays tribute alongside the rest of its people.[37]

For this tree to pay tribute, it would have to produce something of value. Balsam timber was not considered particularly notable, and contemporary sources typically focus on the oil that balsam can produce.[38] This leads to a tentative identification of *Commiphora gileadensis* L. following Östenberg, although an alternative of *Chrysanthemum balsamita* L., the fragrant leaves of which are used in cooking and medicine, has been proposed by André.[39]

The traditional location for the balsam's housing in Rome after its display as the Templum Pacis reinforces this identification, given the proximity of the complex to the Horrea Piperataria, a spice market built by Domitian at the close of the Flavian dynasty.[40] This identification rests on the Marble Plan of the Templum Pacis, which contains six unusual markings in a colonnaded courtyard outside the main building, as well as a brief mention of the construction of the temple in Josephus' *Jewish War*. However, excavations have indicated that the unusual markings on the Marble Plan are not, in fact, beds of plants, but water features. Amphorae were found in the excavation, but analysis of the roots revealed these held roses.[41] Any physical trace of the balsam within the Templum Pacis complex, if it was ever there at all, has yet to be discovered. Meanwhile, Josephus' brief mention of the Temple of Peace in fact identifies that it houses all manner of riches from across the world, 'which before men had wandered all the world to see'.[42] Josephus does include the gold from Herod's Temple in the spoils displayed in this temple, but tells us that other items were displayed in 'the palace', and this could have been the eventual location of the balsam, although such a placement is entirely hypothetical. This makes tracing the balsam harder: it could have been distributed among the spoils, and found a home elsewhere. In spite of its absence from the archaeological record, the balsam's role in paying tribute could suggest that it did remain in Rome, as does Pliny's comment that it was cultivated by the 'treasury' (*fiscus*),[43] and Pliny reports that in the five years following its import, its cuttings and shoots had sold for 800,000 sesterces, indicating some sort of record keeping was going on in regard to the balsam's 'tribute' to Rome.[44]

This record keeping does not indicate that the balsam was in Rome, and the usual habitat of the *Commiphora gileadensis* offers further indication that any balsam that existed in Rome following the triumph was only a token representative of the full amount of trees. Manolaraki, in a study of the balsam's history and its context as a triumphal import, asserts that the balsam was not moved to Rome on a large scale, if at all, and that Roman management of the balsam took place in its original Judaean habitat of Ein Gedi.[45] This, and Pliny's description of the triumphal display (not import), suggest an entirely different motive to that of Pompey's display of the ebony.

With all of the uncertainty around the balsam's display in Rome, questions have to be raised regarding whether it actually was introduced to Rome in the triumph of 71 CE. Did it make sense as an import? The cherry and the ebony of Lucullus and Pompey respectively made a statement: they were new trees from the eastern reaches of Rome's conquered territories, but the balsam was already known by the Augustan period; it appears in Vergil's *Georgics*, a full century before the 71 CE triumph.[46] While the earlier imports make geographical statements, this import is one with deep roots in Jewish history, and one which had already been co-opted into Roman control when Pompey first subdued the region in 63 BCE.

The fact that this region had already been subdued complicates the nature of the Flavian triumph. It is no longer a simple statement of geographic conquest, and Manolaraki presents it as a triumph with a fiscal purpose: to demonstrate the acquired wealth of the region. This makes the balsam's financial benefit a focal point of the triumphal procession, and the association that Pollard made with the Horrea Piperataria, while not necessarily helpful in determining the eventual location of the imported balsam, does point us toward the emphasis of the triumph: the demonstration of this conquest's financial benefit to the city of Rome. This, Manolaraki argues, is why Pliny dwells in his section on the balsam on the economic benefit. This section, she proposes, offers a potted biography of the tree, leading us from its earlier cultivation before Vespasian and Titus' conquest to its 'enhanced productivity' under new Roman rule.[47]

How were trees imported?

Bringing trees to Rome from India or Jerusalem respectively is no mean feat; the journey alone would have put the life of the tree at risk, and the display of a tree may have proved challenging once it had been successfully brought to Rome. For Lucullus, this is likely to have proved unproblematic, since the cherry tree would have been long established before his static triumph in the Circus Flaminius years later. The import and display of the ebony and balsam involved a journey across or around the Mediterranean, followed by a triumphal procession through the streets of Rome, and these two steps require two different solutions.

The consensus from Östenberg, Stackelberg, Kuttner, and others is that these trees were imported with the intention of planting them, even if this is as a representative sample of a larger whole, as in the balsam.[48] As a result, it should be assumed that they were imported and displayed as trees, possibly even as living trees, as Östenberg proposes. The import of trees over long distances is not a novel idea in the ancient world, and Pliny tells us of a usual practice by which the citron tree was imported and attempted to be replanted:

> Peoples have tried to import it [the citron tree, perhaps *Malus medica*] because of its excellent medicinal value to their countries in earthenware pots, with holes drilled through the pots for roots, just as all plants about to be transported a particularly long distance are planted as tightly as possible.[49]

Comparative examples of the display of a tree in a procession have been found by Östenberg in a number of places, including Egyptian paintings which depict trees being displayed 'upright in carrying devices, which were suspended on poles carried by men'.[50] In the Roman tradition, there is a mural from an *oecus* in Pompeii which shows an alternative method, in a wedding procession, with the bride and groom portrayed as Iuventas and Hercules. On the left-hand side of the fresco, two men carry a tree on a *ferculum*, and Östenberg again notes that this tree is carried upright.[51]

Assuming that the display of a tree in the Pompeian wall painting is a close representation of the actual mechanics of carrying a tree in a procession (a similar representation is found in the display seen on the pediment of the Temple of Apollo Sosianus), there is clearly no room for the roots of the tree.

As a result, we could conclude that the trees actually displayed in the triumph were part of a larger import, the majority of which were retained as living trophies for future planting. By planting the trees, they would then be able to act alongside the other permanent displays of *spolia*, as arboreal representatives of the land from which they originated.

Case study: Trajan and Dacia

While there are only the two literary examples of trees displayed in the triumphal procession, there are other means by which arboreal imports might be identified, and an example of this can be found in the overarching motifs within triumphal Trajanic architecture, specifically the 235 trees on the Arch of Trajan at Beneventum, the Great Trajanic Frieze, and the Column of Trajan.[52] While not the only pieces of Trajanic sculpture, or even of Trajanic triumphal sculpture with trees on, these three monuments can form the basis of a case study of the influence of the Dacian landscape in celebrations of the region's conquest in the second century CE, and of the potential involvement of this landscape in the triumphal procession as well. Other instances of trees on Trajanic architecture include the Plutei of Trajan, which depict a tree in the Forum Romanum, possibly the Ruminal fig tree, and the Trophaeum Traiani at Adamklissi, the trees of which are too weathered to identify with any accuracy. The Plutei will not be discussed in this case study as they are not triumphal architecture, nor do they depict a foreign landscape. The Trophaeum friezes will be useful to a limited extent here, and will be referred to occasionally.

Each of the three main monuments in this case study have significant amounts of arboreal imagery, and each depict events of the Dacian conquest, maintaining a consistent triumphal message throughout – a common theme of Trajanic architecture.[53] The column, erected in the emperor's forum complex by 113 CE as a monument to his successful Dacian Wars, depicts Trajan in a foreign landscape, and is decorated with a helical relief that shows the events of these campaigns and the land in which they were fought.[54] The Arch of Trajan, erected at Beneventum, south of Rome, at the northern end of the Via Traiana (where it joined the Via Appia), commemorates two conquests, over the German and the Dacian territories, with a focus on the Danube region, and particularly the confluence with the Tisa, a tributary in Romania.⁵⁵ The dating of the arch is uncertain, but it is generally accepted to have been dedicated at a similar time to the column.⁵⁶ The Great Trajanic Frieze, however, is far more challenging to date, but Leander Touati has attempted to fix it.⁵⁷ It survives in the form of eight slabs, which were adapted and incorporated into the Arch of Constantine in the fourth century CE, and a number of fragments. Like the arch, it is assumed to have been a commemoration of the Dacian Wars, and may have been housed in Rome, possibly in the Forum of Trajan itself.

This case study will first examine the trees to identify the types that are present on the friezes, and to assess whether they are trees of special significance to Dacia in particular, as the cherry, ebony and balsam were to their respective regions. It will then explore how the trees are deployed on the friezes in order to understand their importance in the narrative of Dacia's subjugation, before discussing how they might have been linked to Dacia in Rome's cityscape.

Identification

The 224 trees on the Column of Trajan have highly individualized and stylized leaves, which enables their easy identification. These leaves are amplified and highly likely to have been painted, making them prominent features on the column's helical frieze. They have been identified as being carved by at least two sculptors, one of whom injected more vigour into their carving, and their intricacy remained regardless of the height that they were positioned on the column's frieze.⁵⁸ The trees themselves have 37 different leaf variations, as identified by Christian Stoiculescu (see Figure 2). The level of detail in the carving of these leaves invites the viewer to consider the broader role and significance of trees on this iconic early imperial monument, and the types identified by Stoiculescu can be identified on both the Arch of Trajan and on the Great Trajanic Frieze (see Tables 4 and 5). The 37 leaf varieties are separated into seven groups, and resinous trees form one large, almost indistinguishable group.

These trees are typically evergreen and identifiable by their straight trunks, growing from a singular point. The trunks are almost invariably more than half the height of the tree (some allowance must be made for the two trees in

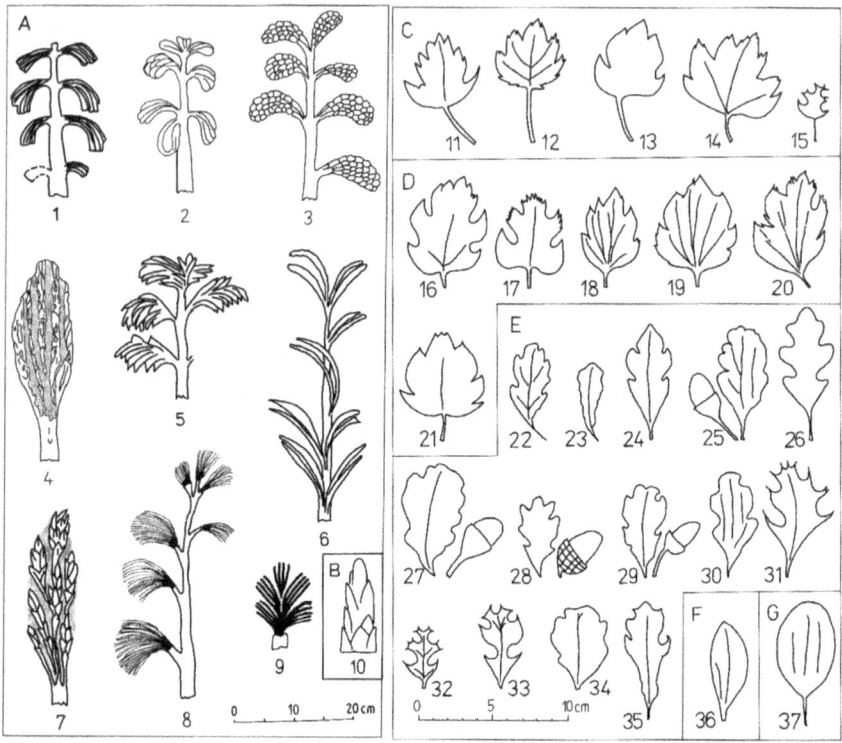

Figure 2 Leaf types on Trajan's Column, as identified by Stoiculescu (1985, figs 4 and 5) and redrawn by author. Stoiculescu describes the resinous leaf types (A and B) as follows: 'Resinous species types included in the A and B species subgroup according to the crown and needle forms. Columnary crown: type 1 – long and pendent needles; type 2 – revolute, semilanceolate needles; type 3 – short and scaly needles; type 5 – needles grouped in pendent fascicles; type 6 – slightly revolute, lanceolate, big needles; type 7 – scaly and oblong needles; Pyramidal crown: type 10 (suggesting a primitive form of the actual pyramidal black poplar – Populus nigra L. cv. Italica – or the cypress – Cupressus sempervirens L.) Semipyramidal crown: type 8 – needles grouped in short fascicles; Rhomboidal crown: type 4 – long and scaly needles, catenary disposed; Ovate crown: type 9 – erect, fanned, exclusively disposed at the tree top.'

The leaf types of the deciduous trees (C – G) are listed thus: 'Foliaceous species types divided in five subgroups according to their form of leaves: C – pentapalmary lobate leaves (suggesting Acer genus), D – broadly ovate leaves, with 3–5 triangular lobes slowly decreasing to the top (suggesting Sorbus torminalis L.), E – unregularly obovate and pennate lobate leaves (suggesting Quercus genus), F – oblong leaves (suggesting Prunus genus), G – elliptic leaves (suggesting Fagus genus).'

Table 4 The trees on the Arch of Trajan at Beneventum

Tree location	Identifications in other literature	Identification following Stoiculescu's drawings
Arch: *Cbr* – Country (NE) facing, bottom row, right pillar.	Two pear trees.[62]	F.36 (*Prunus*) – contrary to Rotili's identification.
Arch: *Cbl* – Country (NE) facing, bottom row, left pillar.	Oak.[63]	E.31/32/33 (*Quercus*).
Arch: *Ctr* – Country (NE) facing, top row, right pillar.	Oak.[64]	E.24 (*Quercus*).
Arch: *As* – Vault, South side.	Vine.[65]	D.16/21 (*Sorbus torminalis*). Could also be an *Acer*.

Table 5 The trees on the Great Trajanic Frieze

Tree location	Identification by Leander Touati (1987)	Identification following Stoiculescu's drawings
Frieze: Slab 2	Pine.[66]	Adapted A.1 – added fruit.
Frieze: Slab 3	Oak, from lacinated outline of foliage.[67]	Impossible to achieve without detailed foliage.
Frieze: Slab 6	Oak.[68]	E.30 (*Quercus*), possibly adapted with fruit.
Frieze: Slab 7	Pine.[69]	Adapted A.1 – added fruit.
Frieze: Slab 8	Sycamore.[70]	C.13 (*Acer*).
Frieze: Fragment P	Oak.[71]	E.29 (*Quercus*).

scene III, given that they are at a significant distance from the scene's action) and are topped with a narrow excurrent crown, which typically only has a few branches, often with the tree's needles directly attached to the trunk. It is through these needles that Stoiculescu divides the resinous trees into subspecies. The trunks of the deciduous trees, which account for five of the groups, are twisted and 'full of imperfections', which are particularly noticeable given that they usually lack branches on the trunk's bottom half. Further, these trunks are fluted, pitted, and with visible loose knots, an indication of the dedication of the sculptors to projecting an appearance of reality.[59] The expectation would be for branching, particularly on deciduous trees, to start earlier on the trunk, as opposed to the column's depictions, in which the spreading branches of the deciduous trees are restricted to the top of the relief. The knots on the trunks suggest that the lower branches expected on these trees have been removed. The crown of these deciduous trees is described by Stoiculescu as either umbelliform (with laterally spreading branches) or obovate (with branches spreading from a central point).⁶⁰

Depictions of the beech, or *fagus*, are unexpectedly rare: the tree, found across modern-day Romania, only appears in one form (Type G.37), and is only seen once on the column. The motivation for this, Stoiculescu argues, is that 'the beech was much too common', and he goes on to suggest that Trajan aimed instead to impress his audience with a conquest over an exotic and foreign land, populated with strange-leafed trees. While the level of control that Trajan exerted over the frieze's arboreal contents is unclear, it is widely accepted to expect that his account of the wars, the highly fragmentary *Dacica*, would have had some influence in the overall intentions of the column, if not its individual components.⁶¹

The five trees on the arch and the six identified by Leander Touati on the frieze can generally be identified by the drawings of Stoiculescu. These trees, like those found on the column, have a variety of functions, including as architectural features of the scene: the pine on Slab 7 of the frieze acts as a central spine of a scene, while the sycamore at the close of the scene, on Slab 8, ends the action, although it should not be considered the end of the frieze as a whole, which would surely have continued.⁷² While the majority of the trees on the Trophaeum Traiani at Adamklissi are too damaged to determine species, the continuity of stylistic features and the species depicted on the arch and the frieze suggests that they would have been of a similar form.

The trees depicted on these monuments are reasonably representative of the forest at the time, and care should be taken to treat them as such. Unlike the monumental fig tree on the Plutei of Trajan, the trees on these monuments have no known real-world equivalent, contrary to earlier suggestions that they might be used to specifically place the scenes they feature in.⁷³ The unusual inclusions and exclusions are the beech, addressed above, and the two non-Dacian trees (Type B.10), which are found on the Roman side of the Danube at the start of the relief, in a walled city. Oak, the most common tree on the monuments, is one of the more dominant trees of central European forests at the time, and features in Pliny's description of a nearby region as 'acorn-bearing'.[74] The impressive variety of foliage on the column and (by extension) the other monuments is hampered by the problems of visibility, and a number of solutions have been proposed to address the traditional questions of how the column in particular was interacted with.[75] The problem of visibility here is not in understanding the narrative, however, but in identifying the trees on the column's scenes: there is an assumption that a Roman observer would be able to identify the type of tree depicted, and to associate it with Dacia.

The oak, one of the more common species on the frieze, was found across Europe at this time, and the same can be said for the other two dominant foliaceous trees: the service tree (a type of wide-ranging *Sorbus* genus, which includes mountain ash and rowan in its variations) and the sycamore.[76] Similarly, Romans would have been familiar with a variety of resinous trees, evidenced through poetic record stretching as far back as Ennius' *Annals*,[77] and the agricultural handbooks of the mid to late Republic and early Principate, written by Cato the Elder, Varro and Columella, discuss a large number of resinous trees. While these texts would only have been read by a small proportion of the population, the implication of their coverage is that there would have been some degree of familiarity with the trees in Rome and its surrounding territories among the wider community without knowledge of specific species group. Additionally, the content of these works may have been disseminated by the educated elite, typically landowners such as Pliny the Younger, to their workforce. To what extent it matters, however, that these trees and their species group may have already been familiar by sight to the Roman people will be dealt with in the context of tree felling on the column and the triumphal procession in the next section.

Through identifying the different varieties of trees, a study of Trajanic architecture, and particularly the column, reveals an almost complete depiction of the (expected) Dacian landscape of the time. The absence of the beech is particularly important, since it reveals that the sculptors were selective over what trees they carved, and the range of leaf types shows a concern for individualized depictions, as in the human figures on the relief. Clearly, they were carved with this much care for a purpose, and that purpose may become clear as we explore the different functions of the trees on the monuments.

Deployment

Trees are used to narrate the conquest of Dacia on the column, although they have historically been dismissed as 'scene dividers' on the column, and the trees that divide scenes are often performing dual functions on the frieze.[78] Here, two examples of the functions of trees will be examined: their presence in tree-felling scenes, and their associative role in the portrayal of Dacians, especially the Dacian king, Decebalus. Understanding the role of trees on the Great Trajanic Frieze is obviously very difficult, as the frieze rarely shows a full scene, and trees feature only in small fragments. As such, this section will focus on depictions on the arch, the column, and the Trophaeum at Adamklissi.

There are forty-eight trees in tree-felling scenes on the column, and the column is the only monument discussed in this case study on which there is direct interaction between the human figures and the arboreal elements.[79] This frequency of depiction makes it one of the most common contexts in which trees appear on the relief, and these scenes are found from the column's opening. The first example of the practice is in scene XV, and the activity continues to appear up to the final tree-felling scene (CXXXVII). The usual content of these scenes is exceptionally revealing: beyond three instances of Dacian tree felling, all within the same scene (LXVI), Roman soldiers are felling Dacian trees, in line with the general theme of industry on the column's relief.[80] The absence of warfare and the prominence of construction scenes is, for Davies, part of an effort to portray a mechanized Roman army, in complete control of both their surroundings and the war.[81] In this reading of the column, the tree-felling scenes are key, and when this is put in the context of the Romans' relationship with the environment in times of war, a fresh understanding of the usage of trees on Trajan's Column begins to emerge. However, challenges arise when tree felling on the column is considered within the broader tradition of tree felling in Greek and Roman myth and history, and there has typically been an assumption made by modern scholars that any tree felling is a sacrilegious act.[82] Recently, Hunt has revisited this assumption, and has explored the possibilities of sacrality in trees beyond a wholesale attribution.[83] This leads to a challenge in identifying which trees are sacred, which prompted Thomas to earlier conclude that 'any tree felling [is] potentially hazardous'.[84] The consequences for such a felling are usually severe.[85] The felling of the trees on the column operates alongside this rich literary tradition of tree violation, but also engages with a cultural tradition with its roots in the late Republic and the conquest of foreign nations.

The deployment of trees that are associated with areas is a common theme in Trajanic architecture, and the images on the Trophaeum include trees in association with Dacian soldiers. On the Arch of Trajan as well, the oak is found in the *Cbl* and *Ctr* reliefs, which are commonly understood to represent the pacification of Germany and the submission of Dacia respectively, two regions linked to the oak tree.[86] In the representation of this tree, its symbolic association with foreign lands at the outer reaches of the empire, established in part by the contemporaneous column's relief, and other factors such as the reference of Pliny, the treatment of the oak as a forest tree (it is presented as the seminal forest tree in the *Natural History*), and its status as the uncultivated source of food to early man in Lucretius, may have superseded its actual geographic spread, which reached into Italy. The couple of trees on each of the arch's friezes might have been used to represent nature, as they are understood in the Great Trajanic Frieze,[87] and broadly 'convey the region', as on Trajan's Column.[88] The specificity of trees depicted across the monuments and their shared triumphal context lead us to assume that the trees depicted are intended to represent the region.

Every felled tree is in Dacian territory, and many felled trees are oak – a tree associated with Dacia by modern scholars, as noted above. In scene XV, the trees are identified by Lepper and Frere as being exclusively oaks, although Stoiculescu's analysis of the foliage proves otherwise.[89] Regardless of their error in this particular scene, oaks are prominent on the column, and the argument of Lepper and Frere that certain trees can be considered characteristic of Dacia is useful. While the trees in scene XV are not exclusively oak, they are all trees which Stoiculescu identifies as being typical of a Romanian forest, and he adds that 'the priority cutting of the deciduous trees suggests the preponderant waging of the two Dacian wars just in this vegetation-zone type, where resinous trees existed only sporadically'.[90] These authors direct us to the conclusion that the forest depicted on the column is both authentically and symbolically Dacian, being composed of trees that were both theoretically common to the area and traditionally associated with it.[91]

In the broader context of the role of trees in triumphs as imports and representatives of a land and its people, tree-felling scenes take on a particular significance, and a depiction of Roman war on the landscape is revealed.[92] In the opening tree-felling scene on the column's relief, Trajan ratifies the industry that continues through the relief, and the continued action between scenes XV and XVI (Trajan looks across Cichorius' border) could be read to imply that the trees felled in XV are used for the wooden Roman fortifications in XVI. The Roman soldiers are seen taking control of the foreign landscape, moulding it to their purpose, and in doing so urbanize their rural surroundings, in contrast to their Dacian enemies.[93]

War on landscape is a common theme in contemporary Roman descriptions of the Dacian Wars, particularly in the accounts of Pliny the Younger. Control of the landscape is a key component of Trajan's portrayal in contrast with Decebalus in the *Panegyricus*, Pliny's only surviving speech, written and delivered prior to Trajan's first Dacian War. In this panegyric, written in the expected hyperbolic fashion,[94] Pliny describes the land of the 'barbarian king' and its betrayal of the native ruler. It prefers to part for Trajan to advance, before turning and fighting for the emperor.[95] Here, a good emperor is seen in complete mastery of the forces of nature, in contrast to the negative portrayal of Domitian later in the speech, which has been argued to be artificial and incomplete compared to the willing submission of the landscape to Trajan.[96] Moving genre, to Pliny the Younger's *Letters*, and a letter to Cannius Rufus, the theme continues. Here, Pliny relates Trajan's command of the landscape, his creation of new rivers and the subsequent bridging of these rivers, an echo of the bridging of the Danube at the base of the column's frieze.[97]

Linking these trees with Dacia is not only seen through the Roman war on the landscape, but also in the depictions of the two leaders on the column. Decebalus' first and last appearances isolate him within and under trees respectively, while a Dacian envoy approaches Trajan across the forest line. The two leaders are found among trees and forests elsewhere on the column's frieze.[98]

The Dacian association with landscape, and with forests in particular, is established in part by the appearances of the Dacian leader, Decebalus, who is ten times more likely to appear in a forest setting than his Roman counterpart, Trajan. In his first scene (XXIV), Decebalus is hidden deep in an isolated forest, and only his face is visible.⁹⁹ Viewers are directed to him by the (conjectured) angle of Jupiter Tonans' thunderbolt and his gaze, fixed on the Dacian king in the woods.¹⁰⁰ The previous scene is one of tree felling, and Decebalus' first appearance, watching a battle from the forest, is followed immediately by Trajan overseeing construction, the heads of Dacians (perhaps those displayed to the emperor in scene XXIV itself) mounted on stone battlements. The trees that shelter Decebalus have been identified as scene dividers in the past, and while this is one of their uses in this scene, they serve a greater purpose, linking the conquest of the Dacians to a conquest of the land of Dacia itself.¹⁰¹

By the end of the war, Decebalus is no longer hidden deep within the forest, but is instead isolated from his sons by it, forced into a prone position by a rare low branch as he commits suicide, his sons on the other side of the tree, and no Dacian army between him and the oncoming Roman forces (scene CXLV). Here, the oak tree might be taken to reflect the anger of Jupiter Tonans (with whom the oak is linked) in the Dacian king's first scene (XXIV), which is positioned lower on the same vertical axis.¹⁰² In addition to isolating and identifying the figure of Decebalus, this oak tree forces him from the shadows of his first appearance and thrusts him to the foreground at the moment of his death. At this, the climactic moment of the Dacian Wars, and of the column's relief, the landscape of Dacia, represented by the tree most commonly associated with Dacia, betrays the Dacian king and works for the Romans, thus paralleling the rivers and mountains in Pliny the Younger's writing. Thus, the scene not only shows the defeat of the Dacians, but also the subjugation of Dacia itself, and the Romans' war on the landscape, begun by felling trees in scene XV and bridging the Danube at the base of this vertical axis, is complete.

The moment that the power over the landscape begins to shift is not Decebalus' death, however, but can be found several scenes earlier, in a scene with Trajan and a Dacian embassy (scene LII). Like all of Trajan's appearances on the column, he is not in a forest, and is instead facing the trees. Here, the embassy approaches the Roman emperor, and reaches across the treeline towards him. The tree frames the distinction between the two, and the Dacian must enter the recently urbanized landscape (the other trees of the scene are being felled by the Roman forces) to treat with Trajan. This positioning of the Roman emperor as outside the wood is echoed in Trajan's other appearances near trees on the column.¹⁰³ It also mirrors the role of the emperor on the arch, where he is never in the forest, which is always associated with those approaching him, whether in battle or peacetime.[104] In this victory monument, the rusticity of the Dacians and the Germans is contrasted with the urban sophistication of the emperor, which has been a common theme throughout the monuments of this case study. But while the forest is inherently linked with the Dacians, and to some extent the Germans, there remains a question of whether the average onlooker would know that the trees on the column or the frieze were representative of the Dacian landscape, and how the association might have been enforced within the city's layout.

Dacia in Rome's cityscape

At this point, it might be helpful to remind ourselves of the point we are at in terms of evidence. There is no precise evidence of an arboreal triumphal import in Trajan's pacifications of Germany or Dacia, in literature or in visual or material culture. However, there is some archaeological evidence that suggests that trees were used not only in the depiction of the conquest, but also in its memorialization. Like the Flavian triumph over Judaea, the conquest depicted by these monuments was not the first conquest of Dacia, which was accomplished by Domitian, but this earlier conquest was portrayed as incomplete in a contemporary literary account.[105] The conquest was incomplete because of a lack of control over the landscape, and the landscape features prominently in the monuments discussed here, as well as in a panegyric on the conquest.[106]

If Trajan were to have displayed the landscape and the trees in the triumphal procession, or amongst the *spolia* otherwise displayed, then he would likely have followed precedent and housed them in his manubial construction, his forum complex. This complex is likely to have housed the statues of Dacians, possibly in the attics of the porticoes.[107] In addition to these statues, Trajan may have continued the tradition of arboreal triumphal imports, and a small excavation in 1982 revealed a potential planting pit corresponding to one of the markings on the twelfth-century sketch of the Severan Marble Plan.[108] These markings show a double colonnade extending into the Area Fori, as well as a border to the otherwise open space (aside from the equestrian statue of Trajan in the centre). Packer's excavation focused on one of the markings from the outer row of the double colonnade, and the archaeological report expressed a hope that future excavations would reveal further details on the spacing and species of the trees in the planting pits. Future excavations did not reveal that the pavement on the outer edge of the Area Fori was interrupted by planting pits, although whether there was planting corresponding to the inner row of dots remains unclear.[109]

Contemporary literature about the Dacian wars, such as Pliny the Younger's *Panegyricus* and his letter to Cannius Rufus, suggests the important role that certain Romans ascribe to the landscape in times of war. In these pieces, the mountains, seas and rivers are presented as active participants in Pliny's description of the war, which is often assumed to be hyperbolic as a result of their genre. However, the frieze on Trajan's Column demonstrates the boundless nature of this hyperbole, which transcends genre. Nature plays an active role in the column's relief, and is crucial in communicating its message of Roman dominance and superiority over a foreign enemy and their land. Trees formed a similar function throughout the triumphal procession alongside other natural features, such as mountains and rivers. There is some evidence to indicate that they were also used narratively in the commemoration of conquest, and to illustrate the breadth of Roman expansion. This use of trees as representative of both a geographic location and of Roman control over that location is replicated elsewhere in victory displays, in the crowns awarded throughout Roman history.

Crowns

While trees are imported in the triumph as representatives of a place, either fiscally as in the balsam, or geographically as in the plane and the cherry, foliage can also be used in a triumphal context to act as a metaphor for a country. This section will explore three crowns: the grass, triumphal and civic crowns, their uses of foliage, and their long-term impacts on the city of Rome.

Grass crown

The first crown to be explored is also reckoned by Pliny to be the oldest of the crowns to be awarded in Rome: the grass crown or *corona graminea*, also known as the *corona obsidionalis*.[110] To be eligible for this crown, the recipient would have to save either an army or a city from total disaster, and be unanimously awarded the crown by those he had saved, unique among the Roman victory crowns.[111] It was constructed from the foliage available at the site of the victory, and was only awarded ten times by Pliny's reckoning, and to nine people.[112] The construction of the crown, of its immediate foliage, makes each *corona graminea* individual, and is a key attraction of the crown to Pliny. He notes that whatever plants were nearby, however ignoble or worthless, were used, and this lends the crown nobility.[113] This comment precedes an invective against luxury and the abandonment of the pursuit of knowledge, as Pliny segues into a discussion on medicinal plants. It is perhaps telling, then, that the grass crown had not been awarded in almost a hundred years at the time of Pliny's writing, and appears to have been phased out of use.

The construction of the grass crown may have been borne out of necessity of constructing a makeshift crown out of whatever material was to hand, but Pliny links it to an ancient tradition, which he recalls is still practised in Germany at the time he was writing.[114] By Pliny's account, this tradition involved handing over the *flora* of a particular location as a sign of total surrender, giving up your burial place and your homeland. This representative quality of *flora*, linking it to a land, is a common element with the trees of triumphal imports, which the crown predates. The display of trees in the triumph over a nation could, therefore, be taken as a sign of that region's total and utter conquest, further advancing the argument that monuments like Trajan's Column depict a conquest not only over the Dacians, but over Dacia itself.

The *corona graminea* was last presented by Marcus Tullius Cicero the Younger to Augustus on behalf of Rome, on 13 September 30 BCE, and after this it disappeared from public record. There are perhaps political motivations for this: it was the only crown that placed authority in the people of the city as opposed to a benefactor of higher or equal position, and as such the receipt of it could not be controlled by Rome's imperial families, who were able to impose themselves on the other crowns and the triumphal processions. As a result, the grass crown was amalgamated into the civic crown, which had already undergone a shift in its construction during its history.

Civic crown

The *corona civica* passed through three phases, from *ilex* to *aesculus* to *quercus*, according to Pliny's undated sequencing of the crown's variation.[115] André identifies a different species of oak tree, which can be differentiated by their leaves and acorn sizes, for each of these terms.[116] Pliny tells us the focus in the *quercus* phase was on the fruit of the tree, the acorn, and there will be some discussion later in this section on the implication of the changes between foliage types, and in the crown's construction and depictions. Like its construction, the means by which the *corona civica* was achieved changed over time. Originally, the crown was awarded to a citizen for the saving of another citizen's life and the killing of an enemy, before holding the spot against the enemy on which these events occurred for the remainder of the day.[117] However, Pliny, who outlines these conditions of the crown's acquisition, earlier states that it had become a symbol of 'the clemency of the emperor' a long time before the *Natural History* was written.[118] This section will consider the implication of this shift, which allowed the *corona civica* to be awarded to the saviour of a citizen body, rather than limiting it to an individual citizen. The redefinition of the *corona civica* corresponds to the *corona graminea*, the difficulty of its acquisition, and the subsequent construction of the *corona civica*.

Pliny explicitly links the second iteration of the *corona civica* to Jupiter, identifying that the *aesculus* (which André identifies as the *Quercus farnetto* L.) is held to be sacred to the god.[119] This did not halt the crown's development, and in its third and final iteration the *corona civica* closely resembles the *corona graminea* in its construction; Pliny reports that 'a variety was further made with *quercus*, likely the *Quercus robur* L., combined with whichever tree grew where the crown was given, the honour being linked solely to the acorn'.[120] The shift from a species apparently sacred to Jupiter is perhaps not as great a concern as might be inferred from a reading of Pliny's account, since the *quercus* is more commonly associated with Jupiter in a wide variety of Latin literature.[121] The species type, then, is hardly important, given the general association between all varieties of oak and Jupiter. However, the distinction between type of leaf is crucial, since the final iteration of the crown took the emphasis away from the foliage and placed it upon the fruit.

The civic crown was well exploited in Augustan ideology and iconography, frequently appearing on coinage (worn or unworn) with the phrase *ob cives servatos* (for saving the citizens),[122] and hanging above the door of Augustus' house, as recounted in the *Res Gestae*, and by Ovid.[123] In the *Res Gestae*, Augustus directly links the civic crown with the people's gratitude to him for establishing peace, and this message is spread through the coinage that bears the crown during Augustus' reign. Such prevalence of the wreath ought to be seen in comparison to that of the *corona graminea*, of which no easily identifiable representation exists in either coins or relief, and no mention of it in the *Res Gestae*. Building upon the legacy of the grass crown, the *corona civica* became synonymous with acts that saved the city under Augustus, often accompanied by the legend *ob cives servatos* or similar, although it was bestowed upon an individual rather than awarded up to an *imperator*.

The movement to composing the crown of whatever foliage grew in the area where it was given further invites the comparison to the *corona graminea*, which fell out of use, and the association between the *corona civica* and the Augustan linking of the phrase *ob cives servatos* to the *corona civica* further shows the extent to which the *corona civica* overtook the role of the *corona graminea*. The inclusion and prominence of fruit, however, distinguishes the *corona civica* from the *corona graminea*, and influences the interpretation of the crown.

The lack of dates in Pliny's account of the composition of the *corona civica* causes us to have to identify the oak used in depictions of the crown, in order that the intended symbolism of the crown can be deciphered. For the Augustan period, compital shrines offer frequent depictions of the *corona civica*, and one of the best-preserved examples is found, in situ, on the corner of the Piazza della Bocca della Verità in Rome, opposite the Temple of Portunus (see Figures 3 and 4). This altar clearly depicts the pinnately lobed leaves of either the *aesculus* or the *quercus*, emphasizing the fruit, with the acorn being placed centrally in the leaf, in an entirely manufactured position.[124] The prominence of the fruit indicates that the emphasis of the Augustan wreath had moved from the foliage to the fruit, and that the *corona civica* depicted in the Augustan period was the replacement for the *corona graminea*.

Figure 3 Front view of the compital shrine, Forum Boarium, Rome. Photo taken by Andrew Fox (26 April 2016).

Figure 4 Detail of oak wreath on compital shrine, Forum Boarium, Rome. The stalks on the acorns suggest the *Quercus robur*, while the leaf maintains similarities to the *Quercus petraea*. Photo taken by Andrew Fox (26 April 2016).

To understand the importance of the fruit's symbolism, and how nature has been manipulated to convey one message over another, the wreath's frequent appearance on compital shrines must be addressed. Lott argues that the regularity of the crown's presence is an effort on the part of Augustus to place himself as a symbolic resident of every *vicus* in Rome. This argument recalls the crown above Augustus' door, and Lott suggests that the extension of Augustus' liminal honours, the *corona civica* and the *Laurus nobilis* L. branches, which are less frequently found on compital shrines, extends the reach of his *domus*.[125] Through such a manipulation of the honours given to him by the Senate and the people of Rome, Augustus finds himself able to have a presence across the city, with permanent depictions of mortal, natural honours giving his status as the saviour of the citizens a legacy not afforded by the extensive coinage.

The superimposition of the fruit over the leaf in the crown coincides with a transition from the Jupiter-associated *aesculus* to the *quercus* and indicates a distancing from the divine implications of the wreath under Augustus towards continued fertility. This aspect of the *corona civica* is repeated in the *corona triumphalis*, which also places a fruit at the centre of its leaves, unlike the leaves in reality. Fertility imagery is crucial in Augustan art, and Caneva's work on the botanic imagery of the Ara Pacis serves to emphasize the rich tapestry of botanical life that was used by the Augustan sculptors.[126] Drawing attention to the fruit in depictions of the *corona civica*, possibly an Augustus-inspired transition, promoted the image of the fresh growth of Rome, which had been ravaged by the civil wars previously and was now able to flourish, with no small thanks owed to the fertile influence of the city's new emperor, now found in every neighbourhood of the city.

Triumphal crown

The triumphal crown, or *corona triumphalis*, is very well known in antiquity, and is composed from the leaf of the *Laurus nobilis* L., which was known as a *laurea*, while the tree is a *laurus*, which became an early epithet for crown in Latin literature. The wreath's nature did evolve, and Aulus Gellius relates that the *laurus* was replaced by a gold crown by the second century CE.[127] The standard award procedure was to present it to any general celebrating a triumph, and in the Imperial period this presentation was exclusively reserved for members of the imperial family. Unlike the *corona graminea* and *corona civica*, the *corona triumphalis* is exclusively bestowed upon an individual, rather than being awarded upwards, from soldier to general, or laterally, from citizen to citizen. Depictions of the crown give the fruit prominence, in a similar fashion to the later iteration of the civic crown, and through this added element in the crowns, and their use in the architecture of the city of Rome, there was the potential for the crowns to be exploited for their symbolic value, which was reliant upon the trees that comprised them.

The identification of the crown's composition as *Laurus nobilis* is one of the most certain identifications of crown foliage in the ancient world, and the leaf is identifiable by its obovate structure with crenulations around its edge.[128] The ripened fruit of the *Laurus nobilis*, a dark purple berry,[129] will have suited the typical associations of the triumphal dress, which is often characterized as being purple and gold, and is likely to have been exploited in the composition of the crown.[130] Bradley's brief comments on the colours in the triumphal procession, however, suggest a general lack of focus on colour in descriptions of the procession, although the colour that is most commonly attested to identify the *triumphator* is purple.[131] As a result, and from the limited information we have concerning the actual events of the Roman triumph, the purple of the ripe *Laurus* berry would have complemented the prominence of purple in the ceremony itself, and the berries would have served as a powerful contrast in the crown's composition, and in its depiction on the Arch of Titus and the large wreath at the base of Trajan's Column (see Figures 5 and 6). Like the acorn on the *corona civica*, the fruit takes a prominent position, and is superimposed against the leaf on Trajan's Column, and between the leaves in the crowns on the Arch of Titus.

The contrast of the fruit is only possible in the context of the ripe fruit, since the unripe berry of the *Laurus nobilis* is green and pointed, a shape which is replicated by at least one Augustan sculptor (see Figures 7 and 8). In the winter months, when the fruit of the *Laurus nobilis* is green and contrast with the leaves is impossible, a new berry might offer such a distinction between leaf and fruit. The carving of the Augustan sculptor suggests that there may be a

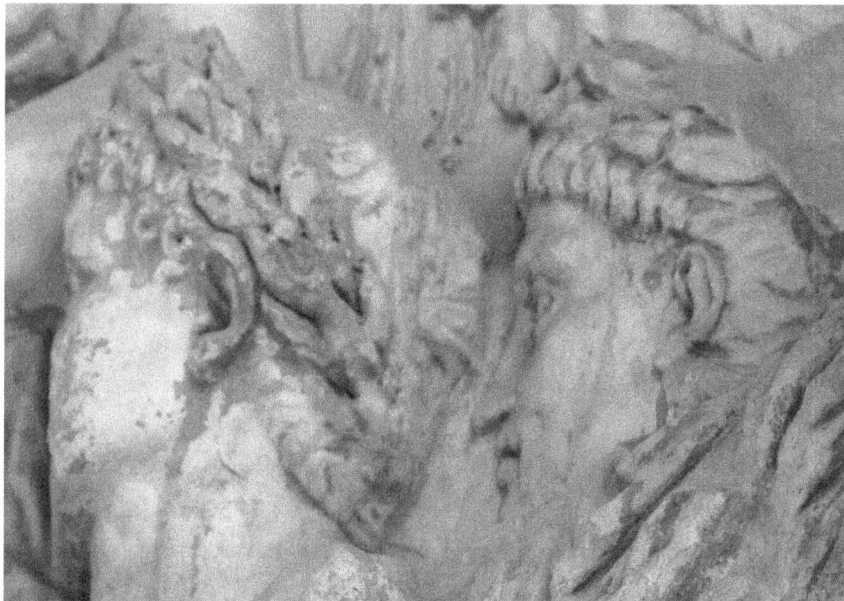

Figure 5 A wreath of *Laurus nobilis*, on the head of a soldier directly below Titus on the northern internal frieze of the Arch of Titus (post 81 CE). The berries of the crown can be seen between the leaves. Photo taken by Andrew Fox (2 May 2016).

Figure 6 Wreath of *Laurus nobilis* around the base of Trajan's Column. A mixture of pointed and rounded berries can be seen. Photo taken by Andrew Fox (27 April 2016).

Figure 7 The fruit of the *Laurus nobilis*, Isola Sacra, Portus. Photo taken by Andrew Fox (12 May 2016).

Figure 8 Fragment of frieze with *Laurus nobilis* branches. Augustan Age (first century BCE–first century CE). Church of Santa Maria Antiqua, atrium (inv. no. 593994). By concession of the Ministry for Cultural Heritage and Activities and Tourism – Archaeological Park of the Colosseum.

tendency towards realism in the carving of the fruit, and this is not replicated in the carvings of wreaths of *Laurus nobilis*, which universally show round berries. There is, then, potential for a new berry, similar to the ripe berry of the *Laurus nobilis* in both shape and colour, and able to be manipulated for its ability to contrast with the green leaves of the *Laurus nobilis*.

The possible aetiologies of the crown offered by Pliny neglect to mention any berry, in line with his assertion that the *Laurus nobilis* lacks one, and he identifies the purificatory properties of the *laurus* as being the genuine aetiology.[132] This is taken from a passage by Masurius, and is a popular one in modern scholarship.[133] The association of the *laurus* and purification is not unique to Pliny's citation of Masurius, a first-century CE author, and can also be found in Festus' epitome of the Augustan dictionary of Verrius Flaccus.[134] When it comes to the role of *laurus* as a tool to expel pollution, Pliny repeats himself at the close of Book Fifteen of the *Natural History*, this time without a citation, simply stating 'it is also employed for purification'.[135] Other trees with similar triumphal connotations are also found to be used for purification, and the most obvious, the myrtle, whose dark fruits ripen in the months while the *Laurus nobilis* berry is green, is found immediately before Pliny's chapters on the *laurus*.[136]

The role of the myrtle as a vehicle for purification is well attested, and it is employed in Rome's early myth-history as a purificatory element at the shrine of Venus Cloacina in the Forum Romanum, used to purify combatants of both sides in the peace after the war with the Sabines, an association shared with the *Laurus nobilis*.[137] It is again recognized in association with Venus Cloacina in Servius' *Commentary on the Aeneid*, where she is identified as a purificatory goddess. Servius gives Venus Cloacina three epithets: (i) *Myrica* (of the tamarisk),[138] (ii) *Myrtea* (of the myrtle) and (iii) *Purpurissa* (highly coloured, and closely associated with purple), and indicates the close link between the deity, purification and the myrtle. The epithet *Purpurissa* explicitly highlights the purple fruit of the tree.[139] Linking myrtle and *Laurus nobilis* in a triumphal context, outside of purificatory themes, has one precedent in Roman history, and a Marcus Valerius is reported by Pliny as triumphing with two wreaths, one *Laurus nobilis*, one myrtle.[140]

If there were an intent to maintain the purple berries throughout triumphal crowns, maintaining the contrast that is implied by the prominence of the fruit in depictions of the crown, then the myrtle berry would provide a useful substitute while also adding an additional, olfactory purpose. Plants were often used for their scent in the ancient world, and the deployment of them for their scent is sometimes portrayed as an expression of control over the plant itself: scent, like timber, is a product.[141] The leaf of the *Laurus nobilis*, better known as bay leaf today, has a scent familiar to a kitchen, and was recognized by Vergil:

> And I will take both you, *Laurus nobilis*, and you, neighbouring myrtle,
> Since when you are planted together, you mix your sweet scents.[142]

Vergil puts the *Laurus nobilis* and the myrtle together, as two harmonious scents, and this will have had an added benefit in the context of the triumphal procession. Here, the foliage of the *Laurus nobilis* and the myrtle, placed on the head of a triumphing general and rubbing against his head with every small movement, will have provided an aura of 'sweet scent' around him. In treating the general as a participant of the triumph, and not as a detached figure, we place him directly in the sensory assault of the procession of soldiers, captured people, and animals (with all their associated excrement), entering a city that exceeded a million population in the early Principate.[143]

However, the triumphing general will have needed to maintain a degree of separation from this smelly onslaught as he processed through the streets as either a king or a god. The triumph was a veritable riot of senses, and the odours of the triumphal *spolia*, from animal dung to the sweat of the soldiers and captured people who proceeded the general, will have only been one side of the olfactory onslaught that awaited him in his attempt to appear distant from the celebrating crowd in a Roman winter, all of which will have combined into a potentially overwhelming stench, only to be mitigated by the sweet scent of the *Laurus nobilis* crown, dressed in myrtle berries. This may have promoted the continued use of *Laurus nobilis* in the triumphal crown, and the potential use of myrtle berries to augment the scent.

As well as its benefits in changing the smell around the general, the myrtle adds a symbolic value to the triumphal decoration, one of particular resonance in the Augustan period. The myrtle was employed at the shrine of Venus Cloacina in the aftermath of the rape of the Sabine women to unify the two sides of the conflict, a process which led to Rome's expansion and the incorporation of the Sabine people and territories into Rome. So too, the triumph involves the leading of new territories into Rome, and the myrtle, sacred to Venus, promotes this unification. Through this manipulation of the symbolism of the trees in Rome, Augustan and early Imperial depictions of the *corona triumphalis* subtly lead to both the implications of fertility in the inclusion of a fruit, and the unification associations of the myrtle berry, a unification dependent upon the victory and peace symbolism of the *Laurus nobilis* foliage attached to it.

In these three crowns, trees are exploited for their physical properties: in the case of the *Laurus nobilis* (and possibly the myrtle) for their smell; their value as rooted representations of location, the *corona civica* being comprised of the foliage from the site at which it was won (following the precedent of the *corona graminea* in this regard); and the fruit of the tree being used to emphasize fertility. It is in depictions of the crowns that we can observe them being exploited for their symbolic value, particularly in the spread of the *corona civica* around Rome. Here, we can see an awareness of arboreal imagery in Augustan architecture, and the harnessing of nature, and specifically trees, to communicate Augustan policy, which emphasized fertility and growth, much as the acorn's emphatic position in the centre of the leaf in the *corona civica* on compital shrines implied fertility and placed the stress on the fruit as opposed to the foliage. Like the arboreal revolution in Augustan Rome, highlighted in the floral imagery on the Ara Pacis, the planting of evergreen trees around the Mausoleum of Augustus, and the treatment of the *ficus Ruminalis*, the changing nature of the *corona civica* promoted unity and fertility in Rome. The crown's presence on compital shrines, placed at crossroads across the city, made sure that this message was communicated throughout the city as opposed to the exclusive monuments mentioned above, and ensured that the effects of the arboreal revolution were felt in all quarters, rather than being reserved for those who interacted with the isolated monuments of Augustan Rome. The stress on fertility is apparent in the *corona triumphalis*, on which the berries again take prominence. This crown is symptomatic of a further manipulation and exploitation of trees, here for their olfactory qualities. In this instance, the leaves of the *Laurus nobilis* and its possible supplementation with myrtle berries become a tool for the *triumphator*, and are exploited to isolate the general from his rowdy and pungent surroundings, while also promoting unity through the combination of two trees.

Tropaea

Before the triumphing general entered the city, shielded by the harnessed aromas of the *Laurus nobilis*, the spoils of his victories were displayed to the people of Rome. From Pompey's time, trees were a part of this procession, and natural representations such as river deities had been an integral feature of the exhibition for several years before.[144] But trees had had a role in the procession since its inception, although not as a direct import. Instead, they were employed for their physical capabilities, particularly their strength and size, bearing the armour of fallen victims as *tropaea*.

These *tropaea*, or occasionally *trophaea*, were not exclusively triumphal, nor entirely arboreal. Some, like the Tropaeum Traiani at Adamklissi, were constructions outside Rome, temporary or otherwise,[145] while others were holdings for enemy armour within the triumphal procession and subsequently housed in the city. The holdings for armour and the temporary constructions were made from the wood of the local area, and arranged in such a way as to house armour, in a similar pose as a scarecrow.[146] Since the evidence for temporary constructions outside the city is limited to only a few pieces of literature, this section will only address representations of the housings for armour. Well-preserved depictions of the armour housing can be found on Trajan's Column, flanking the Victory shown halfway up the relief (see Figure 9).[147] These depictions show a tree-like structure bearing armour, although the nature of the structure makes the identification of it as a definitive tree challenging. The bases of the trophies on Trajan's Column are shrouded by shields, although the visible features of the wood are similar to those of the trees discussed earlier: knotted and weathered, following the deciduous type. Similarly, the other *tropaea* are questionable in terms of whether they are living trees, although for other reasons.

While the Trajanic trophies are clearly thrust into the ground, these others are depicted balanced on a *ferculum*, like the tree carried in the fresco from Pompeii depicting the marriage procession of Hercules and Iuventas discussed

Figure 9 *Tropaea* on Trajan's Column, Scene LXXVIII. Source: Cichorius 1896: plate LVII.

above. Earlier artistic precedent suggests that realism is not at issue in portrayals of trees on litters, evident in a red figure Attic *krater* from the fifth century BCE (see Figure 10).[148] Here, the tree offers visual cues such as foliage and a slightly flared base which indicate that the tree is alive and the potentially problematic felling of a tree in a ritual context is avoided. While realism is then superseded by the need for space in these artistic contexts, numismatic images cause confusion as to whether a *tropaeum* should be considered as a living tree. Greek numismatic representations indicate that the trophy was constructed from a living tree, with the characteristic flaring of the root at the base of the trunk, or foliage lower than the armour in some instances.[149] Roman depictions on coins are less ambiguous, showing the trophies as being less elaborate structures, more akin to a log thrust into the earth, with armour fixed to it, a depiction which remains consistent throughout the body of evidence.[150] Roman literary accounts complicate the simple Roman numismatic evidence, particularly in two representations of trophies from Vergil's *Aeneid* and Lucan's *Civil War*.

In Book Eleven of Vergil's *Aeneid*, Mezentius' armour is arranged on an oak trunk by Aeneas. This account has been treated as a *locus classicus* for the

Figure 10 Attic red-figure *krater*, fifth century BCE, housed in the Louvre, Paris (G 496).

construction of a *tropaeum*, and the trunk as representing the body of the fallen Mezentius.[151] This passage describes Aeneas lopping the branches off the trunk of the tree and arranging the armour on it, before pronouncing the structure to be Mezentius:

> Stripping a huge oak of all its branches,
> He thrusts it into the ground of a hill, and dresses it in shining arms,
> Stripped from the commander, Mezentius,
> A trophy to you, great god of war …
> '… These are the spoils and the first yield, taken from a proud king.
> This is Mezentius, made by my hands.'[152]

Here, there is no question that the oak is dead; there is no other explanation for Vergil's statement that it is 'thrust' (*constituit*) into the ground. This is in contrast with other *tropaea*, which are sometimes arranged on living trees. In Statius' *Thebaid*, Tydeus erects a trophy to his protector, Pallas Athena, and arranges armour both on and around an ancient oak.¹⁵³ Similarly, in the *Aeneid*, Pallas, the son of Evander, promises to arrange the armour of Halaesus on the Tiber's oak tree,¹⁵⁴ and in Lucan's *Civil War*, Pompey is compared to an aged oak tree, laden with the spoils of conquest:

> He stands, a shadow of his great name;
> Just like a lofty oak in a fruitful field,
> Bearing the aged arms of a people,
> And consecrated gifts of leaders, no longer
> Standing from the strength of its roots, fixed by its own weight,
> Casting bare arms through the sky, it makes shade
> From its trunk, not its leaves;
> And although it sways, about to fall under the first breeze,
> And many trees grow up around it with strong timber,
> It alone is worshipped.¹⁵⁵

This simile, which presents Pompey as a static general, significantly past his prime and without a future, reveals the continued life of a *tropaeum*, while the dedication of Mezentius' armour before showed us the creation.¹⁵⁶

These two accounts, from two closely related poems, offer differing versions as to whether the trophy is constructed of a tree or of timber. Mezentius' armour, as we have already discussed, is arranged on a piece of timber, while the trophy Pompey is compared to is a tree. However, this tree is clearly no longer alive, and is held upright solely by its own weight. The death of the tree is underscored throughout the simile, by the fertility of its surroundings (*frugifero ... in agro*), by the implications of weight (through the use of *pondere*) which call to mind Lucan's description of Pompey's corpse, and the *truncus* of the tree echoing his decapitated body.¹⁵⁷

Both of these literary *tropaea* subvert the triumphant nature of the structure in different ways. Pompey is a fallen icon, and the tree that is harnessed for *spolia* and used as a *tropaeum* indicates this. Similarly, Vergil's presentation of Mezentius' *tropaeum* is highly negative, a brutal anthropomorphization of a dead trunk. Other *spolia* in the *Aeneid* are more positive, while the *tropaeum* of Mezentius brings the action of the preceding books to an abrupt halt, and forces Aeneas to reflect on the cost of war.¹⁵⁸ The lopping of the branches, the insistence that this tree is dead, and the stained and broken *spolia* all create a gruesome trophy, and its dedication to Mars (evident from *bellipotens*) highlights its role in warfare,[159] particularly when juxtaposed with the oak tree, which is associated with Jupiter, sometimes in terms of sacrality.[160] This is a trophy of contradiction, celebrating a tragic victory.

The oak *tropaeum* is often associated with the *spolia opima*, and the deliberate dedication of Mezentius' arms on an oak to Mars rather than Jupiter Feretrius, the traditional recipient deity of the *spolia opima*, invites the comparison. The *spolia opima* was awarded following the defeat of an enemy commander by their opposite Roman commander.[161] Like the grass crown, the *spolia opima* is both rooted in Rome's earliest history and rarely awarded. They are distinct from the typical *tropaeum*, although the construction of the *spolia opima* as dedicated is similar. The typical *tropaeum* is erected on a hill: Mezentius' armour is arranged on a *tumulus*, the oak trophy that simulates Pompey is notable for its prominent position surrounded by smaller trees, and Servius tells us that this is typical, highlighting a trophy set up by Pompey in the Pyrenees;[162] the *spolia opima* are dedicated in the Temple of Jupiter Feretrius on the Capitoline, and are substantially rarer in Roman tradition. The *tropaeum* is permitted to any military commander and they are numerous in the Republic and the Empire. However, the *spolia opima* were traditionally only set up on the Capitoline three times in Roman history: by Romulus, Cossus and Marcellus.

Once the *spolia opima* had been obtained, the tree harnessed for their display is composed of oak, like the other *tropaea* in this chapter. This is not a compulsory feature of the trophy, and although several accounts of generic *tropaea* refer to the wooden frame, only the few referred to above mention the wood used.[163] The use of the oak is similarly inconsistent in the *spolia opima*, being employed twice out of the three times the spoils were dedicated: by Romulus in 752 BCE and by Marcellus in 222 BCE.

In the case of the *spolia opima* set up by Romulus, there are two variant traditions, put forward by Livy and Plutarch. Livy relates that Romulus, after killing Acron, the king of Caenina, during the Sabine women episode, stripped his foe of his armour, arranged it on a *ferculum*, and deposited the armour 'at an oak held as sacred by shepherds' on the Capitoline, before marking out the temple of Jupiter Feretrius.[164] The account of Plutarch, however, differs slightly, and Romulus cuts down an oak tree in the camp, fashions it into a *tropaeum*, arranges Acron's armour on it and carries it to Rome, there dedicating it to Jupiter Feretrius.¹⁶⁵ In both accounts, an oak is present, and Plutarch parallels his version of Romulus' dedication in the *Life of Marcellus*, the final time that the *spolia opima* were dedicated, in 222 BCE.¹⁶⁶ The statue of Romulus outside the Temple of Mars Ultor in the Forum of Augustus is described in brief by Ovid as 'bearing the arms of the conquered leader on his shoulders', and the inscription indicates that these arms were clearly those of Acron.¹⁶⁷ Further, the statue is believed to have been replicated in a painting in Pompeii, which shows Romulus bearing a trophy on his shoulder, which is a clear stump, from the texture of the tree.¹⁶⁸ Meanwhile, in Plutarch's account of the third dedication of the *spolia opima*, Marcellus arranges the armour of Viridomarus of Insubria on an oak and again carries it to Rome, dedicating it to Jupiter Feretrius.¹⁶⁹ The two oak trees are different from each other: Romulus' is described as 'exceedingly difficult' to fell, while Marcellus' oak is 'slender'.

The difference between the two types of oak (only in form: δρῦς is used for both trees by Plutarch) may serve to highlight Romulus' immense power, as a demi-god, compared to the merely human Marcellus, or perhaps to resemble their opponents. From a practical perspective, a more robust trophy would be required to carry larger armour, and a 'slender' oak would suffice as a trophy for a smaller man and lighter armour. In both examples from Plutarch, the tree does not equate to a figure that is ambiguously dead and alive. They have been definitely felled and are no longer alive, and there is no evidence that these trunks were treated as representative of the enemy whose armour was arranged on them.

Unlike other monumental trees, any tree harnessed for the display of the *spolia opima* potentially posed a significant threat to Rome, due to Roman attitudes to the armour taken from a dead enemy. Enemy armour, Versnel tells us, is considered to be a taboo item in Rome, and he argues that this taboo applies not only to the majority of armour, burnt outside the city as an offering to Vulcan, but also to the more distinguished armour dedicated as *spolia opima*.¹⁷⁰ At this point, Versnel invites us to consider that a *piaculum*, perhaps included within the dedication of the *spolia opima*, would lead to the power of the armour being bound to Jupiter Feretrius, and further directs us to Plutarch for an explanation as to why the spoils of war were not renewed or moved, and left to decrepitude.¹⁷¹ Plutarch hypothesizes two answers. First, perhaps the spoils are not cleared as a reminder that all men must die, and that when they die, their glory will fade. Or his second – and favoured – opinion is that restoring the armour of a fallen enemy would be to tempt fate, and a restoration of their power rather than the glory of the victor. The Temple of Jupiter Feretrius is not a crowded space for dedications, and the three *spolia opima* would not be jostling for space if they were present at the same time, as Propertius implies they were.[172] The unusual mention of the tree type in accounts of the *spolia opima* compared to the paucity of precise references to the material used for general *tropaea* is telling, since the oak is associated with Jupiter.[173] From the moment that the *spolia* are placed on the oak, be it branch or tree, it is linked to the deity, although a restoration of the *tropaeum* would restore the power of the conquered rather than the conqueror. The tree is employed and subjugated, with the intention to channel the power of the armour to the god, just as the oxen directs the power of the plough. The tree is a particularly useful vehicle for the potentially hazardous armour, since its mortal lifespan allows the power of the armour to dissipate without any adverse effects for the city, or any concern for the vitality of a tree which stood for a now long-dead foe.

Livy's account of Romulus' dedication of the *spolia opima* is unusual. Here, the tree is alive, and Romulus carries the armour to the Capitoline, dedicating it to Jupiter Feretrius by depositing it at (*ad*) an oak tree. This presents a fresh dilemma. In previous chapters, we have explored Hunt's re-examination of the opening to Pliny's *Natural History*, in which he refers to the *numen* of particular trees. This tree, we can assume, did not survive the building projects on the Capitoline with its status intact throughout the remainder of Rome's semi-legendary regal period, and the Republic, until 222 BCE, when the *spolia opima* were dedicated for the final time. Numismatic evidence for Marcellus' dedication indicates that there was a temple here, and the tree is not evident in these depictions.[174] Pliny relates, at the opening of the *Natural History*, that trees were once considered the temples of the gods. Hunt has challenged this as a blanket statement, arguing that there were degrees of sacrality, and that some trees are, ultimately, just trees. However, there will have been no temple for Jupiter Feretrius on the Capitoline for Romulus to dedicate the seminal *spolia opima* in, and perhaps this oak, historically associated with Jupiter and equated in the Augustan period with buildings, as in Propertius' description of the Porticus Pompeiana, could have been briefly repurposed as a makeshift temple by Livy, who wrote in the afterglow of Republican arboreal displays.

***

These arboreal displays, which lasted from the Republican triumphs of Pompey and Lucullus to Vespasian and Titus at the end of the first century CE, and perhaps beyond that, were used to demonstrate a total conquest and control over a foreign landscape. Like the river gods, displayed on litters, or the captives paraded through the streets of Rome, the trees of the conquered land were now brought under Roman control. For some trees, this was purely symbolic: the ebony imported by Pompey did not remain in Rome for long, and the plane became the tree associated with the victory instead. For others, Roman control was felt as a fiscal duty, and the balsam paid its dues to Rome each year, just as Juvenal reports that the grove at the Porta Capena paid rent to its new masters, the Jewish market. The trees displayed following the triumph were not used in an effort to push for geographical accuracy, but to evoke an idea of the far-off lands that had been subdued, and Trajan's Column shows us this departure from realism to establish a setting for a total conquest in a forest. Using trees to communicate ideas of conquest to future generations is not an unusual concept in Rome, and resembles the Julio-Claudian exertion of control over the triumph, and Roman attitudes towards their own immediate landscapes, as in the example of Pollius Felix from the start of this chapter. Trees were exploited to communicate key ideas annd ideals, and the initial use of trees in the *tropaea* is a particularly simple and compelling one, as a physical frame for the armour; the *tropaeum* echoes the size of the armour's original wearer: Pompey's oak towers above its rivals, belying its feeble root system and lack of offspring; the oak for Mezentius is monstrous; and Acron's armour needs to be displayed on a tree which befits its size. Elsewhere in the triumphal context, the deployment of trees is more complex, and the crowns of the period employ different foliages and fruits to adapt their messaging. The grass crown, barely seen in the Republic and defunct after Augustus, reflects the display of trees as a statement of total conquest, and this message is passed to the civic crown over the course of the latter's lifespan, which can be traced through visual representations that would have had a more lasting impact over Rome's populace than the brief display of a crown in a public space. Augustus' influence, and his consistent pressure for fertility and rebirth throughout the city, will have been felt at every crossroads, his civic crown displayed for all to see, carved into compital shrines across the city.

4

Keeping Trees in the City

Once trees had been imported to Rome, they needed to be planted, whether they were a triumphal import, like Lucullus' cherry may have been, or the plane tree, imported for its shade. Some of these trees will have found homes in the *horti* around the city or in private gardens, but others put down their roots in the city's urban spaces. These trees were rarely solely planted for their symbolic value; they had more tangible impacts on Rome's cityscape, and were planted for more than just their aesthetic qualities. This chapter begins by exploring one Roman's conceptualization of why trees should be planted in the city's ideal spaces, and will discuss how these trees would impact activities within these places. The chapter will then move to consider three complexes and buildings in the city of Rome, each of them suspected to have contained trees, but none of them with individually important trees, or trees planted as a result of a triumphal import. These sites are all impacted by the nature of the plantings within them, and the plantings engage in a dialogue with these buildings, in turn dictating the use of the site and being dictated by the intended use of the place. These interactions with the building and with visitors are influenced by the species of tree used, and in each instance the species planted in these sites will be identified and the potential planting discussed. After these three case studies, the evidence for which is brought from literature and Rome's Marble Plan, the chapter will close with an overview of how trees can control spaces in the Roman city, and a case study of the Mausoleum of Augustus' trees, replanted in the twentieth century. This case study will focus on the Augustan planting of the mausoleum and its surrounding areas, first identifying the trees that may have been planted there, and then examining the symbolic and topographical consequences. Through identifying the importance of these trees and the roles that the species of tree played in defining these spaces in the centre of Rome's cityscape, we can reframe Rome's

Vitruvius on porticoes

> The central areas, bounded by porticoes, should be decorated with greenery (*viridia*). This is because walking in the open air is very healthy, especially for the eyes, because from the plantations, a fresh and rarefied air flows into the moving body, sharpens the vision, and thus clears the eyes of the thick humour, and leaves the gaze clear and acute. Moreover, since the moving body heats up by walking, the air extracts the humours from the limbs and diminishes their repletion, dissipating what the body has, more than it can carry.[1]

Vitruvius places *viridia* at the heart of his ideal porticoed place, and links their inclusion to the health (*salubritas*) of the visitors. He expands that, by necessity, these green spaces have to be 'in the open air', and their ability to rarify the air is vital to the continued health of a body in motion. Davies has identified that air quality was a concern for a number of Roman authors, and that Horace encourages visitors to the city to put the smoke and din to one side, and to focus on other aspects.[2] The smoke was likely a result of the chief fuel of the city, wood, and the creation of open public spaces in the first century BCE such as the Porticus of Pompey and the *Horti* formerly owned by Caesar in Transtiberim will have created zones which might have provided some separation from the smells and sounds of the city.

Vitruvius' interest in the creation of the *viridia* is not, like his account of the lead workers' struggles with air quality, concerned with the creation of impurities of the blood in visitors, but instead presents a green space in a complex as a place for cleansing 'the thick humour' from the eyes of the visitor. Whether this 'humour' (*umor*) corresponds to a humour in the Hippocratic (or later Galenic) sense is unclear, and Vitruivius could have been using *umor* to refer to a 'liquid'. In this instance, it could be taken that the 'thick humour' (*crassus umor*) that greenery cleanses are reflex tears, created in response to a foreign irritant.[3] It would then be reasonable to assume that the foreign irritants are elements such as the smoke generated by Rome's fuel and other particulates that would be carried in the air in an urban space.[4]

The cleansing nature of green spaces is not unique to Vitruvius' writing in the ancient world. Herodian reports that the emperor Commodus was, in the late second century CE, sent by his physicians to Laurentum, to walk among the laurel groves. Herodian further tells us that Commodus was expected to benefit from the refreshing shade of the trees, and the purifying scent of the laurel trees themselves.[5] Conversely, too much shade could be understood as a negative thing for a tree, and Pliny tells us that the fir tree (*abies*) drips poison from its branches, preventing any growth beneath them.[6]

Vitruvius' focus on the moving body and repeated references to walking in the space tells us something about the expected activities of the area, specifically that they were expected by the architect to be primarily peripatetic (at least in the case of the Porticus of Pompey, which is Vitruvius' ideal building in Book Five). That porticoes are used for walking should be of little surprise; it is well attested in ancient sources, and walking is often linked with good health.[7] Celsus ranks the locations for walking for the purpose of exercise as follows:

> Walking up and down hill varies the movement of the body ... but it is better to walk under the sky than in a portico; better if your head permits it, to walk in the sun than in the shade, better in shade cast by a wall or trees than under a roof; it is better to walk in a straight line than a winding wander.[8]

Celsus' account tells us two things: first, that walking was known to be a healthy activity in the first century CE; and second, that walks in natural surroundings were particularly healthy. The inclusion of *viridia* in the urban porticoes of the late Republic and the early Imperial periods are unsurprising then, at least from a public health standpoint. But public health was not the typical use of a tree-lined porticoed space, and while Celsus advises immediately after the above passage that the ideal walk should build up a sweat, the amblers of a portico are unlikely to have done that.

Instead, porticoed spaces were primarily used as venues for discussion.[9] In the second book of Cicero's *On Oratory*, Catulus and Crassus walk and talk in a portico,[10] Pliny relates a meeting held in the Porticus of Livia,[11] and reports that his friend Spurinna held conversations or listened to books as he took his morning walk of three miles.[12] Meanwhile, Ovid directs men to porticoes to find a date,[13] and it is hard to imagine the public (and private) porticoes of Rome as being anything other than an ambulatory venue, whether the purpose of this was to discuss business, hold serious conversations with friends, or simply to wander aimlessly – the hallmark of a wealthy man.[14] It is possible, as well, that a portico may have contained different 'zones' which encouraged different types of walking; on the Marble Plan, the central avenue of Pompey's portico appears to have ended at the theatre with an arch, implying a more efficient, processional type of movement, while the circumnavigatory promenades could have been more ambulatory.[15]

As a venue within the ancient city for walks, either for business or for leisure, the porticoes of the first century had to remain pleasant places to be, and shade features in descriptions of porticoed places.[16] By making this shade greenery, per Celsus' advice, walking in these areas becomes a healthy activity, not just one with a commercial benefit. However, while Vitruvius identifies his ideal building and sets out a blueprint for its design, very few buildings actually seem to follow his vision, and this leads to trees being planted in a variety of ways around the city of Rome.

Three urban forests

The mechanics of how trees were physically planted in private Roman peristyle gardens has been examined before, and these techniques do not differ substantially from the techniques that appear to have been employed in public spaces.[17] Typically, these trees would have been planted in a series of planting pits or larger beds among the paved areas, and designs prioritized features such as shapeliness, symmetry and correctness. In terms of sustaining the trees in public spaces, trees typically only require watering when they are establishing, and Jansen suggests that domestic trees would be catered for simply by a cistern or a nearby fountain.[18] Given the ease in incorporating trees into paved urban spaces, it is unsurprising that they were present in complexes across the city, although their inclusion was rarely incidental. In the following three examples, different trees will be seen to be planted in different contexts, and each planting will have a different effect on interactions within and with the space in which the trees appear.

The Porticus Europae and the Porticus Vipsania

The Porticus Europae is a building with a complicated past, if it even existed at all. It is unclear where this building was in Rome, or when it was built, and its history has been broken down before by Prior.[19] The Porticus Europae is referenced in only one place, Martial's *Epigrams*, and Prior has identified it as a colloquial name for the Porticus Vipsania, following previous approaches, although Rodriguez Almeida has linked the Porticus Europae with the *dromos* of the Iseum Campense, on the Campus Martius.[20] The Porticus Vipsania, which was known by a number of different names in its lifetime, could be found on the Campus Agrippae, on the eastern side of the Via Lata. It was completed by Vipsania Polla, and begun by her brother, Agrippa, so its completion can likely be dated to the late first century BCE.[21] It was home to a map of the Roman world, perhaps similar to the *Tabula Peutingeriana*, and housed detachments of the Illyrian forces in 69 CE.[22] This section will treat these two sites as separate places, whether two parts of a larger complex (which may explain the feasibility of housing an army within the Porticus Vipsania), or as two separate porticoed sites on either side of the Via Lata.

Both sites are reported by Martial as containing greenery: the Porticus Vipsania contains laurels, while the Porticus Europae is populated with box hedging:

My attic looks out over Vipsanian laurels; I have grown old here.[23]

He runs back to the box hedging of warm Europa.[24]

Does he sit or amble in delicate Europa's sunshine among the box trees, warm in the afternoon, free of niggling concerns?[25]

The laurels in the Porticus Vipsania correlate with its triumphal imagery exemplified by the map reported by Pliny, and the purificatory nature of the laurel made it a popular choice in Augustan Rome.[26] There is the added factor to the laurel in Rome that it grows well enough to be ubiquitous on the Palatine today, and was widespread in the Augustan city.[27] It is entirely plausible that the laurels in the Porticus Vipsania are nothing more than incidental laurels that have self-seeded, and are not a part of any larger architectural plan. Without further evidence, the only conclusion that can be drawn is that there were laurels in the Porticus Vipsania, and that they would not have been detrimental to either the triumphal imagery or the typical Augustan deployment of trees.

The Porticus Europae, meanwhile, offers some greater indication of the role of trees in a built space. In *Epigrams* 2.14, Martial describes Selius' route around the Campus Martius, beginning with the Porticus Europae, where he praises Paulinus' feet, 'fast as Achilles'.[28] Later, in 7.32, Martial returns to the running track of the Porticus Europae, where he praises Atticus for neglecting the other pursuits of the sports ground in favour of running.[29] It is in *Epigrams* 2.14 that Martial introduces the box hedging (*buxeta*) of the Porticus Europae, alongside the reference to Paulinus' swift running. He returns to them in 3.20, this time as a potential venue for Canius Rufus to sit or stroll in 'delicate Europa's sunshine among the box trees'. The Porticus Europae, then, has two distinct uses in Martial's poetry, and three types of motion: sitting, strolling and running. This has the potential to create a complex space if not properly separated, and the box hedging identified in 2.14 is the ideal tree for this purpose.

In his letter to Gallus, Pliny the Younger describes his Laurentine villa and estate, and a *gestatio* partitioned, in part, by a box hedge.[30] His uncle, the elder Pliny, informs us that box is used in ornamental gardening, and that the native box forms the thick box hedge that we recognize today.[31] A space such as the one Martial describes would benefit from the division that a programme of box hedging would provide, and such a division finds precedence in other Roman green spaces with multiple intended uses. Further, while the box trees that Canius Rufus would have walked among are likely to have been taller than him – shade, after all, is a valuable commodity in the Roman city – the hedging would not need to have been. We might imagine, then, a track like Pliny's *gestatio*, running in a circuit around the edge of the porticoed space, partitioned by low box hedging, while in the centre of this circuit, as in Pliny's Laurentine garden, a small cluster of trees to stroll through or sit in.

Adonaea

The Adonaea is an unusual building, and the only comprehensive evidence we have for its design comes from four fragments of the Marble Plan (see

Figure 11). These fragments, 46acd and 46b, depict three sides of a possibly T-shaped building. These fragments were originally one whole, discovered in 1562, and there is a missing fragment of that original piece preserves in Cod. Vat. Lat. 3439, which extends the surviving inscription. In fragments 46acd and 46b, 167 smaller drilled dots are visible in the formation directly surrounding the central markings, which may indicate flower beds or water features. These drilled dots are likely to correspond to trees: they are too closely grouped together to realistically relate to columns. In the reconstruction presented in Lloyd's 1982 article, there are a total of 319 smaller drilled dots, although some

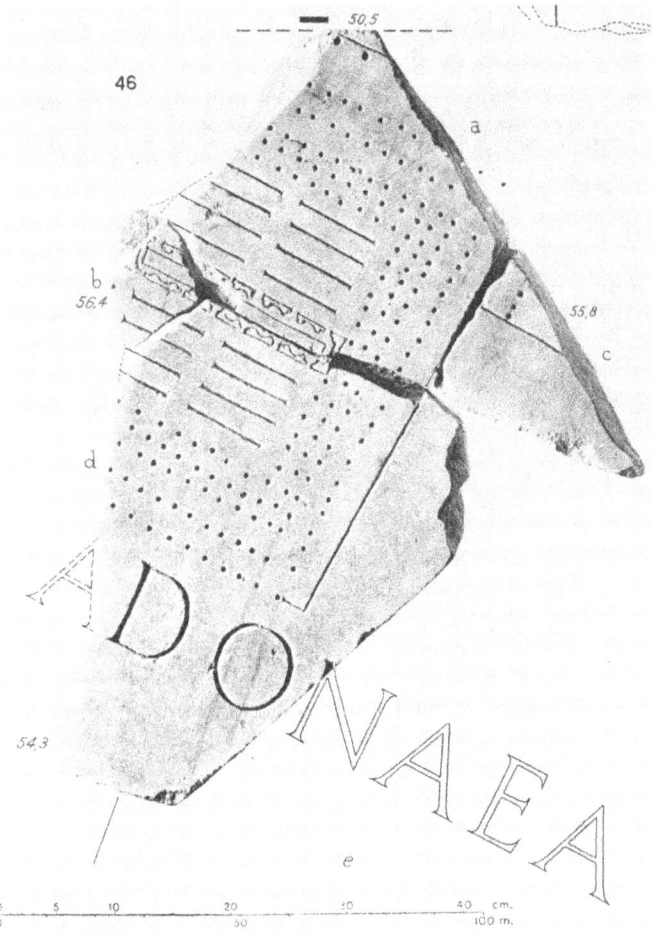

Figure 11 The Adonaea on the Marble Plan (Carettoni et al. 1960: Tav. 34). © Sovrintendenza Capitolina ai Beni Culturali.

elements of the reconstruction are conjectural and divert from other reconstructions. I follow Lloyd in discounting the larger drilled dots on the outer edge of 46acd, since these dots are distanced from the tightly gathered smaller dots, are of a different size, and a different spacing. The sketch from Cod. Vat. Lat. makes it clear that there is no division between the smaller dots of 46a and 46d, gathered in a tight square around the central markings, and the three additional dots of fragment 46c. As a result, we can surmise that there were a minimum of 170 small drilled dots in the original image of the Adonaea, and extrapolate that there were more on the corresponding opposite sides of the complex, perhaps aligning with Lloyd's reconstruction. The precise location of the Adonaea is unknown. Early attempts to place it on the Palatine have proven to be inconclusive, and despite a tentative identification of the site following an excavation of the Vigna Barberini in the 1990s, this garden has been reassessed as belonging to a temple of Elagabal from the third century CE.[32]

In terms of literary evidence, the Adonaea is only indirectly referenced by Ovid, who directs readers of the *Ars Amatoria* to the Adonaea as a good place to take a date, and lists it alongside a number of other venues we might recognize:

> Only walk slowly under Pompeian shade [the Porticus of Pompey],
> When the sun comes to the back of Hercules' lion,
> Or where the mother adds her gifts to her son's,
> A work rich in marble cladding [the Portico of Octavia].
> You shouldn't skip over the Porticus of Livia either, which
> Littered with antique paintings, keeps its founder's name:
> And where the daughters of Belus dare to plot death for their pitiable cousins
> And their fierce father stands, sword drawn [the Portico of the Danaids].
> And don't let Adonis, lamented by Venus, pass you by [the Adonaea],
> Nor the seventh day, held sacred by the Syrian Jews.[33]

These locations are noted for their shade, their wealth and their history, while all being porticoed spaces. As we have already discussed in this chapter, porticoed spaces are ideal for leisurely strolls in the city, but could also have involved sitting and taking rest. It is this latter use that the Adonaea lends itself to; the plan suggests a space too crowded for functional walking, especially in the three innermost rows. This crowding gives us some hints as to what planting we might expect in this location, as does the canonical description of worship of Adonis in a built-up space, from Theocritus' *Idylls* 15, which describes temporary arbours draped in dill, casting a shade in a courtyard setting, ideal for the romantic strolls of Ovid's *On the Art of Love*.[34]

The crowded depiction of the space clearly shows that any trees that may have been planted there are unlikely to have been mature trees, the roots of which would have competed against each other, and are more likely to have been a permanent arbour, which would have had plants grown up it to provide shade.[35] This is not a unique feature in the Roman city, and Pliny describes another porticus, the Porticus of Livia, as being shaded by a huge vine on trellises.[36] This, perhaps with the additional placing of pools in the central space (as indicated by the unusual markings on the plan), would make the Adonaea design resemble an artificial *locus amoenus* in the cityscape, a trope typically associated with rural landscapes, and an attractive location for both the worship of Adonis and for the more casual activities referenced briefly by Ovid.

Porticus Philippi

The Porticus Philippi neighboured the Porticus Octaviae in the Circus Flaminius, and surrounded the Aedes Hercules Musarum. The Marble Plan depiction of this building is highly fragmentary, and is found on fragments 31bb, cc, dd, eeff and ggz (Renaissance drawings) and hh (see Figure 12). It is a complex building, and appears to consist of two distinct phases. The oldest part of the complex is the round temple at the centre, the Aedes Hercules Musarum, and a rectilinear porch coming from it with a series of niches, four on either side.[37] This was built by Marcus Fulvius Nobilior, probably in the 180s BCE, following a triumph in 187 BCE. This dating places it as the oldest round temple in Rome. Surrounding this temple and porch, a second phase is found, of a more typical Roman design for the traditionally accepted construction date of 29 BCE by Lucius Marcus Philippus.[38] This colonnade is depicted as two concentric rectangles of dots, separated by a solid line, and excavations have revealed that the space between this solid line and the rectilinear porch was approximately three metres lower than the outer

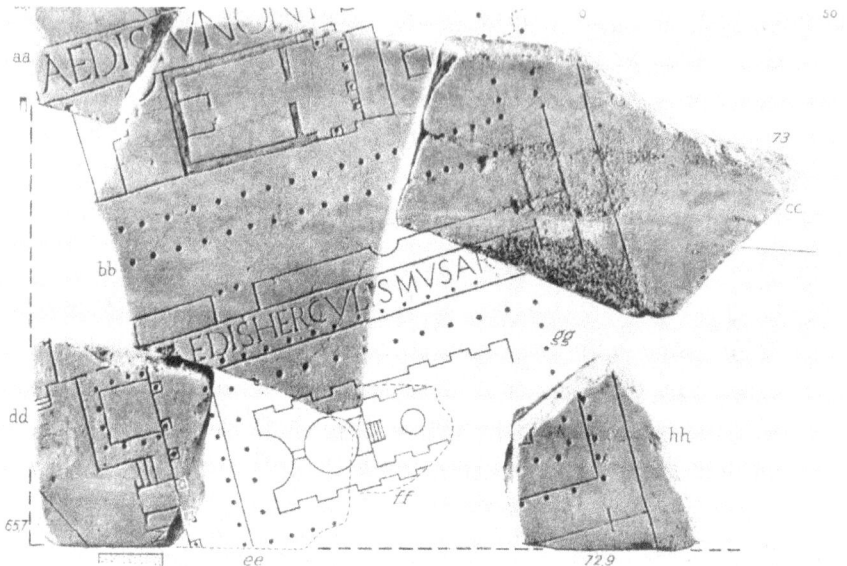

Figure 12 The Porticus Philippi on the Marble Plan (Carettoni et al. 1960: Tav. 29). © Sovrintendenza Capitolina ai Beni Culturali.

colonnade. It is unclear what the inner row of dots, in this depressed space, might represent, since dots can depict a number of features on the Marble Plan and the excavations were not conclusive. Coarelli proposes trees in his rendering of the space, and this leads to the concept of a treetop walkway in Augustan Rome.

The ancient testimony for this space is sparse, and none of the sources refer to trees in the space, only other activities, such as hairdressing,[39] and the artwork housed in the complex.[40] The space near the temple was used as a meeting place for the *collegium poetarum*.[41] There is a possible reference to this space being used for leisure, in Martial's whistlestop tour of the city, in the same epigram that looked for Cannius Rufus in the Porticus Europa.[42] Despite the paucity of evidence, however, we do have one indication that Coarelli's identification of the inner square of drilled dots might be accurate:

> Numa built a small bronze shrine for the Camenae-Muses, which, after it was struck by lightning and was moved into the Temple of Honos and Virtus, Fulvius Nobilior transferred to the Aedes Hercules, which is now called the Aedes Hercules Musarum.[43]

This passage, from Servius' *Commentary on the Aeneid*, links this potential urban forest with a story rooted in Rome's mytho-history, Numa and the Camenae. When we have discussed this before, the grove of the Camenae, outside the Porta Capena, was in its afterlife, the gods had moved on, and it was occupied by a Jewish market – an emblem of all that Juvenal's Umbricius believed was wrong with Rome. Here, we see Numa installing a shrine for the Camenae, at an undisclosed location, which was then moved to the Temple of Honos and Virtus, near the Porta Capena, and the same area as the Camenae grove. This shrine was then transferred by Nobilior to his new temple, the Aedes Hercules Musarum, and installed there. To plant a grove at this temple and around this relocated shrine would echo the original context, and could reinforce the transference of the shrine.

In the reconstruction depicted in Figure 13, we can see the space as defined by Coarelli's guide.[44] The trees chosen are poplars, which are linked to Hercules, the beneficiary of the round temple in the centre of the complex.[45] Other trees would cast more shade, and would create a more clear division between the two areas, colonnaded and sunken, and there is no indication that the bridging space between the temple and the Porticus was exclusively associated with one or the other. If we take Coarelli's reconstruction to be accurate, trees in the

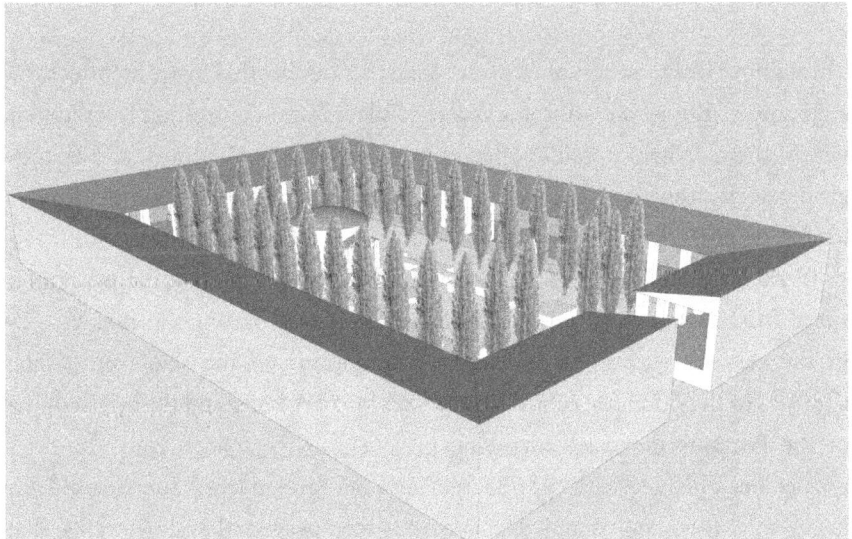

Figure 13 Digital reconstruction of the Porticus Philippi. SketchUp model.

depressed area would have a profound effect on the entire complex. As we have already established, the space underneath a tree's canopy is quiet, the canopy mitigating sound as well as air pollution, and the space between the portico and the porch would provide a sensible arena for, for example, poetry recitals. The sound from the upper level would be unlikely to carry down into the space below, and the noise from outside the complex would be deadened as a result of the canopy and the enclosing walls. If the lower area was used for the *otium* that Cannius Rufus was suspected of in Martial's *Epigrams*, then the upper area may have been used for *negotium* and the hairdressers identified by Ovid. This colonnade would have been less shaded than the traditional portico underneath a tree canopy, and the natural light may have helped with a trade based around appearance. The promenade that the portico offered, three metres above the base of trees in the complex, would have additionally provided an unusual perspective on the interior of the complex, and on the trees themselves. In addition to providing a place for *negotium*, it also defines a fixed boundary to the internal grove, potentially distancing uninvited visitors from it, and preventing any of the violations that Ovid advises shepherds to pray for forgiveness for.[46]

Controlling spaces

Throughout this monograph, we have seen trees embedded in the architectural cityscape of Rome, dictating the usage of places, and controlling interactions within them. Where possible, species types have been identified, and Rome's arboreal cityscape has become a cosmopolis of trees from across Rome's territories and beyond them.

In each example of trees discussed above, the trees dictate the usage of a space, from Pompey's Eastern planes in a complex celebrating a Roman victory in the east, mirroring his Alexandrian ambitions, to the shade-producing climbers of the Adonaea, echoing early worship of Adonis, and the box hedging of the Porticus Europae, mirroring private exercise spaces. Had Pompey's portico been planted with cypress trees, another foreign tree,[47] there would not have been the same dappled shade that encouraged the slow walks that characterized porticoes. The Porticus Pompeiana, as home to a double grove of plane trees, four rows of them, had to be large enough to fit the trees. The *Platanus orientalis*, which is the most likely candidate for the variety of plane tree employed in the portico, would have grown to a substantial size in the century since its planting, to a potential height of 30 metres, and with a typical spread of 8 to 10 metres. To accommodate four trees across the four colonnades, rising in 'strict order' as Propertius tells us they did,[48] and with symmetry prioritized in the design of Roman green spaces, the central zone of Pompey's portico had to be wide enough. Plane trees do not grow well in shade, so the space on either side of the plantings had to be substantial, but not so substantial as to negate the shade that the mature trees would eventually cast. This requirement establishes the need for the wide promenades of Pomepy's portico, and the inclusion of the trees, following Pompey's desire to compete with Lucullus, directs the portico's use as a shaded avenue for the slower walks established earlier.

The trees of Pompey's portico, at their full maturity, will have been visible from outside the compound, and while height has not been an often-discussed aspect of this study, which has typically focused on the role of trees from ground level, we might now appreciate the impact of a tall tree in a short building. The scale of the plane, like the trees on Trajan's Column, would have allowed for Pompey's complex to be experienced without impeding lower lateral branches. The tall, straight trunks would have framed the entire portico, and housed Pompey's displayed *spolia* under a shady canopy. They would have allowed different levels to be appreciated, and each trunk could more comfortably act as a stand in for a column, breaking and framing different views throughout the portico, just as the trees of Trajan's Column functioned as occasional scene-dividers.

Elsewhere around the city, trees such as those of the Porticus Philippi echoed the original trees of the Camenae grove, and sanitized the worship of the Camenae in their new home, while the laurel grove of the Caesars at the Villa of Livia commanded the landscape and reminded visitors to the city in the early Principate of the dynasty's power. Trees echo throughout Rome's toponyms, used by Romans to navigate and understand their monumental cityscape as a site of continued reception, from the pear tree that loaned its name to Martial's building to grander names, such as the Vicus Aesculeti and the Mons Querquetulanus. Working alongside these trees, the compital shrines, with their leafy crowns, reminded Romans of the foliage that once covered their city, and of the trees that still stood in the bustling metropolis.

At Rome's heart, trees were more likely to take on a monumental role, and when the Ruminal fig was moved to the Comitium during Augustus' reign it helped to redefine this as the new focal point of the city, moving away from the Lupercal. This movement was part of a broader programme of centralization within the Augustan cityscape, reorienting the foundational monumental history of Rome on the Forum, and the Comitium, with the Lapis Niger, Ruminal fig, and the statue of Attus Navius, in close proximity to the Lacus Curtius and overlooked by the Rostrum, was the focal point. Rome's leafy canopy spread from the administrative centre of the city, right out to the extreme edges and beyond, into groves just outside the city walls, and while archaeologically fugitive and difficult to track with a high degree of certainty, the impact of these trees on the cityscape cannot be underestimated.

Case study: Trees on the Mausoleum of Augustus

The Augustan period has been a constant presence throughout this study, from the Ruminal fig to the compital shrines to the Julio-Claudian laurel grove, and Augustus' impact on the arboreal cityscape can be felt even today, in the trees that surround his mausoleum, which were influenced by Strabo's description of the site:

> The most noteworthy is what is called the Mausoleum, a great mound near the river on a lofty foundation of white marble, thickly covered with evergreen trees to the very summit. Now on top is a bronze image of Augustus Caesar; beneath the mound are the tombs of himself and his kinsmen and intimates.[49]

Strabo does not specify a species of tree that cover Augustus' tomb, and excavations at the site have not indicated what type of tree was planted there. However, it is planted with cypress trees (*Cupressus sempervirens*) today. This tree, which Pliny tells us was an import from Crete to Tarentum at some point prior to the second century BCE,[50] was closely associated with funerary practices, and a branch was hung from the doors of households suffering a loss where the corpse was laid within.[51] Cypresses are routinely associated with death in Latin literature, and they are a logical choice for the Mausoleum, fitting the only descriptive requirement that we have: evergreen trees.[52] Reproductions of this site in Renaissance maps of the city rarely incorporate trees, and where they do, as in Pirro Ligorio's *Antiquae urbis imago accuratissime ex veteribus monumenteis formata* (1561), it is not clear what species of trees are being shown, and they should not be taken to be realistic depictions of the site in any instance. It was not until the latter half of the twentieth century, after the site had been cleared as preparation for the Mausoleum to one day house Mussolini's body, that it was planted with the cypress trees that surround it today.

This is not to say that there is not some debate about which trees were originally planted on the Mausoleum. Strabo specifies that the nearby *ustrinum* was planted with black poplars, but for the Mausoleum, the only specification is that they are 'evergreen'.[53] Claridge does not speculate on the tree type, and simply calls them trees, and Coarelli makes no mention of the trees at all.[54] Meanwhile, Carandini and Richardson speculate. Richardson suggests that the traditional cypresses would have grown too large and posed a risk to the structure, as well as obscuring the statue. As an alternative, he proposes low-spreading junipers – a tree with no association with death in Latin literature.[55] Meanwhile, Carandini tentatively suggests laurels in the caption to his diagram, although he has previously indicated cypresses.[56] Of these alternative suggestions, only laurel has any potential. Richardson's suggestion that the trees would grow too large is quickly countered by Roman engagement in *ars topiaria*, especially with cypress trees.[57] His concerns regarding root damage are slightly more challenging to address, although Roman adaptation of trees is not unusual; the creation of a dwarf plane, by a friend of Augustus, was roughly contemporary with the construction of the Mausoleum.[58] Carandini's tentative suggestion of the laurel would also address Richardson's concerns, being shallow-rooted and not too tall. It would also serve to echo Augustus' house and his perpetual triumph. However, the early date of the Mausoleum, before Octavian was Augustus and before an Augustan style had truly been developed, make this echo unlikely to be intentional, if there even was one, and the cypress remains a more likely candidate.

During Augustus' lifetime, his house had become an arboreal monument to his success, an oak wreath above his door, and laurels planted outside it.[59] To enter his house in Rome was to be reminded of his victories and his importance to the city, and this messaging was continued outside of Rome, in the Villa of Livia. After death, the mourning process was similarly perpetual, and the evergreen cypress trees as opposed to the transitory branches typically hung on doors continually reminded Rome of its loss. However, only planting trees on the Mausoleum itself would not be enough to establish a state of perpetual mourning; Romans must have been encouraged to use the space to make the plantings effective, and Augustus' efforts to bring people to the Mausoleum are evident from its surroundings and its prominent position on the bank of the Tiber, from where visitors to the city would be able to see the tall cypress trees as they arrived.

The broader landscape of the Mausoleum served a similar purpose to the shady plane colonnades of Pompey's portico, which encouraged visitors to enjoy the space and to appreciate the scale of Pompey's conquests and subsequent beneficence. Augustus populated the immediate area with *silvae* and *ambulationes*, and it had been established as a public park since 28 BCE, when Augustus began the construction of the Mausoleum.[60] While no trace of the design of these parks has ever been found, and no clue as to the design of them ever made apparent, they housed a number of sites that would have reminded Romans of the Julio-Claudians' importance to the city, and more specifically Augustus'. These included the Ara Pacis, the *ustrinum* and the Horologium, alongside many more altars.[61] This grand public park formed part of Augustus' large-scale re-landscaping of Rome, which included a renovation of Pompey's portico.[62] This renovation may have only been a renewal of materials and movement of Pompey's statue (which will have lessened the political impact of the place) to an arch which may have also been added by Augustus. As a result, the planting of the plane trees is unlikely to have been affected, but the reinvigoration of Rome's Campus Martius as a place to walk and talk is apparent.[63]

***

Green spaces abound in the ancient city, and were designed to encourage socialization and healthy activities within an environment where communications could be actively controlled by the builder. These urban green spaces were laid out to strict designs, and sometimes resembled the fixed, controlled nature of the buildings they were found within. Different species were used to communicate different messages, and to change the atmosphere of a place. In the Adonaea, shade was a priority, while the Porticus Europae may be focused on the development of a carefully designed and regimented exercise space, using formal hedging to establish a boundary between an exercise area and a more leisurely space. Designs did not only focus on the ground plan, however, and locations such as the Porticus Philippi demonstrate that consideration was given to utilizing different levels in the city's buildings. Elsewhere, trees were employed with the priorities of symbolism and larger topographical influence. The movement of the Ruminal fig to the Comitium enhanced the foundational symbolism of the space and complemented the monuments already there, while the cypress trees on Augustus' Mausoleum exploited traditional funerary practices to suggest Rome should be in perpetual mourning for Augustus and his dynasty.

Conclusion

A New Leaf

This book opened with a single tree in Rome's centre, and one overarching question: what was the impact of trees in the Roman city? We began with Rome's engagement with its historical trees, and how the memory of Rome's wooded past affected the cityscape of the late Republic and early Principate. This was sometimes evident in neighbourhood names, and other times in the depictions of mytho-historic Rome, as in Evander's tour of the forest cityscape. Trees were used publicly and privately to control a message beyond one lifetime, although that message was corruptible, evidenced by the grove of the Camenae, a result of public accessibility and the evolution of a site. As trees were introduced to the city of Rome, Romans like Pliny had to reckon with the morality of these introductions. The Roman natural historian considers characteristics such as utility, luxury and commercial benefit alongside his desire to establish Rome as a world city, and to pursue Roman dominance over the natural world.

This theoretical introduction of trees in the *Natural History* becomes reality in the context of triumphal imports, where trees were introduced as captives, and were depicted as adversaries in Trajanic triumphal artwork. As part of the conquered contingent in the triumphal procession, trees featured alongside rivers and mountains to represent the total conquest of a region, as the local foliage did in the *corona graminea*. Crowns and trophies employ leaves and trees to communicate across the city, both during the triumphal procession and beyond, in depictions on compital altars. These trees displayed Roman conquest with a greater sense of permanence than the transitory triumph, and their growth in the Roman city advertised the extent of Roman influence, whether through military conquest or through exploration and diplomatic ties, and a Roman arboreal cosmopolis could be established in actuality, beyond the confines of texts such as the *Natural History*. Outside of the boundaries of this triumphal context, trees are evident in Rome's wider cityscape. Typically planted in strict symmetrical designs within buildings, these trees reflected contemporary Roman desires to connect with the natural world around them on their strictly ordered terms, and to engage with the control and conquest of a landscape that was idealized in foundational poetry such as Vergil's *Aeneid* as being wild and untamed

Green spaces in the ancient city had an impact on reducing pollution within key ambulatory sites, both air and sound, and Romans will have found these sites to be sanctuaries from the noise and din of the city. Several of these trees have not been examined here: the Capillata of the Vestals, the laurel trees that likely surrounded the Temple of Caesar in travertine planters, the trees of the various *Horti*, and the other trees of the Roman Forum, the Lacus Curtius trio of fig, olive and vine being the most famous example. Trees were found across the ancient city, and directly affect the architecture of buildings such as the Porticus Philippi and Adonaea, adding shade and framing features to otherwise open spaces, directing activities within them, from worship to walking to reciting poetry. Inclusion of these trees into urban spaces enhances our understandings of these locations. Future examinations of nature in the Roman city could look to these trees, and others, to understand their role in a city that, while it continually evolved and re-evolved, maintained its connection with its natural origins, and preserved the memory and vitality of trees throughout its congested landscape.

Appendix: Categorized List of Contents for Books Twelve to Seventeen of Pliny's *Natural History*

All translations of specific species types are led by those proposed by Jacques André (1985).

Book Twelve.
Key: **Trees**; *Plant/fruit/other product*; **Historical reference**; General/Other

Chapter	Topic: The nature of trees		
1	<u>The grace of trees</u>		
2			
3		**Plane**	***When it first came to Italy, and from where.***
4			Its nature
5			Miracles concerning it. Dwarf plane
6		**Who was the first to decide to prune tree gardens**	
7		The Assyrian apple. How it is planted.	
8		Trees of India	
9	**On Foreign Trees**	Trees of India	**When ebony was first seen in Rome. Of which *genera***
10			Indian thorn tree
11			Indian fig
12			Forms of Indian trees without names. Flax-bearing Indian trees. The *pala* (Borassus/Palm). *The ariera fruit.*
13			Forms of Indian trees without names. Flax-bearing Indian trees. The *pala* (Borassus/Palm). *The ariera fruit.*
14			*The pepper trees. The genera of peppers. Bregma. Zingheri or Zimpheri.*
15			*Caryophyllon, Lycium, or Chironian pyxacanthus*

Chapter	Topic: The nature of trees		
16			Achir
17			Sugar
18		The trees of the Abianan people, the same of the Gedrosians, and the Hyreanians	
19		The same of the Bactrianans, Bdellium, or Brochon, or Malacha, or Maldacon. Scordastum. *Adulterations used in all the odours and condiments, experiments, values.*	
20		**Trees of Persis**	
21		**Trees of the islands of the Persian Sea. The cotton tree.**	
22		The tree called *cyna* (**Kapok**). From which trees cloth is made in the Orient.	
23		In which places no leaves fall from the trees.	
24		*How the fruits of the trees are used.*	
25		*About the costus.*	
26		*About the nard. The twelve different types.*	
27		*About the hazelwort.*	
28		*About the cardamom.*	
29		Cardamomum	
30		About a region producing incense	
31		About a region producing incense	**About which trees bear incense**
32			*The nature of frankincense and the varieties*
33		*About myrrh*	
34		*About myrrh*	**About which trees bear it**
35			*The nature and types of myrrh.*
36		**About cashew**	
37		*About pink rock roses, and stobolon*	
38		*Gum procured from the olive tree.*	
39		**The Savin Juniper**	
40		**The stobrum**	
41		On the happiness of the Arabians	
42		**On cinnamon, *cinnamomum, xylocinnamum*.**	
43		On Chinese Cinnamon	
44		Commiphora and Agarwood.	
45		Serichatum and gabalium.	

Appendix

Chapter	Topic: The nature of trees	
46		**Moringa**
47		**The Egyptian Date**
48		*About the scented reed*
49		*Hammoniacum*
50		*Scented moss*
51		**The Cyprus tree**
52		**Clovers (with long leaves) or the camel thorn**
53		*Oriental Oregano?*
54		*On Balsam (3 types)*
55		**The styrax officinalis**
56		*The Galbanum*
57		*On Opopanax*
58		*Spignel/Baldmoney*
59		**Indian Cassia**
60		*The oil or juice of unripe olives or grapes*
61		*Moss, wild vine, grapes from wild vines*
62		**Palmetto or the spathe**
63		**Cinnamon, or *Comacum***

Book Thirteen.
Key: **Trees**; *Plant/fruit/other product*; ***Historical reference***; General/Other

Chapter	Topic: On foreign trees		
1	On perfumes		***When they were introduced***
2			*The varieties and 21 compositions*
3			*Scented powder, mixtures. The test of unguents*
4			*The quantity of luxury in unguents*
5			***When they were first used by Romans***
6	**On the palm**		
7		**On the palm**	On their nature
8			How they are planted
9			The varieties of the fruit and 49 signs
10	**Syrian trees. The Pistachio, Syrian fig, Damascan prune, the Sebesten**		
11	**Cedar.** Which trees bear three years' worth of fruit simultaneously.		
12	**Terebinth**		
13	*Sumac*		
14	**Egyptian trees. The Alexandrian fig.**		
15	**The Cyprian fig.**		
16	*Plant pod*		
17	**Persian tree.** On which trees fruit regularly grows beneath each other		
18	**The doum palm**		
19	**The Egyptian thorn**		
20	*The eight varieties of gum. The Astragalus*		
21	On Papyrus		On the use of paper. ***When it was created***
22			How it is made
23			Their 9 varieties
24			The testing of paper
25			The defects of paper
26			***On the past of paper***
27			***On the books of Numa***
28	**Ethiopian trees**		
29	**A tree of Mount Atlas. On the citrus tree**	*On citrus tables*	

Chapter	Topic: On foreign trees	
30	**On the citrus tree**	*What things are good or bad in these tables*
31		*The citrus fruit*
32	**Lotus**	
33	**The trees of Cyrenaica. The Paliurus**	
34	*Nine varieties of the Punic apple.* **The pomegranate**	
35	**Asian and Greek Trees**	*The smooth rupturewort. The heather tree. The Cnidian grain or the flax leaved Daphne*
36		*The tragion, the astragalus gummifer*
37		*Ephedra,* **Tamarisk, the Hop Hornbeam**
38		***Euonymos***
39		**Broomrape tree**
40		**The Greek Strawberry tree**
41		**The Smoketree, the strawberry tree**
42		**The giant fennel**
43		*The deadly carrot*
44		*The caper*
45		*Nutsedge*
46		*Mugwort*
47		*Cytisus (could be moon trefoil)*
48	**Trees** *and Fruits in our sea*	
49		
50	**The same in** *the Red Sea*	
51	**The same in** *the Indian ocean*	
52	**The same in** *the Troglodytic sea. Neptune grass, marine algae, the hair of Isis, Charito-blepharon*	

Book Fourteen.

Key: **Trees**; *Plant/fruit/other product*; **_Historical reference_**; General/Other

Chapter	Topic: Fruit-bearing trees
1	
2	On the nature of the vine
3	How fruits are harvested. On the nature and care of grapes.
4	91 varieties of vines and grapes
5	Distinctions regarding the cultivation of vines
6	On the creation of mead
7	On the nature of wines
8	50 distinguished wines
9	38 noble foreign wines
10	7 types of salted wines
11	On 18 types of boiled and sweet wines
12	3 types of second best wine
13	***When distinguished wines began to be grown in Italy.***
14	***Observations on the wine from the reign of Romulus***
15	***Which wines were used in antiquity***
16	On Opimian (Falernian) wine. Notable facts around storehouses.
17	***When four types of wine were first served***
18	5 uses from the wild vine. Which wines are, by nature, the coldest.
19	66 types of fictitious (artificial) wine
20	Honey mead, or lesser honey mead, or water-mead
21	Vinegar honey mead
22	12 types of marvellous wines
23	On which wines might not be used for the sacred rites
24	By what means unfermented wine is made
25	By what means unfermented wine is made.	On the pith, resins
26	On vinegar. On the lees of wine.
27	On vessels for wine. On store rooms.
28	On drunkenness
29	Things with the strength of wine derived from water and fruits.

Book Fifteen.

Key: **Trees**; *Plant/fruit/other product*; **Historical reference**; General/Other

Chapter	Topic – On the nature of fruit bearing trees		
1	**On the olive**		***For how long it was only in Greece***
2			***When it first came to Italy, Spain, and Africa.*** **On the nature of the olive** *and the creation of olive oil*
3			*On olive oil. Types and excellences of olive oil.*
4			*15 types of olive*
5			*On the nature of olive oil*
6			*The growth of olives. On harvesting olives. How they become olive oil.*
7			*48 types of artificial olive oil.* **The Castor tree.**
8			*On the dregs of oil.*
9	*The varieties and natures of every fruit.*		*4 types of pine nut.*
10			*4 types of soapweed.* **4 types of quince.**
11			*9 types of Carthaginian fruit. 7 types of Persian peach.*
12			*12 types of prune*
13			*On the Mimusops*
14			*30 types of apple.* **At what time foreign apples came to Italy, and from where.**
15			*Which are newest*
16			*41 types of pear*
17			On varieties of grafts and repairing lightning
18			On harvesting fruits and grapes
19			*29 types of fig.*
20			**On the history of figs**
21			On caprification[1]
22			**3 types of hawthorn**
23			**4 types of mountain ash**
24			*9 types of nut*
25			**8 types of chestnut**

Chapter	Topic – On the nature of fruit bearing trees		
26			**The Carob tree**
27			**On the mulberry tree**
28			**On the strawberry tree**
29			*On the nature of berries.*
30			*9 types of cherry.*
31			**The cornel. The mastic tree**
32			*13 differences between juices*
33			*13 differences between juices*
34	*The varieties and natures of every fruit.*		
35	**On the myrtle**		
36			*History of the myrtle*
37	**On the myrtle**	**11 varieties of it**	
38			*History of the myrtle*
39	**Laurel. 13 types of it.**		
40	**Laurel. 13 types of it.**		

Book Sixteen.

Key: **Trees**; *Plant/fruit/other product*; **Historical reference**; General/Other

Chapter	Topic – **On the nature of forest trees**		
1	Countries without trees		
2	Miraculous trees in the northern regions		
3		On the civic crown	
4		**On the origin of crowns**	
5		Which leaves are used for crowns	
6		*13 types of acorn*	
7		**On the beech**	
8		On the other acorns. On fuel.	
9		On the gall nut.	
10	**On acorn bearing trees**	The multitude of other things except acorns that are borne on the same trees	
11		The multitude of other things except acorns that are borne on the same trees	*The catkin*
12		The multitude of other things except acorns that are borne on the same trees	*Oak galls*
13		The multitude of other things except acorns that are borne on the same trees	*Fungus*
14	*Of which trees the bark is used*		
15	*On shingles*		
16	**On the pine**		
17	**On the wild pine**		
18	**The pitch pine. The fir.**		
19	**The larch. The pitch pine.**		
20	**The yew tree**		
21	*The means in which liquid pitch is made. How cedar oil is made*		
22	*How thickened pitch is made, which resin is cooked.*		
23	*Waxy pitch*		

Chapter	Topic – **On the nature of forest trees**	
24	Of which trees the wood is valued	4 types of ash
25		2 types of lime tree
26		10 types of the maple tree
27		*Growths on the maple, and the bladdernut*
28		3 types of box
29		6 types of elm
30	The nature of trees according to site.	On mountains, on fields
31	The nature of trees according to site.	Dry soil, wet soil, both equally.
32	**Division into species**	
33	**On which trees leaves don't fall. On the rhododendron on which not all the leaves fall. Places in which there are no trees**	
34	On the nature of falling leaves	
35	**Trees which have varying colours of leaves. 3 types of poplar. The trees of which leaves change shape**	
36	Leaves which turn round every year	
37	The care and use of the leaves from palms	
38	Miraculous facts about leaves	
39	The natural order in crops	
40	**Which trees never flower. About the juniper**	
41	**On the conception of trees. On their germination. On their flowering.**	
42	**In what order they flower**	
43	**On the cornel. At what time trees bear fruit**	
44	**Trees which bear through the whole year. Trees which bear three years' worth of fruit simultaneously**	
45	**Trees which do not bear fruit. Trees which are reckoned unlucky**	
46	**Trees which lose their fruit and flowers most easily.**	
47	**Trees which do not bear fruit in particular places.**	
48	**How trees bear fruit.**	
49	**Trees on which the fruit precedes the foliage.**	
50	**Twice and thrice bearing trees per year**	
51	**Which trees grow old very quickly and which age very slowly.** *The Apricot fruit.* The late season.	
52	**Trees on which several other things are produced.** *The kernel of the box tree fruit.*	

Chapter	Topic – **On the nature of forest trees**	
53	**Differences between the trunks and branches of trees**	*Jujube or Greek beans*
54	**Differences between the trunks and branches of trees**	**On the branches**
55	**Differences between the trunks and branches of trees**	**On the bark**
56	**Differences between the trunks and branches of trees**	**On the roots**
57	**Trees which spontaneously grow from the ground**	
58	**How trees are born [spontaneously]. The differing natures of trees not growing everywhere.**	
59	**The differing natures of trees not growing everywhere**	**Where no trees are born**
60	**The differing natures of trees not growing everywhere**	**On the cypress**
61	Things often born from the earth that it has not given birth to before.	
62	*On ivy. 20 types of it.*	
63	*Thorny bindweed*	
64	*On water plants*	*On reeds. 28 varieties of the reed. On reeds used for writing*
65		*On reeds used for arrows*
66		*Reeds used for pipes. Reeds of Orchomenos and reeds used for fowling and fishing*
67		*On the reeds of vine-dressing.* **On the alder.**
68		**On the willow. 8 varieties of it.**
69		**Trees used except for the willow for binding**
70		*On rushes, candle-rushes, reeds, and thatching reeds*
71		**On elder trees,** *on bramble bushes*
72	*On the juices of trees*	
73	**On the nature of materials of the trees**	
74	**On the felling of trees**	
75	**On the felling of trees**	
76	**On the size of trees.** *On the materials used for building.* **On the spruce**	
77	Methods of obtaining fire from wood.	
78	**Trees which do not feel dry rot, trees which do not crack.**	
79	*Historical facts on the durability of wood.*	
80	The types of boring worm	

Chapter	Topic – **On the nature of forest trees**	
81		
82	<u>On the materials used by carpenters</u>	
83	*On wood glued together*	
84	*On veneering*	
85	The age of trees	*A tree planted by Africanus. A 500 year old tree in the city of Rome*
86		*Trees from the founding of the city*
87		*Trees older than the city in the suburban districts*
88		*Trees planted by Agamemnon. Trees from the first year of the Trojan war. Trees from that place called Ilium ad Troy older than the Trojan war*
89		*The same in Argos. Trees planted by Hercules. Trees planted by Apollo. Trees older than Athens.*
90	**Which species of trees age the least**	
91	*Trees that have been rendered famous by events*	
92	*Plants which do not have a set location for growth.*	
93	*Plants which live on trees and cannot grow on the earth. 9 varieties of them. The cassytha vine, mistletoe, knapweed. On mistletoe and similar plants.*	
94	*On the growing of mistletoe.*	

Book Seventeen.

Key: **Trees**; *Plant/fruit/other product*; ***Historical reference***; General/Other

Chapter	Topic – **On the nature of cultivated trees**	
1	**Incredible prices of trees**	
2	**The effect of weather on trees.** *Which part of the skies vines ought to see.*	
3	What kind of earth is best	
4	On the eight types of the Earth, which are enjoyed by Greeks, *Britons* and Gauls.	
5	On the use of ashes	
6	On dung	
7	Which crops make the earth more fruitful, what exhausts it	
8	How manure is used	
9	**How trees are planted**	
10		**Grown by seed**
11		**Which trees never degenerate**
12		**Grown by sprout**
13		**Grown by graft and cuttings**
14		About nursery plots.
15		**On the growth of the elm**
16	How trees are planted	On ditches
17		**On the intervals to be left between trees**
18		On shade
19		On dripping from the leaves
20		**Trees which grow slowly, which grow quickly**
21		**Trees grown from layers**
22		*How it was discovered*
23		By inoculation
24	On grafting	The varieties of grafting
25		On grafting the vine
26		By the insertion of bark
27	*Plants born from a branch*	
28	*Plants which grow from cuttings and how they are planted*	
29	**The cultivation of the olive**	

Chapter	Topic – **On the nature of cultivated trees**	
30	**The cultivation of the olive.** <u>An enumeration of the work required for producing young shoots throughout the year</u>	
31	<u>On loosening the earth around trees and heaping it up</u>	
32	**On willow groves**	
33	*Reed beds*	
34	*On others which are cut for poles and stakes.*	
35	The culture of vines and of their shrubs	
36	*The culture of vines and of their shrubs. The grapes not disturbed by animals*	
37	**The diseases of trees**	
38	**Prodigies from trees**	
39	**Treatment of trees**	
40	Treatment of trees	How they are irrigated
41		**Miraculous facts about irrigating**
42		On incisions made in trees
43		**How they are pierced with holes. The gelding of trees**
44		*Caprification*
45		**Treatment as a result of pruning**
46		**Faults found with the manuring of trees**
47		*Medicaments of trees*

Notes

Introduction

1 Plin. *HN* 15.77.
2 Livy 10.23.12.
3 Dion. Hal. *Ant. Rom.* 1.32.4–5. Cf. Livy 1.4.5; Varr. *LL* 5.54; Ov. *Fast.* 2.411–12.
4 Ovid's etymology of the tree, at *Fast.* 2.411–12, offers some idea as to this conflicting history: *arbor erat: remanent vestigia, quaeque vocatur / Rumina nunc ficus, Romula ficus erat.*
5 Dion. Hal. *Ant. Rom.* 1.79.
6 Conon, *Narr.* 48 (πρὸ τοῦ βουλευτηρίου).
7 Dion. Hal. *Ant. Rom.* 3.71.5 (πρὸ τοῦ βουλευτηρίου). The identical phrasing of Dionysius' and Conon's descriptions may be an indication that the two fig trees are identical.
8 Plin. *HN* 34.21. Had the Navian fig been damaged in the burning of the Curia Hostilia, it is not unlikely to expect it to have been mentioned in Cicero's *Pro Milone*, particularly since the razing of groves is a negative trope that he exploits in this speech.
9 For the Silvanus fig, see Plin. *HN* 15.77. The first source to name the *ficus Navia* is Festus' second century epitome of Verrius Flaccus' Augustan work, and all contemporary sources distance the Comitium fig from the Navian myth, using it as a geographical placeholder, as in Dion. Hal. *Ant. Rom.* 3.71.5, or not mentioning it in the context of the Navian memorials, as in Livy 1.36.5, and Cic. *Div.* 1.31–3. Given the complete absence of named references to the *ficus Navia* prior to a second century attribution, which Evans (1991) and Hunt (2012; 2016) both ignore, alongside several others, it seems unnecessary to complicate the already crowded memorial arena of the Comitium with a second monument to a lesser myth, especially when this monument can quite simply be explained by an accumulation of cultural attribution from the statue (which is present in ancient sources) to the Ruminal in its later life.
10 Livy 1.4.5 on the site of the Lupercal, *ubi nunc ficus Ruminalis est*; Ov. *Fast.* 2.411–12.
11 The transfer of arboreal identity is found echoed at the opening of Cicero's *De Legibus* (1.1–5), when Quintus recalls an oak named the Marian Oak from his

youth, the identity of which is transferred to a new tree on the same site, regardless of its relationship to the original tree.
12 Tac. *Ann.* 13.58.
13 Syme (1958: 745) dismisses the death of the tree as 'brief, isolated, and meaningless' in Tacitus' *Annals*, although Segal (1973: 108) argues that the tree's isolation 'make[s] it stand out all the more ominously.'
14 Segal 1973: 113–15.
15 Hunt 2012: 122.
16 Dion. Hal. *Ant. Rom.* 3.71.5.
17 Conon, *Narr.* 48.
18 This shift may have occurred during a centralization of Roman memorial tradition under Augustus, or to distance the location of Augustus' house on the Palatine from the mythical site of Romulus' exposure, in a move of false modesty.
19 Fest. 168L–170L.
20 See Hunt 2016: 116–19.
21 Varro, *Rust.* 2.11.5. It is also possible that these priests were responsible for the movement of the Ruminal from its Palatine location to the Comitium, which occurred with minimal disruption to its identity.
22 Varro, *LL* 5.152.
23 Stearn's *Botanical Latin* (1966: 84; 387; 582) is similarly blunt in its definition of *arbor* as a tree.
24 Plin. *HN* 14.9.
25 Columella, *De Arboribus* 1.1.
26 Verg. *G.* 2.9–34.
27 Isid. *Etym.* 17.6.1.
28 Verg. *Aen.* 9.115–16.
29 Ap. Rhod. *Argon.* 1.527.
30 Broise and Scheid 1993: 151.
31 Dumezil 1975: 43.
32 Quint. *Inst.* 1.6.34; Serv. *Comm. Aen.* 1.441.
33 Isid. *Etym.* 14.8.30, 17.6.7. Hunt reads this artificial form of light as candles (2016: 150).
34 Hunt 2016: 148–50.
35 *CIL* i^2 366; xi 4766. Panciera (2006: 903–19) identifies variant language in the inscription, of *caidito* and *caidere* for *cedito* and *cedre*, a dialectal difference in early Latin (Sandys 1927: 163). To accommodate the ambiguity between 'enter' and 'cut' or 'slaughter', Dowden (2000: 108) includes 'cut' in a parenthesis, while Hunt (2016: 128) questions her translation.
36 Ov. *Fast.* 4.749–55.

37 Hunt (2016: 132) examines this complexity in a religious context, and refers to the navigation of sacrality and the destruction of potentially sacred trees a 'live and ambiguous issue'.
38 Hunt (2016: 137–40) refers to a practice of 'piacular pruning' in the Arval grove, translating *coinquere*, only found in the Arval inscriptions and in Festus, as 'to prune'. For an alternative reading of these inscriptions and this passage, see Fox (forthcoming).
39 Plin. *HN* 16.132.
40 Hughes 2014: 235.
41 Hughes 2014: 226–8.
42 Meiggs 1982: 372, citing Lucr. 5.1370–1. Later, at 374, Meiggs also reminds his readers of Tertullian's comment that 'woods have given way to the plough' (Tert. *De anim.* 30.3).
43 Meiggs 1982: 1–3. Meiggs memorably recounts his journey to trees in the opening pages of his monograph, and reflects on the movement away from 'the mainstream of Roman history' (he had already produced works on Roman Ostia (1960) and the Athenian empire (1972)) so as to 'luxuriate in a comparatively untrodden field', specifically the timber trade.
44 Meiggs 1982: 27–8, citing Verg. *Ecl.* 7.65–6, Mart. 3.58.1–5 and 12.50.1–2, with comparison to landscape painters, who use the tree for its ornamental appearance.
45 Wilson 2012: 139–40. The brevity of Wilson's engagement, which does introduce a new source, is replicated in the essays in *Ownership and Exploitation of Land and Natural Resources* (Erdkamp, Verboven and Zuiderhoek 2015), where woodlands are only briefly mentioned, and timber not at all, despite being identified as 'crucial' in a chapter on villa production (Marzano 2015: 187–8).
46 Barlow 1866: 97.
47 Tylor 1871: 197–201.
48 Thiselton-Dyer 1889: 1–2. This is only one example of nineteenth-century ideas about the animism of trees, which pre-dates Tylor's influential study. See Philpot 1897: 1; Jennings 1890: 2; Barlow 1866: 84; and Boetticher 1856: 313.
49 Baddeley 1905: 101; 103.
50 Lewis and Short 1897.
51 Rose 1948: 13; Wagenvoort 1947: 75.
52 Baddeley 1905: 101.
53 Ov. *Fast.* 3.295–6.
54 Plin. *HN* 12.3.
55 For the Ovid passage, see Granger 1895: 95; Bailey 1932: 41; Rose 1935: 237 among others. For the Pliny passage in the period concerned, see Granger 1895: 96; Pfister 1937: 1280.

56 Bailey 1932: 44.
57 Dowden (2000: 66–78; 108) produced the most sustained discussion of sacred trees in the intervening years, although the influence of the comparativists is evident: trees are 'appreciated', and are given rights, as well as the death of trees being universally condemned. Beard (1998) makes no mention of trees, and neither does Rüpke (2012).
58 Hunt 2016: 62–3.
59 Ferguson 1970: 66. Cited by Hunt 2016: 16. The passage is identified by Hunt as being from Verg. *Aen.* 8.351–2, although it is unreferenced by Ferguson.
60 Hunt 2016: 1–9. The broad approach to sacred trees in the Roman world is found in Bodel (2009: 24), who argues for the auto-consecration of natural settings and phenomena, as well as Turcan (2000: 39), who proposes a 'frisson of the supernatural' in any forest. Other broad strokes include Rives' assertion (2012: 178) that 'the grove was simply perceived as sacred', regardless of any formal consecration. Hunt's opening chapter offers a detailed survey of the academic environment that preceded her, and sets herself apart from this environment (2016: 29–71).
61 Warde-Fowler 1911: 118.
62 Hunt 2016: 178.
63 Hunt 2016: 116–17. Hunt extends this discussion to other trees from the foundation of Rome, including Romulus' spear. For more on both these trees, see the final chapter of this thesis.
64 A more recent counter example (Giesecke 2022) prioritizes the religious against the backdrop of polyvalent botanical symbolism, and does not engage with Hunt's nuanced approach to the sacred trees of the Roman world, taking a more wholesale approach to sacrality.
65 Austen 2023: 1–9.
66 Austen 2023: 12–13.
67 Larmour 2007: 11.
68 Hunt 2016: 100, citing Plin. *HN* 16.241; 130; and 17.155. This is replicated in an earlier contribution to an edited volume by Hunt (2012: 112).
69 Beard 1996: 167–210.
70 Edwards 1996: 45–7.
71 Livy 5.52.2.
72 For discussion of this, see Edwards 1996: 33–42.
73 Spencer 2010: 161–71. For specifics on the difference between the two, see 167.
74 Spencer 2010: 168; Gleason 1994. The Porticus Pompeiana will be examined in the fourth chapter of this thesis.

75 Mart. *Ep.* 12.57.21. Watson and Watson (2003: 156) compare this passage to Mart. *Ep.* 4.64.25 and Plin. *Ep.* 5.6.35. Purcell (1987) presents the difficulties of definition in *rus*, *urbs*, and related terms. Spisak (2007: 74–81) comments on the frequent use of the country and the city as oppositional elements in the *Epigrams*, with particular reference to the different lifestyles in the territories.
76 Von Stackelberg 2009: 76–9. At 79, Von Stackelberg provides a helpful summary of the *Horti* of Rome coming under imperial control in the early Principate.
77 Stat. *Silv.* 2.2.52–62.
78 Von Stackelberg 2009: 80.
79 The interaction of the *hortus* with its accompanying construction and decorations within it has been a popular topic: Jashemski's early work on Pompeiian gardens (2002) used frescoes to help direct garden archaeology, while Bergmann's more recent scholarship (2017) has examined the relationship between artwork and idealized gardens.
80 McEwan 2003: 301.
81 Leach 1973: 84.
82 Östenberg 2009: 184–8.
83 Plin. *HN* 12.112; Östenberg 2009: 187.
84 Luc. *Bell. civ.* 3.394–452.
85 Phillips 1968: 296.
86 Phillips 1968: 300.
87 The communicative qualities of civil war landscape in Lucan's poetry are further explored by Spencer (2005).
88 See Bradley (1969) for further on the Augustan links between farming and warfare, alongside the links to Hesiodic tradition. Gale (2000: 252–9) explores the idea of the farmer as a general, with the land acting as both his ally and his enemy, and focuses on Verg. *G.* 1.95–105. For further Greek precedent, see esp. Gale (2000: 253–4).
89 Edwards 1996: 40.
90 The exploitation of plants in politics has very recently been explored by Marzano (2022). Regrettably, this monograph was published days before the final manuscript for this one was prepared, and it was impossible to include it here.
91 Watkins 2016: 12. The holistic approach of Watkins in the monograph can be found replicated in his earlier co-authored work, *The British Arboretum* (2011), with Elliot and Daniels, and in the recently published *Trees in Art* (2018). It is particularly evident in the opening chapter of *The British Arboretum* (11–36), which addresses the British tree culture of the nineteenth century, and incorporates social and cultural approaches to trees alongside timber production.

92 The broad engagement with trees outside of the classical world has been remarked on by at least one reviewer (Houlbrook 2017) of Hunt's monograph (2016). Houlbrook (2017: 323–4) struggled with Hunt's early assertion that trees had been relegated to a 'funny old world' approach, and subsequently neglected in scholarship, citing a number of examples of engagement with our arboreal neighbours outside of the classical world, beginning with Davies (1988), and ending with Watkins (2016).
93 Watkins 2016: 275.
94 Watkins 2016: 11–12.
95 Whyte 2013: 500–3.
96 Whyte 2013: 500.
97 Bradley 2000: 34–5.
98 Whyte 2013: 500–3.
99 See Thomas (2007) and Meyers (2012).
100 Thomas 2007: 3–4.
101 Thomas 2007: 11.
102 Meyers 2012: 8–10. She cites a number of sources, and Horace's hope that his poetry becomes 'a monument more lasting than bronze' (*Carm.* 3.30) is the most helpful for relating *monumentum* to non-architectural forms. An example left uncited by Meyers is that of Paul, in his epitome of Festus' abridgement of the Augustan Verrius Flaccus' *De significatu verborum*. Here, Paul defines a *monumentum* as being either funerary or 'anything to conjure a memory of someone, from shrines, to a porticus, to writings and poems' (Fest. 123L).
103 Meyers 2012: 11.
104 Zanker 1997: 186; Edwards 2003: 46.
105 While Augustan sources associate foreign statues with the rise of luxury in Rome, Gruen (1992: 116) argues that the attempt to pinpoint the origin of this, and to lay the blame at the base of particular Greek statues is 'hackneyed' and 'devoid of historical value'.
106 Representations of geographical areas is a well-known use of statues in Rome (Toynbee 1934: 7–23).
107 Plin. *HN* 12.3.
108 Edwards 2003: 59.
109 An overview of Rome's collections, and their desire to conquer and catalogue the known world can be found in Rutledge (2012).
110 Meiggs 1982: 15.
111 Dinsmoor 1950: 241; Meiggs 1982: 213.

112 Meiggs 1982: 32–4. Meiggs precedes his critique of the Latin poets with praise of Homer and Hesiod, who provide better evidence for his purpose. This intertextuality is briefly noted by Coleman (1977: 71), and more thoroughly treated by Jones (2011: 29–32), who also explores the prevalence of beech trees in Vergil's *Eclogues*.
113 Verg. *Ecl.* 1.1–2.
114 Theoc. *Id.* 12.8.
115 Meiggs 1982: 34.
116 Meiggs 1982: 32. Also see Ulrich 2007: 3.
117 Landgren 2016: 78.
118 Plin. *HN* 19.39.
119 Miski 2021; Grescoe 2022.
120 Keshri et al. 2004. Nelson 2009 provides a good overview of efforts to identify historical contraceptives.
121 A work-in-progress open access database, the *Roman Trees Database* (Fox 2018: http://www.nottingham.ac.uk/roman_trees), has so far catalogued 45 different species terms occurring 1,855 times.
122 These observations are taken from the evidence gathered in the *Roman Trees Database* (Fox 2018).
123 Verg. *Aen.* 2.16. Austin's (1964: 69) suggestion that the later contradiction, where Sinon identifies that the horse is made of *acer* at 2.112, is a deliberate misidentification by Vergil, in order to further characterize Sinon as dishonest, is reasonable. Both *abies* and its adjective or rare poetic form *abiegnus* have been catalogued in the *Roman Trees Database*, and appear 35 and 24 times each respectively.
124 Verg. *Aen.* 5.663; 8.91; *G.* 2.68.
125 Verg. *Aen.* 9.85–7.
126 Theoph. *Hist. Pl.* 5.7.1–3. Meiggs (1982: 118) cites this passage when discussing ship building, and Theophrastus lists fir as best for warships, pine for merchant ships, and cedar when there is no fir available.
127 Prop. 3.1.25; 4.1.42. The use of *abiegnus* rather than the traditional *abies* is stylistic rather than functional, being a rare poetic form of the latter (Fedeli 1985: 76; Fedeli, Dimundo and Ciccarelli 2015: 231; Coutelle 2015: 399).
128 The use of *abies* also works with the rationalist tradition that the horse actually functioned as a battering ram, in part preserved by the Propertius passages cited above (following Heyworth and Morwood (2011: 150), and also found more explicitly at Plin. *HN* 7.202 and Paus. 1.23.8. *abies* is used in the context of a battering ram by Ammianus Marcellinus (23.4.8).
129 Bernabei et al. 2019. Strabo, *Geographia* 5.3.7.

Chapter 1

1 Plut. *Rom.* 20.5–6.
2 Verg. *Aen.* 8.342–61.
3 Spencer (2010: 50–1) on this tour being of both pre-Rome and *ur*-Rome.
4 Livy 1.4.5; Ov. *Fast.* 2.411–13.
5 Prop. *El.* 4.4.28, 48. At 4.4.3, Propertius also describes a grove in the Roman Forum.
6 Vitr. *Arch.* 4.8.4 relates that this area was the home to a Temple of Veiovis, and the phrase also appears in Livy 1.8.5, Dion. Hal. *Ant. Rom.* 2.15.5; Vell. Pat. 1.8.5. When Cicero was writing, the area was open, and no longer wooded (*Div.* 2.40).
7 Liv. 1.8.5.
8 Dion. Hal. 2.15. The historic site of the two groves is also described by Velleius Paterculus (1.8.5).
9 Kondratieff 2015: 199; Boyle 1999: 152.
10 O'Sullivan 2015: 120. Ovid employs a similar technique in the *Tristia* (3.1.27–35), linking the foundation of Rome with the site of Augustus' house, which is the crescendo point of a tour of historic sites of the city, including Numa's house (the *regia*). Armstrong (2019: 91) also highlights this equal weighting of present and past Rome in the *Aeneid* passage, drawing attention to the repeated use of *iam tum* (now, then) in the description.
11 Varr. Ling. 5.152.
12 Plin. *HN* 16.37
13 Varr. *Ling.* 5.51. Spencer (2019: 146) identifies that this etymology is 'tersely expressed' when compared to others, and is a relatively simple statement: 'there were willow groves there'.
14 The Vicus Aesculeti is also identified in *CIL* vi 30957.
15 Varr. *Ling.* 5.49.
16 Varr. *Ling.* 5.54.
17 Varr. *Ling.* 5.154.
18 Plin. *HN* 15.121; Serv. *Comm. A.* 8.636.
19 Festus 135L; Tert. *Spect.* 5, 8.
20 Tac. *Ann.* 4.65 is the only direct reference to this alternative name for the Caelian hill.
21 Mart. 1.117.6. The identification of this as a reference to an apartment block originates with Friedländer (1886: 234 n.6) and Jordan (1842: 71), who took it as a building name, following the standard location setting of *ad* plus a noun. Since this, Ad Pirum has not concerned readers.

22 Spencer (2019: 129–59) examines some of the passages of Varro explored in this section in more detail, alongside other etymologies found in Varro's tour of Rome.
23 Conon *Narr.* 48; Varr. *Ling.* 7.9.
24 Freud 1985: 257.
25 Edwards 1996: 28–32.
26 Larmour and Spencer 2007: 3–4.
27 Dupont 1989: 74.
28 This tree group is unusually not mapped by Carandini (2017), although he usually includes the trees of Rome on the maps in the atlas.
29 Dupont 1989: 74.
30 Plin. *HN* 16.234–40.
31 Plin. *HN* 16.234.
32 Plin. *HN* 16.234. The dragon, which may have been the focus of Pliny's source material for this tree, is briefly discussed by Ogden (2013: 206) in a section regarding the reincarnation or transformation of heroes into snakes after death. Pliny is clear here that the *draco* is not Scipio reincarnate, but is instead a guardian of Scipio's shade (*manus eius custodire*) similar to the serpent guarding the Golden Fleece in the *Argonautica*.
33 Sen. *Ep.* 86.14–21.
34 Henderson 2004: 122.
35 Verg. *G.* 2.58.
36 Sen. *Ep.* 86.14. Henderson 2004: 122.
37 Henderson 2004: 122.
38 Henderson 2004: 122; Plin. *HN* 16.234. In his second *Georgic*, Vergil explores the means by which nature can be tamed, directly contradicting the altruism of tree planting advocated by Seneca, who has cherry-picked the quote from 2.57–8 in order to lend credence to his argument (by reverting to the tales of 'our Vergil'), while utterly divorcing the quote from its wider, contradictory context.
39 Pliny's use of Vergil's poetry, particularly the Georgics, as a practical handbook has been well documented, however, by Doody (2007) among others.
40 Plin. *HN* 1. *Summa: res et historiae et observationes*.
41 Locher 1986: 24. For a discussion of this categorization as an expression of authorial control and a part of the process of constructing a totality, see Carey 2003: 30–2.
42 Plin. *HN praef.* 23.
43 Lao 2011.
44 Hunt 2016: 99.
45 Nora 1989.

46 Quite what occurred in this 'carrying' (*defertur*), and what the purpose of the act was is unclear, and Pliny makes no effort to clarify his statement to this end. However, we can surmise, as Hunt does (2016: 90 n.35), that it is not necessarily in order to make an offering of the hair to the tree, since the language used is ambiguous. That the Vestals had a connection to the trees in Rome is evident from both their interactions with this tree, and their intervention with the fig tree uprooting the statue of Silvanus (Plin. HN 15.77), although Pliny fails to offer an explanation as to why they were so involved with Rome's arboreal residents. It can, therefore, be surmised that either Pliny was ignorant of their link, or it was so widely understood at the time that it did not warrant further discussion in the *Natural History*. Hunt draws on a marble relief depicting the temple of Vesta with an oak branch protruding from behind, and tentatively suggests that 'the combining of the oak, often associated with Jupiter, and the Vestals' temple aimed to articulate in arboreal terms how worship of Vesta stood at the heart of Rome's divinely favoured strength and supremacy' (Hunt 2016: 282 fig. 14).
47 Plin. *HN* 16.236.
48 Plin. *HN* 16.237.
49 Hunt 2016: 100.
50 Plin. *HN* 16.236. McCulloch (1980: 239), in an effort to establish a Tacitean focus on the *annus horribilis* (Gowers 2011: 87–8) for Rome's trees in 68 CE, links this omen with the omen of the cypress tree in Tacitus' Histories which portended the rise of Vespasian. For the portent, see Tac. *Hist*. 2.78.2; Suet. *Vesp*. 5.4; and Cass. Dio 66.1. This cypress tree is the same one that Suetonius reports withered before Domitian's assassination (Suet. *Dom*. 15).
51 McCulloch 1980: 239–40.
52 Tac. *Ann*. 13.58. Morgan (1996: 47 n.21), responding to McCulloch's abbreviated argument (1984: 163–5), points to the Julio-Claudian laurel grove at the Villa Prima Porta as a more fitting comparison to the Flavian cypress to indicate the withering of the Julio-Claudian line and need for a new dynasty. To some extent, this is a reasonable criticism, and the laurel grove (which was synonymous with the Julio-Claudian line), withered closer to the resurgence of the Flavian line than the 58 CE withering of the *ficus Ruminalis*.
53 Sen. *Ep*. 86.6–13.
54 Suet. *Galb*. 1; Cass. Dio 63.29.3.
55 The story is found in two other sources, Cass. Dio 48.52.3–4, and Plin. *HN* 15.136–7.
56 Macaulay-Lewis 2018: 99–100.
57 Klynne 2004; Reeder 1997a, 1997b, 2001.
58 Klynne and Liljenstolpe 2000: 226; Pinto-Guillaume 2002.

59 For discussion on this, see Kellum 1994: 222; Klynne 2004; Klynne and Liljenstolpe 2000; Reeder 1997a; 1997b. There is no evidence to confirm the presence of the laurel grove, and no archaeological evidence has directly linked this villa to Livia.
60 Suetonius (*Galb.* 1) and Pliny (*HN* 15.137) both agree on this usage of the grove.
61 Suet. *Galb.* 1.
62 Plin. *HN* 15.136–7.
63 This idea is expressed in the context of cameo portraits of Livia by Flory (1995).
64 Zachos 2003: 81 fig.24.
65 There is no archaeological evidence available to determine what plant was grown in these pots.
66 The association of the laurel with the Julio-Claudian household has been discussed in Flory (1995: 52–5), and Kellum (1994: 211–13).
67 Suet. *Vesp.* 5.2. Tacitus (*Hist.* 2.78.2–3) and Cassius Dio (*Xiphilinus* 66.1.3) tells us that another tree, this one a cypress, is regarded as an omen by Vespasian, and this has been examined by Vigourt (2001: 346–7), Wardle (2012), Morgan (1996), who compares this cypress tree to an elm tree at Nocera, and Ash (1999: 132), who explores the choice of tree, which is linked to death.
68 Fest. 57L. Violation is a key theme of this definition, in both the Latin and the English.
69 Dowden 2000: 108.
70 Hunt 2016: 128. Relating the challenge of navigating which *luci* were *capitales* (which Ovid cautions his shepherd over) to a religious context, Hunt explores the challenges that would be faced when distinguishing between the levels of holiness accorded to each tree, and questions how this would have affected everyday Roman life, particularly since Rome had a substantial timber trade.
71 There is some debate as to the location of this grove, particularly in Juvenal's poetry, and this has been discussed by Kraan 2001, Nisbet 1988: 92–3, and Pearce 1992.
72 Livy 1.21.3; Juv. 3.17. Livy 1.21.3 offers the dedication, while Juv. 3.18 refers to the *sacer fons* in the location. For more on Egeria and the grove, see Oglivie (1965: 102) for Livy and Courtney (1980: 157–9) for Juvenal.
73 Livy 1.19.5.
74 Livy 1.21.3.
75 Juv. 3.12–16. The alienation of the grove from the spirit of Egeria, which used to dwell within it, is examined by Motto and Clark (1965), who use it and the surrounding dried fountains to show the isolation of the grove from its surroundings. For the difficulties posed by Juvenal's phrase *amica nocturna*, see Hardie (1998).

76 Courtney 1980: 158. See Sturtevant (1911) for further on the rent paid, which is not the levy imposed by Vespasian on the Jewish population.

Chapter 2

1 Whether this view was common in the ancient world is unclear, and is explored by Doody (2007), who addresses Pliny's and Columella's use of the *Georgics* as a practical guide, although Meiggs (1982: 33–4) is critical of the Augustan poet's knowledge and consistency in trees. The relationship between the works of Cato, Columella, Varro, and Vergil is also explored by Dupont (2008) and Spencer (2010: esp. 86–104). The reliance of Pliny on Varro, and the complicated relationship between Varro and his predecessors, Cato and Vergil, is examined in relation to grafting by Lowe (2010), who also explores Columella's views on the same subject, finding similarities in their approaches. That Cato's, Columella's, and Varro's writings remained influential agricultural manuals among the Roman élite is not a recent discovery, and Liu (2010) reflects on eighteenth-century historian Robert Castell's examination in *Villas of the Ancients Illustrated* of planting habits in Pliny the Younger's Laurentian villa, which bear a striking resemblance to those set out by the three authors.
2 Plin. *HN* 21.46. Quite what is meant by luxury in the ancient world, especially in regard to plants, is explored by Totelin (2022) who contrasts trade and exploration.
3 Plin. *HN* praef. 10.
4 Liv. praef. 10; Plin. *HN* praef. 10.
5 De Oliveira (1992) identifies *l'utilité sociale* as a key factor in Pliny's judgement of imperial rule, and focuses on it throughout his monograph.
6 Plin. *HN* 16.78.
7 Lucret. 5.939; Ov. Met. 1.112.
8 Plin. *HN* 12.5.
9 Plin. *HN* 12.6.
10 Plin. *HN* 17.178. Also see Wallace-Hadrill (1990).
11 Plin. *HN* 14.8. On Pliny and perfumes, see Dalby (2000) and Vons (2000).
12 Plin. *HN* 14.9.
13 Wallace-Hadrill (1990: 88–9), citing Plin. *HN* 16.95; 18.154–61.
14 Plin. *HN* 14.4.
15 Plin. *HN* 14.9
16 Plin. *HN* 16.62–73. In this contained treatment of timber, Pliny addresses the timber of five trees: the ash, the lime, the maple (which is second to citrus in cabinet making), the box and the elm.

17. Plin. *HN* 16.62.
18. Plin. *HN* 16.62. This comment refers to Hom. *Il.* 22.133. Elsewhere, Ovid states that Achilles' spear is made of ash (*Met.* 12.122), and Pliny comments that it is the best wood for spears (*HN* 16.228). For the plane tree planted by Agamemnon, see Plin. *HN* 16.238. For more on Pliny's idealization of the past, see Fear (2011).
19. Plin. *HN* 16.62.
20. Plin. *HN* praef. 33.
21. Wallace-Hadrill 1990: 88.
22. As Beagon comments (1992: 191), Vespasian was keen to exploit trade 'as the East became more accessible and its products… easier to acquire', while remaining 'adept at manipulating trade to the advantage of himself and the state treasury'.
23. Hom. *Od.* 5.59–61: πῦρ μὲν ἐπ᾽ ἐσχαρόφιν μέγα καίετο, τηλόσε δ᾽ ὀδμὴ κέδρου τ᾽ εὐκεάτοιο θύου τ᾽ ἀνὰ νῆσον ὀδώδει δαιομένων. Θυώδης, the adjectival form of θύον, is found at *Od.* 4.121 and 5.264, identifying the fragrant scent to Helen's chamber, and to the clothes Calypso provides Odysseus with. Curiously, Pliny identifies three trees that are burnt as being the *citrus*, *larix*, and the *cedrus*, as opposed to only the *citrus* and *cedrus*, as well as mis-identifying the burner in the Odyssey as Circe (*HN* 13.100).
24. Theop. *Hist. Pl.* 5.3.7. Meiggs (1982: 286–7) explores the use of the tree in Egypt, and in Cyrene, with particular attention being paid to the tables within Cleopatra's palace, which he already singled out for its luxurious solid ebony doorposts.
25. Plin. *HN* 13.96–100. Further, Pliny (*HN* 13.101–2) cites Theophrastus' comments on the application of the timber, although Theophrastus makes no mention of the citrus wood tables and prizes the citrus around the Temple of Hannon in Cyrenaica, as opposed to Pliny's preference for the timber of Mount Ancorarius in Mauretania.
26. Fest. 282L.
27. Varro, *RR* 3.2.4.
28. Vell. Pat. 2.56.2.
29. De Oliveira includes Pliny's extensive comments on the value of the tree in his list of diatribes against luxury to be found in the Natural History (1992: 184 n.321).
30. Plin. *HN* 13.91.
31. Plin. *HN* 13.92.
32. Plin. *HN* 13.93–4.
33. Plin. *HN* 16.233.
34. We should not overlook the impact of tree felling and over-zealous tree felling in particular in Pliny's worldview. In the thirty-first book of the *Natural History*, when Pliny's topic is water, he returns to the issue of tree felling and emphasizes over-zealous felling. He comments that 'dangerous torrents converge where woods,

which used to contain and absorb the rain, have been taken away from the hills' (*HN* 31.53). Hughes observes that ancient authors are unafraid to link the negative impact of deforestation with human activity, and it is the overindulgence of man in timber that Pliny now identifies as the cause for flooding (1983: 440). Hughes goes on to cite Vitruvius (*De arch*. 8.1.6–7), who observes the effect that forests have on water supply.
35 Plin. *HN* 13.95.
36 Meiggs 1982: 290.
37 Luc. *Bell. civ*. 9.426–8.
38 Luc. *Bell. civ*. 9.430.
39 Sen. *De Vita Beata* 17.2. Cassius Dio (61.10.3) tells us that the Stoic Seneca, who abhorred luxury in all its forms did indulge in the craze for citrus tables, having a collection of 500 tables with the fashionable ivory legs for dining from. Meiggs, taking his lead from a line of Martial, comments on the symbiotic relationship between the ivory and citrus workers, who formed a guild, the *citrarii* et *eborarii* (1982: 290, citing Mart. 2.43.9, Juv. 11.122–7, and CIL vi 9258 for the guild).
40 Plin. *HN* 13.96–9.
41 Plin. *HN* 13.100; 13.102.
42 Lao 2011: 35.
43 Lao 2011: 35 n.2.
44 Lao 2011: 39–40.
45 Lao 2011: 45.
46 Lao directs her readers to Plin. *HN* 12.128–35, among other ancient authorities. The citrus wood tables are discussed at 13.92–5.
47 Beagon 1992: 190; Sen. *Tranq*. 4.4.
48 Plin. *HN* 13.97.
49 Plin. *HN* 16.198.
50 Plin. *HN* 16.200. It is peculiar that Pliny treats this piece of timber as a tree, referring to it as *arbor*, while it clearly is not, and is referred to later as *trabs*. Perhaps Pliny is pointing to an exhibition of the tree, which was subsequently made into timber for the bridge to the island in the middle of the *naumachia*.
51 Plin. *HN* 12.6.
52 Plin. *HN* 15.29.
53 Plin. *HN* 24.44–5.
54 Plin. *HN* 17.90.
55 Plin. *HN* 12.11–12.
56 Murphy 2004: 29.
57 Plin. *HN* 14.2.

58 For a general comment on Pliny and imperialism, see Fear (2011), for more focused discussion, see Conte (1994), and Carey (2003).
59 Goodyear 1982: 670; Plin. *HN* praef. 13.
60 Plin. *HN* praef. 33. In discounting the contents list from the number of books, I follow Laehn (2013: 7), who takes his lead from the author himself. In his prefatory letter, Pliny identifies 36 volumes of the *Natural History*, and states that the list of contents is appended to the letter. This is a statement which Pliny the Younger does not appear to acknowledge, in a letter to Baebius Macer (*Ep.* 3.5).
61 Healy 1999: 39.
62 Plin. *HN* 16.1.
63 Plin. *HN* 16.6.
64 Plin. *HN* 17.99.
65 Carey 2003: 76.
66 Carey 2003: 34.
67 Naas 2011: 59. See Lao (2011: 41), also Carey (2003: 75–9).
68 Carey 2003: 33.
69 Murphy 2004: 132.
70 Plin. *HN* 6.81–91.
71 Plin. *HN* 12.16–17.
72 Verg. *G.* 2.116.
73 Plin. *HN* 12.14.
74 Fear 2011.
75 Plin. *HN* 12.3.
76 Carey 2003: 32–40.
77 Plin. *HN* 12.1.
78 Plin. *HN* 12.2.
79 On the changeability of Natura in Pliny's *Natural History*, see Beagon (1992: 36–42).

Chapter 3

1 Livy 1.54. This tale was inspired by the Herodotean precedent in Thrasybalus and Periander (Hdt. 5.92)
2 Plin. *HN* 19.50; 19.169.
3 Totelin 2012.
4 Just. *Epit.* 36.4.3.
5 Plut. *Dem.* 20.1.

6 Xen. *Oec.* 4.20–5
7 Stat. *Silv.* 2.2.52–62.
8 Stronach 1990.
9 Plin. *HN* 22.6–14.
10 Plin. *HN* 22.8.
11 Plin. *HN* 15.102.
12 Plin. *HN* 12.20; 12.111.
13 Plin. *HN* 12.111.
14 Ath. 197c–203c = *FGrH* 627 F2. The procession described by Athenaeus/Kallixeinos has been dated by Rice (1983: 5) to the 270s BCE.
15 Probably of the *Diospyros* genus, as identified by Östenberg (2009: 185–6).
16 Solin. 52.52; Verg. *G.* 2.116–17.
17 Plin. *HN* 12.17, citing Hdt. 3.97.
18 Meiggs 1982: 286.
19 For the date, see Broughton 1952: 169.
20 Plut. *Luc.* 37. See Keaveney (1992: 129–42) for the machinations that led to Lucullus' triumph.
21 Possibly the *Prunus cerasus* L. or *Prunus avium* L..
22 Plin. *HN* 15.102
23 Verg. *G.* 2.116–17: *sola India nigrum / fert hebenum*.
24 Totelin (2012: 132), relying on evidence from Mabberley (2008: 277).
25 Kuttner 1999: 345.
26 For more on Pompey's Alexandrian ambitions, see Greenhalgh (1980), and Seager (2002).
27 Plin. *HN* 15.102.
28 Pliny also includes the ebony in his opening arboreal book, on foreign trees, and it is only the second truly foreign tree to be included (the plane not counted among these).
29 Prop. 2.32.11–13; Vitr. *De arch.* 5.9.1.
30 Plin. *HN* 6.197; Luc. *Bell. civ.* 10.304.
31 Prop. 2.32.11–13. Martial also refers to the theatre as a *nemus* (2.14.10), and they are explored periodically by Davies (2017: 226–34). The trees planted here are likely to have been the *Platanus orientalis* L..
32 Carettoni (Cressedi) 1960: 202. Cf. Lloyd 1982.
33 Coarelli 2007: 285.
34 Russell 2016: 163, Beard 2007: 22–31.
35 Mart. 2.14.10
36 A misreading of *arbores* at Plin. *HN* 12.111–12 as being specifically in reference to the balsam, as opposed to 'trees' generally, has led to the balsam being included in

the trees imported and exhibited by Pompey – *RE* II (1896) s.v. 'Balsambaum' (Wagler), 2837 (This was corrected in *BNP* VIII (2000) s.v. 'Opobalsamum' (Hünemörder), 1258); Greenhalgh 1980: 174; Kuttner 1999: 345; Davies 2017: 226 n.78.
37 Plin. *HN*. 12.111–12.
38 Of the 81 references to *balsamum* in the *TLL*, none of them refer to the wood's timber. Other words for the tree are used sporadically throughout ancient literature, but this is the most common term.
39 Östenberg 2009: 186 n.349; André 1985 s.v. 'balsamum'.
40 Following Pollard 2009.
41 *FUR* 77. Lloyd (1982: 91–2 fig. 1) offers the canonical identification of the outlines as garden beds, hedges, or topiary, although Richardson (1992: 286–7) casts doubt on this, focusing on the accessibility of the open space and its lack of concern with regard to its axis. Meneghini and Santangeli Valenziani (2007: 61–70) have identified the marks on the Marble Plan as water features, following excavation.
42 Joseph. *BJ* 7.5.7.
43 Plin. *HN* 12.113
44 Plin. *HN* 12.118.
45 Manolaraki 2015: 647.
46 Verg. *G*. 2.119.
47 Manolaraki 2015: 636–8.
48 Kuttner 1999: 345; Östenberg 2009: 188; Stackelberg 2009: 81; see also Totelin 2012 and Russell 2016.
49 Plin. *HN* 12.16.
50 Östenberg 2009: 188.
51 Ryberg 1955: 169; pl. LXI, fig. 99. Östenberg 2009: 188.
52 The research for this section formed the basis for an article in *Papers of the British School at Rome*, an in-depth case study of the trees on Trajan's Column (Fox 2019). This section will explore other examples of Trajanic architecture alongside the Column.
53 Leander Touati 1987: 79.
54 This is in contrast to the Column of Marcus Aurelius, which focuses more on the individuals, with significantly less concern over depicting the world in which the war was fought, perhaps a symptom of the style change between the two periods.
55 This is judged from the portrayal of these two river deities on the Arch's country facing (northeast) face.
56 Hassel (1966) proposes 114 CE for the dedication, and Lepper's detailed review (1969: 251–3) of this date indicates that the evidence bears this out as a rough date, although there is some degree for variation, of almost two years either side.

57 Leander Touati 1987.
58 Wootton and Russell 2013: 16. Rockwell (1983: 105) agrees that there were multiple groups of carvers who specialized in different aspects of the relief. Wootton et al. 2013: http://www.artofmaking.ac.uk/explore/sources/519/PR205_1_05_20. The two techniques of carving trees, one flat and lifeless, the second vibrant and vivacious, indicate to Wootton and Russell that there were at least two sculptors of the trees on the Column.
59 Stoiculescu 1985: 85. The freer depiction of the trunk of a deciduous tree is replicated in the oak of the *Ctr* relief on the Arch of Trajan. This trunk, which Lepper draws issue with, due to the way it 'swell[s] out on either side of the join [to the neighbouring panel] like flesh round an open wound' (1969: 260). The depiction is consistent with other deciduous trees in the Trajanic architecture, and there is no reason for Lepper's alarm at the shape of the tree trunk.
60 Stoiculescu 1985: 85.
61 Rossi (1972: 56) explores the possibility of the Tropaeum having been composed with direct imperial supervision. Throughout this article, Rossi points to a number of similarities in a disparate range of examples across Trajanic architecture, artwork, and material culture, which indicate a guiding hand across the depictions, and may explain the consistency of the variety of trees depicted. This is not unusual in commemorative architecture from the period, which is known for a unified purpose.
62 Rotili 1972: pl.80. There is some disagreement in the identification of this tree: Lepper (1969: 258) identifies these trees as Spanish olives, following Veyne (1960: 195) and Toynbee (1934: 15 n.5), who both identify the Hercules figure as Hercules Gaditanus, leading to the identification of a Spanish tree, following Strack (1931: 103).
63 Rotili 1972: 89.
64 Lepper 1969: 255.
65 Leander Touati 1987: 17 n.35.
66 Leander Touati 1987: 17; pl.7.1.
67 Leander Touati 1987: 19; pl.2.
68 Leander Touati 1987: 24; pl.1.3; pl.13.1.
69 Leander Touati 1987: 18, 25; pl.4; pl.14.
70 Leander Touati 1987: 26; pl.4; pl.16; pl.17.4.
71 Leander Touati 1987: 108; pl.50.3.
72 Leander Touati 1987: 25; 26; 32.
73 Lepper 1969: 257.
74 Meiggs 1982: 186–7. Plin. *HN* 3.147. This association is in some conflict with the use of the oak on the Arch of Trajan at Beneventum to represent the German

territories (Rotili 1972; further noted by Lepper 1969: 255), and Schama's extensive analysis of Germany's oak fetishism (1995: 75–134). Further, Pliny distances himself from tying the tree exclusively to the province (*HN* 16.17: *cum robur quercumque vulgo nasci videamus*). However, Pliny is being specific in this example, specifying the *robur* and *quercus*, while neglecting the *aesculus* and other varieties of the oak. Additionally, the profligacy of the oak would not prevent it from being strongly associated with more than one region.

75 Lehman-Hartelben (1926) suggests a vertical reading, as does Gauer (1977), while Coarelli (2000) suggests neighbouring viewing platforms. Brilliant (1984: 90–4) criticizes the Column's circular narrative, and the challenges that would be posed in understanding the uppermost scenes on the relief, although this second issue would be resolved by Coarelli's viewing platforms.

76 As to the intricacies of the variety of oak, Lepper queries whether it should be expected that the artist, or the spectators, would have had the necessary botanical knowledge to differentiate between the Mediterranean oak and those from northern Germany (Lepper 1969: 255). This level of detail in botanical knowledge should not be expected from an ancient audience, much as it should not be from a modern one.

77 Enn. *Ann.* Sk. 6.177.

78 Trees as scene dividers have been a well-covered aspect of scholarship since serious study of the Column began in the nineteenth century, leading reviewers of study on the Column to identify them as 'well-known' (Coulston 1990: 296). Cichorius identifies several scenes which he presents as the beginning and end of scenes in his edition of the frieze. He planned to expand on his definition of scene dividers in a second study, but this never materialized (Cichorius 1896: 5). Lehman-Hartelben uses this absence to present a counter argument, focusing on the image of the scene as opposed to the elements which delimit images, although his divisions remain largely the same as Cichorius' (Lehman-Hartelben 1926: 122). This disagreement is picked up on by Gauer, who reduces the number of scenes on the Column to 100, removing a number of Cichorius' divisions (Gauer 1977). Malissard also identifies a number of trees as framing scenes (Malissard 1982), and Leander Touati extends the use of trees framing scenes to the Great Trajanic Frieze (Leander Touati 1987: 32–3).

79 For the sake of clarity, 'tree felling' is being used here as opposed to 'deforestation' due to a definition-based difference between the terms: while the former indicates simply the felling of trees, the latter is defined as the permanent removal of a forested area, for which there is no concrete evidence on the relief.

80 Davies (1997: 63) highlights the peaceful themes of the Column, which focuses on scenes of travel, construction, *adlocutio*, *submissio*, and sacrifice. The lack of battle

scenes has allowed Ferris to identify the warfare shown on the Column as a 'sanitized' version, thus allaying the Roman population's fear of the army, while the possible association of the Dacians with the forest and the Romans with construction presents a clash between nature and culture (Ferris 2000: 61–85).

81 Davies 1997: 63.
82 This assumption is begun by Boetticher (1856: 195. It is continued in modern discussions of the ancient relationship with the tree, from Thomas (1988: 263) to Dyson (2001: 146–7), and beyond, to Hughes (2014: 185). The primary issue for several discussions of the felling of trees is one of inviolability, and this is briefly summarized by Dowden (2000: 108–9). For a thorough discussion of the assumed inviolability of groves and sacred trees, see Hunt's thorough critique of the past two centuries of European arboreal scholarship (2016: 121–9).
83 Hunt tackles the issue of constrictive definitions of *sacer*, such as the legalistic one, in the introduction to her piece (2016: 1–28), 'Rooting in: why give time to sacred trees?', and addresses the issue of felling trees in her fourth chapter, 'Arboriculture and arboreal deaths: rethinking sacrality again' (2016: 121–72). In the fourth chapter, Hunt acknowledges that an unviolated wood, regardless of whether or not it was dedicated, had the ability to provoke a religious reaction (Hunt 2016: 125, citing Ov. *Met.* 3.28; *Fast.* 2.435; Stat. *Theb.* 4.420; Luc. *Bell. civ.* 3.399). The question of how a sacred tree should be defined and cared for will be dealt with in the final chapter of this thesis.
84 Thomas 1988: 263.
85 In myth and history, the punishment is traditionally dismemberment or decapitation, from Halirrhothius' axe rebounding from Athens' sacred olive tree and killing him (Schol. on Ar. *Nub.* 1005; Serv. *Comm. G.* 1.18), to Turullius' execution by Augustus (Cass. Dio 51.8; Val. Max. 1.1.19). In both these examples, the trees felled are sacred ones, to Athena (as in the case of the olive), and to Asclepius (as in Turullius' delayed execution on Cos).
86 Rotili 1972.
87 Leander Touati 1987: 17 n.35.
88 Lepper 1969: 257.
89 Lepper and Frere 1988: 64.
90 Stoiculescu 1985: 84.
91 Here, the absence of the *fagus* proves challenging for Stoiculescu, who appears to have expected it to be far more common on the relief than it actually is, given the tree's prominence throughout. As was discussed above, this can be excused by the need to display trees which would have been considered exotic or particularly Dacian, as opposed to the more common *fagus*.

92 This depiction is replicated in Trajan's mastery of the sea, expressed in Pliny the Younger's *Panegyricus*, and analysed by Manolaraki (2008).
93 The three trees felled by Dacians in LXVI further this idea of the Roman army subjugating the Dacian landscape throughout the Column's relief. The scene in which the Dacians are maintaining their control of the landscape is towards the end of the first Dacian war, and the conquest of the country is not yet complete.
94 The hyperbole of the *Panegyricus* has historically provoked a dismissive response, found throughout readings of Pliny's lengthy speech. Syme comments that, as a speech, it has done 'no good to the reputation of the author or the taste of the age' (Syme 1958: 114), while Radice calls it 'indispensable yet unreadable', adding that 'some of its topics are laboured to the point of obscurity or hidden behind a façade of elaborate rhetoric' (Radice 1968: 169). Recently, the *Panegyricus* has gained more status as a valuable source for senatorial imperial oratory and its themes have been explored in an edited volume (Roche 2011).
95 Plin. *Pan.* 16.5.
96 Hutchinson 2011: 128, citing Plin. *Pan.* 50.1.
97 Plin. *Ep.* 8.4. Control of the landscape is critical to a Roman conquest, and within Roman war. The oldest crown of the Republic, Pliny the Elder tells us, is composed of grass of a conquered site, and indicates the absolute surrender of the territory and the peoples within it (Plin. *HN* 22.8). In the Second Punic War, Fabrizi points to the emblematic significance of Scipio's sea crossing to Africa throughout her chapter, and also suggests the importance of nature in warfare when discussing the role of fog and dust in the Battles of Trasimene and Cannae (Fabrizi 2016: 286).
98 For more, see Fox (2019).
99 The extent of Decebalus' concealment can be seen by the number of trees which surround him, and the shade they typically cast: three resinous trees (all listed as A.5 by Stoiculescu), and two deciduous (the first is catalogued by Stoiculescu as D.18, the second (under Decebalus) is a D.20). With particular regard to the shade of the resinous trees, ancient authors have a great deal to say on the shade cast by them, with particular reference to the *pinus* and the *picea* (Plin. *HN* 17.91; Hor. *Carm.* 2.3.9–11; Serv. *Comm. Aen.* 9.86; Sil. *Pun.* 1.83).
100 Settis et al. 1988: 146.
101 Lepper and Frere 1988: 71.
102 The vertical reading of the Column follows Bianchi Bandinelli 1978: 139; Settis et al. 1988: 202–3; and Coarelli 2000: 19. This particular vertical axis is perhaps the most significant on the Column, containing the crossing of the Danube at the base, the first appearance of Decebalus, being targeted by Jupiter, the Victory

appearing between two Dacian *tropaea*, and the suicide of Decebalus at the top of the Column. In her analysis of Victoria's position on this axis, Kousser comments that the axis can be read as a synopsis for the campaign, from its origins at the Danube to its moment of closure (Kousser 2008: 85).
103 See Fox 2019: 64–6.
104 The North facing Arch relief (*As*) steps outside of this to some degree: this depicts a scene from *institutio alimentaria*, and does not involve enemies to Rome. However, the tree is still found on the opposite end of the relief to the Emperor, and the Beneventines are leaving toward the wooded area (geographically toward the town).
105 Plin. *Ep.* 8.4.
106 Plin. *Pan.* 16.5.
107 Meneghini, Messa, and Ungaro 1998.
108 Packer 1997: 418–19; Packer, Sarring, and Sheldon 1983.
109 Meneghini 2009; Meneghini, Messa, and Ungaro 1990; 1998.
110 The distinction between the two names, of *graminea* (grass) and *obsidionalis* (siege) is not presented as a large enough distinction to necessitate two separate crowns by Pliny (*HN* 22.7). The grass crown is awarded to the sole saviour of an army, the siege to the sole saviour of a town, city, or people.
111 Plin. *HN* 22.7.
112 The recipients were, in chronological order, Lucius Siccius Dentatus, Publius Decius Mus (who was awarded it twice, once by his army, and once by the army he saved), Fabius Maximus (who was awarded it by the whole of Italy, and is the only example of the grass crown being conferred on someone by the state), Calpurnius Flamma, Scipio Aemilianus, Sulla (by his own account, which Pliny questions), Quintus Sertorius, and Augustus.
113 Plin. *HN* 22.14. This is picked up on in Wallace-Hadrill's exploration of Pliny's stance on luxury (1990: 91).
114 Plin. *HN* 22.8.
115 Plin. *HN* 16.11.
116 André (1985) identifies the three different varieties as *Quercus robur* (*quercus*), *Quercus ilex* (*ilex*) and the *Quercus farnetto* (*aesculus*).
117 Plin. *HN* 16.12.
118 Plin. *IIN* 16.7.
119 Plin. *HN* 16.11. This has been advanced earlier by Pliny, at *HN* 12.2, and is corroborated by Vergil (*G.* 2.16). André 1985 s.v. *aesculus*.
120 Plin. *HN* 16.11.
121 Columella, *Rust.* 7.3.24; Ov. *Met.* 7.623; Phaedrus *Fab.* 3.17.2; Serv. *Comm. Ecl.* 1.17, 7.24; Serv. *Comm. G.* 3.332; Verg. *Aen.* 3.680; Verg. *G.* 3.332.

122 Crowned head: *RIC* 1².26a–b, 33a–b, 35, 36a–b, 37a–b, 38a–b, 46, 46A, 47b, 48, 49, 158, 293, 298, 308, 316, 409, 411, 414.

Isolated wreath: *RIC* 1².*29a–b, 30a–b, 40a–b*, 57, *75a–b*, 76, *77a–b*, 78, *79a–b*, 138, 139, 229, 230, 231a–b, 232, 233, 234, 235, 236a–b, 237, 238a–b, 239, 240, 241a–b, 242, 243, 244, 245, 246, 247, 248a–b, 277, *278, 279, 285, 302, 312, 323*, 324, *325*, 326, *328, 329, 330*, 331, 332, 333, 334, 335, 336, *341*, 342, *345*, 346, 347, *348*, 349, 358, *370*, 371, 372, *374*, 375, *377*, 378, *380*, 381, *383*, 384, *387*, 388, 400, 401, 405, 549.

The depictions found with the legend *ob cives servatos*, or an abbreviation of it, are italicized.

123 *RG* 34; Ov. *Met.* 1.563.

124 The average number of lobes on the leaves is seven, which would suggest that the leaf is that of the *aesculus*, or *Quercus farnetto*. However, how this fits with the development of the crown is unclear, since it could be that the *aesculus* was common to the area at which the crown was awarded, and thus included in its composition (Plin. *HN* 16.11).

125 Lott 2004: 121.

126 Caneva 2010.

127 Gell. *NA* 5.6.

128 The term 'laurel' is often misapplied in the UK, where it typically refers to the Cherry laurel, or *Prunus laurocerasus*. In ancient usage, *laurus* refers to the Bay laurel, or *Laurus nobilis*, a tree which bears very little similarity to the Cherry laurel in the size of its leaves, scent, etc.. In order to avoid confusion, this section will use *Laurus nobilis* throughout as a translation of *laurus*.

129 Somewhat bizarrely, Pliny incorrectly informs his readers that the *laurus* has no berry (*HN* 15.130). See Figure 7 for evidence.

130 Beard 2007: 228. This follows a standard depiction of the triumphal procession, which highlights the colour of the ceremony, found from Gibbon (1781: 361–401) onward.

131 Bradley 2009: 215–19.

132 Plin. *HN* 15.134–5. The aetiologies, that the *Laurus nobilis* is sacred to Apollo, that it is a nod to Lucius Junius Brutus kissing the ground of Delphi after freeing Rome, and that it wards off lightning have each been addressed in other studies. Kraft (1952: 28) argues that the *laurus* is as commonly associated with Jupiter as it is Apollo, although Versnel (1970: 76) challenges this, arguing that while the Greek association may be between the *Laurus nobilis* and Jupiter, the Roman one is with oak, citing Ov. *Tr.* 3.1.35–40. Meanwhile, the other two aetiologies are described by Beard (2007: 246) as two of Pliny's 'daft theories'.

133 As identified by Beard (2007: 246).

134 Fest. 104L. Fantham (2012: 64) advises caution in the pursuit of this lead, and suggests we acknowledge the 'eagerness of antiquarians to track down rituals and responses to pollution', linking the citation of Masurius to Ovid's aetiologies in the *Fasti*.
135 Plin. *HN* 15.138: *eadem purificationibus adhibetur*.
136 The long history of the *myrtus* in crowns is well attested, although Pliny and Masurius do seem confused as to the nature of the procession in which the crown is used: Pliny uses both *triumphans* and *ovans* to describe a general who entered for a procession in 503 BCE and wore a crown of *myrtus*. This, he says, became the crown of the generals celebrating an *ovatio*, but identifies Marcus Crassus as an exception to the rule following the victory over Spartacus (*HN* 15.125). Meanwhile Mausurius is cited by Pliny (*HN* 15.126) as claiming *triumphantes* generals wore myrtle crowns.
137 Plin. *HN* 15.119.
138 As there is no known link between Venus and the tamarisk, and given the two epithets listed alongside *Myrica*, it seems reasonable to suggest a typographical error from Servius, who may have intended *Murcia*, a known epithet of Venus, again taken from the myrtle. André (1985, s.v. *myrice*) directs us to the Greek, μυρίκη which translates as tamarisk.
139 Serv. *Comm. Aen.* 1.720.
140 Plin. *HN* 15.126.
141 Draycott 2015: 60.
142 Verg. *Ecl.* 2.54–5.
143 Embedding the *triumphator* in the procession is a key premise of Beard's assessment of the triumph (2003: 29).
144 Östenberg 2009: 215–44.
145 Both of these constructions indicated a point at which the army was turned around, and conformed to the traditional idea of a *tropaeum*: see Serv. *Comm. Aen.* 10.775.
146 Fratantuono 2009: 16.
147 The depictions on Trajan's Column are very similar to the *tropaeum* on the frieze-architrave of the *cella* in the Temple of Apollo Sosianus, which depicts Augustus' triple triumph of 29 BCE (MC2776).
148 For more on trees in Attic vase painting of this era, see Dietrich (2010).
149 *SNG ANS* 670–1; *SG* 974; *SNG BMC* 1605; *SG* 3780.
150 For some early examples: *RRC* 94/1; *RRC* 95/1; and a significantly later one: *RIC* 5 141.
151 Conington (1883) *ad* Verg. *Aen.* 11.5.

152 Verg. *Aen.* 11.5–8, 15–16.
153 Stat. *Theb.* 2.704–14.
154 Verg. *Aen.* 10.423. For a full discussion of this, see Armstrong (2019: 128–31).
155 Luc. *Bell. civ.* 1.135–43.
156 For more on the simile within Lucan's poem, and its representation of Pompey in comparison with Caesar, who is compared to lightning immediately after (1.151–7), see Rosner-Siegel (1983) and Leigh (1997: 105–6).
157 For Pompey's corpse, see Lucan *Bell. civ.* 8.724. The simile is explored by Roche (2009) in his commentary on the opening book of Lucan's poem.
158 Reckford 1974: 77–8; Alessio 1993: 22.
159 This may be a reference to this trophy being an example of the *spolia secunda*, which were offered to Mars (Alessio 1993: 22).
160 For Armstrong (2019: 130), the dedication of the oak to Mars explicitly cuts Jupiter out of the picture, and removes any echo of the *spolia opima*.
161 Conington 1883 *ad* 11.5; Alessio 1993: 22; Fratantuono 2009: 16. These all correctly identify that Mezentius is not the leader of the opposing forces, and that the spoils are not dedicated to Jupiter, thus challenging any identification of Mezentius' trophy as an early example of the *spolia opima*. Livy 4.20.6 defines the *spolia opima* as being spoils exclusively 'taken from a leader by a leader'. This definition underwent some debate in the late Republic after Crassus claimed a right to dedicate the *spolia opima* and is discussed by Rich (1996, 1999), and Flower (2000).
162 Serv. *Comm. Aen.* 11.6.
163 For examples of generic references to trees in the construction of *tropaea*, see Suet. *Calig.* 45; Juv. 10.133; Ov. *Pont.* 3.4.104.
164 Liv. 1.10.5: *in Capitolium escendit ibique ea cum ad quercum pastoribus sacram deposuisset.*
165 Plut. *Rom.* 22.5–6: ἐπὶ στρατοπέδου δρῦν ἔτεμεν ὑπερμεγέθη καὶ διεμόρφωσεν ὥσπερ τρόπαιον, καὶ τῶν ὅπλων τοῦ Ἄκρωνος ἕκαστον ἐν τάξει περιήρμοσε…ὑπολαβὼν δὲ τῷ δεξιῷ τὸ τρόπαιον ὤμῳ προσερειδόμενον ὀρθόν… τὸ δὲ τρόπαιον ἀνάθημα Φερετρίου Διὸς ἐπωνομάσθη. This distinction, between the arrangement of Acron's armour by a live tree and its placement on an uprooted tree, might be attributed to the statue of Romulus in the Forum of Augustus, which had not been built when Livy wrote, while Plutarch was familiar with the statue (*Rom.* 16.8).
166 Plut. *Marc.* 8.2: δρυὸς γὰρ εὐκτεάνου πρέμνον ὄρθιον καὶ μέγα τεμὼν καὶ ἀσκήσας ὥσπερ τρόπαιον ἀνεδήσατο καὶ κατήρτησεν ἐξ αὐτοῦ τὰ λάφυρα, κόσμῳ διαθεὶς καὶ περιαρμόσας ἕκαστον.

167 Ov. *Fast.* 5.565; *ILS* 64.
168 Pompeii Regio IX.13.5.
169 Vergil's account of this event, in the procession of heroes in the underworld, records that Marcellus dedicated the *spolia opima* to Quirinus, and was the third person to do so (Verg. *Aen.* 6.859). For further on this confusion, see Horsfall 2003: ad loc.
170 Versnel 1970: 309–13.
171 Plut. *Quaest. Rom.* 37.
172 Prop. 4.10.45.
173 It could also have been an understood fact that a *tropaeum* should be constructed of oak, thus explaining the lack of references to the tree type.
174 *RRC* 439.

Chapter 4

1 Vitr. *De arch.* 5.9.5.
2 Davies 2012: 74, citing Hor. *Carm.* 3.29.11–12. Davies also cites Strabo's observation that tall chimneys distance harmful gases from the population (3.2.8), and Vitruvius observing that lead workers suffer as a result of the air impurities essential to their profession (*De arch.* 8.6.11).
3 For more on the three varieties of tears, see Murube (2009).
4 For an article on the efficacy of ancient attempts to mitigate environmental pollution with green spaces, see Fox (2021).
5 Hdn. 1.12.2
6 Plin. *HN* 17.91.
7 For examples, see Ov. *Ars Am.* 1.491–6; Mart. *Ep.* 2.57; Plin. *Ep.* 1.5.8–10; Plin. *Ep.* 3.1; and Celsus, *Med.* 1.2.6.
8 Celsus, *Med.* 1.2.6.
9 O'Sullivan 2011: 78.
10 Cic. *De Or.* 2.20.
11 Plin. *Ep.* 1.5.8–10.
12 Plin. *Ep.* 3.1.
13 Ov. *Ars Am.* 1.491–6.
14 Mart. *Ep.* 2.57.
15 *FUR* 39bc.
16 See, for example, Prop. 2.32.11–13.
17 See, for example, Gleason (2016), and Gleason and Palmer (2018).

18 Jansen 2018: 417.
19 Prior 1996: 124–8.
20 Rodrìguez Almeida 2003: 45–64.
21 Cass. Dio 55.8. This is disputed, and Pliny reports (*HN* 3.17) that the portico was designed by Agrippa, begun by Vipsania, and finished by Augustus.
22 Plin. *HN* 3.17; Tac. *Hist*. 1.31.1.
23 Mart. *Ep*. 1.108.3–4.
24 Mart. *Ep*. 2.14.15.
25 Mart. *Ep*. 3.20.12–14.
26 Kellum 1994: 213.
27 See, for example, *Res Gestae* 34; Serv. *Aen*. 6.230, 8.276; Macrob. *Sat*. 3.12.3; App. Verg. *Cul*. 402. Other accounts, such as that of Ovid's *Fasti* (3.137f) intimate that laurel trees are readily available in Rome, through the consistent presence of the boughs, and the depictions of the laurel on the Ara Pacis and the Temple of Apollo Sosianus indicate that it was a reasonably common species in Rome.
28 Mart. *Ep*. 2.14.4.
29 Mart. *Ep*. 7.32.11–12.
30 Plin. *Ep*. 2.17.14.
31 Plin. *HN* 16.70.
32 For the early identification, see Tomei 1992; Villedieu 1992. For the reassessment, see Rizzo 2001; Villedieu 2001.
33 Ov. *Ars Am*. 1.67–76.
34 Theoc. *Id*. 15.119.
35 This has also been suggested by Lloyd (1982: 98).
36 Plin. *HN* 14.11.
37 Coarelli 1997: 479.
38 Suet. *Aug*, 29.5.
39 Ov. *Ars Am*. 3.163–8.
40 Plin. *HN* 35.66; 114; 144.
41 Val. Max. 3.7.11; Plin *HN* 34.19.
42 Mart. *Ep*. 3.20.9.
43 Serv. *Aen*. 1.8.
44 Coarelli 1997: 474–5.
45 Plin. *HN* 12.3.
46 Ov. *Fast*. 4.749–55.
47 Plin. *HN* 16.139–40.
48 Prop. 2.32.11–13.
49 Strab. 5.3.8.
50 Plin. *HN* 16.141.

51 Serv. *Aen.* 3.64; 681; 4.507.
52 For links between the cypress and death, see examples at Hor. *Carm.* 2.14.23; Luc. *Bell. Civ.* 3.442; Ov. *Tr.* 3.13.21; Verg. *Aen.* 3.64.
53 Strab. 5.3.8.
54 Claridge 2010: 205; Coarelli 2007.
55 Richardson 1992: 247.
56 Carandini 2017(2): Tab. 231; cf. Carandini 2012: Tav. 231.
57 Plin. *HN* 16.140–1.
58 Plin. *HN* 12.13.
59 Ov. *Tr.* 3.1.
60 Suet. *Aug.* 100.
61 Macaulay 2021.
62 Suet. *Aug.* 31.
63 Gianfrotta, Mazzucato, and Polia (1968–9). This excavation also revealed the presence of planting beds in the portico, although no conclusions could be drawn as to the plants within them.

Appendix: Categorized List of Contents for Books Twelve to Seventeen of Pliny's *Natural History*

1 The process of caprification, for Pliny, is one in which the unripened fruit of a fig tree (fruit which will never ripen) is used to fertilize other fig trees.

Bibliography

Alessio, M., 1993. *Studies in Vergil: Aeneid Eleven. An Allegorical Approach*. Montfort & Villeroy, Québec.

André, J., 1985. *Les noms des plantes dans la Rome antique*. Les Belles Lettres, Paris.

Armstrong, R., 2019. *Vergil's Green Thoughts: Plants, Humans, and the Divine*. Oxford University Press, Oxford.

Ash, R., 1999. *Ordering Anarchy: Armies and Leaders in Tacitus' Histories*. Bloomsbury, London.

Austen, V., 2023. *Analysing the Boundaries of the Ancient Roman Garden: (Re)Framing the Hortus*. Bloomsbury, London.

Austin, R. G., 1964. *P. Vergili Maronis: Aeneidos liber secundus*. Clarendon Press, Oxford.

Baddeley, W. St C., 1905. The Sacred Trees of Rome, *Nineteenth Century and After* 58(19–20), 100–15.

Bailey, C., 1932. *Phases in the Religion of Ancient Rome*. Oxford University Press, London.

Barlow, H. C., 1866. *Essays on Symbolism*. Williams and Norgate, London.

Beagon, M., 1992. *Roman Nature: The Thought of Pliny the Elder*. Oxford University Press, Oxford.

Beard, M., North, J., Price, S., 1998. *Religions of Rome*. Cambridge University Press, Cambridge.

Beard, M., 2003. The Triumph of the Absurd: Roman Street Theatre, in: Edwards, C., Woolf, G. (eds), *Rome the Cosmopolis*. Cambridge University Press, Cambridge, pp. 21–43.

Beard, M., 2007. *The Roman Triumph*. Harvard University Press, London.

Bergmann, B., 2017. Frescoes in Roman Gardens, in: Jashemski, W. F., Gleason, K., Hartswick, K., Malek, A-A. (eds), *Gardens of the Roman Empire*. Cambridge University Press, Cambridge, pp. 278–316.

Bernabei, M., Bontadi, J., Rea, R., Büntgen, U., Tegel, W., 2019. Dendrochronological Evidence for Long-Distance Timber Trading in the Roman Empire. *PLOS ONE* 14(12) 1–13.

Bianchi Bandinelli, R., 1978. *Dall'Ellenismo al Medioevo*. Editori Riuniti, Rome.

Bommas, M. (ed.), 2011. *Cultural Memory and Identity in Ancient Societies*. Bloomsbury, London.

Bommas M., Harrison, J., Roy, P. (eds), 2012. *Memory and Urban Religion in the Ancient World*. Bloomsbury, London,

Bodel, J., 2009. 'Sacred dedications': A Problem of Definitions, in: Bodel, J., Kajava, M. (eds), *Dediche sacre nel mondo greco-romano: diffusione, funzioni, tipologie*. Institutum Romanum Finlandiae, Rome, pp.17–30.

Boetticher, K., 1856. *Der Baumkultus der Hellenen nach den gottesdienstlichen Gebräuchen und den überlieferten Bildwerken dargestellt*. Weidmannsche Buchhandlung, Berlin.

Boyle, A. J., 1999. Images of Rome, in: Perkell, C. (ed.), *Reading Vergil's Aeneid: An Interpretive Guide*. University of Oklahoma Press, Norman, pp. 148–61.

Bradley, A., 1969. Augustan Culture and a Radical Alternative: Vergil's *Georgics*. *Arion* 8(3) 347–58.

Bradley, M., 2009. *Colour and Meaning in Ancient Rome*. Cambridge University Press, Cambridge.

Bradley, R., 2000. *An Archaeology of Natural Places*. Routledge, London.

Brilliant, R., 1984. *Visual Narratives: Storytelling in Etruscan and Roman Art*. Cornell University Press, Ithaca.

Broise, H., Scheid, J., 1993. Étude d'un cas: le lucus deae Diae à Rome, in: de Casanove, O., Scheid, J. (eds), *Les Bois Sacrés. Actes du Colloque International Organisé par le Centre Jean Bérard et l'École Pratique des Hauts Études (Ve Section), Naples, 23–25 Novembre 1989*. Centre Jean Bérard, Naples, pp.145–57.

Broughton, T. R. S., 1952. *The Magistrates of the Roman Republic*. American Philological Association, New York.

Caneva, G., 2010. *Il codice botanico di Augusto: parlare al popolo attraverso le immagini della natura*. Gangemi Editore, Rome.

Carandini, A., 2012. *Atlante di Roma Antica: Biogradia e Ritratti della Città*. Electa, Milano.

Carandini, A., 2017. *The Atlas of Ancient Rome: Biography and Portraits of the City*. Princeton University Press, Princeton.

Carettoni, G., 1960. *La pianta marmorea di Roma antica*. Ripartizione del commune di Roma, Rome.

Carey, S., 2003. *Pliny's Catalogue of Culture: Art and Empire in the Natural History*. Oxford University Press, Oxford.

Cichorius, C., 1896. *Die Reliefs der Traianssäule*. Verlag von Georg Reimer, Berlin.

Claridge, A., 2010 2nd edn. *Rome: An Oxford Archaeological Guide*. Oxford University Press, Oxford.

Coarelli, F., 1997. *Il Campo Marzio: Dalle Origini alla Fine della Repubblica*. Quasar, Rome.

Coarelli, F., 2000. *The Column of Trajan*. Colombo, Rome.

Coarelli, F., 2007. *Rome and Environs*. University of California Press, Berkeley.
Coleman, R., 1977. *Vergil: Eclogues*. Cambridge University Press, Cambridge.
Conington, J., 1883. *P. Vergili Maronis Opera. The Works of Virgil with a Commentary* (rev. edn). Whittaker & Co., London.
Conte, G. B., 1994. *Genres and Readers: Lucretius, Love Elegy, Pliny's Encyclopaedia*. Johns Hopkins University Press, London.
Coulston, J. C. N., 1990. Three New Books on Trajan's Column. *JRA* 3, 290–309.
Courtney, E., 1980. *A Commentary on the Satires of Juvenal*. Athlone Press, London.
Coutelle, E., 2015. *Properce, Élégies, livre IV*. Latomus, Brussels.
Dalby, A., 2000. *Empire of Pleasures: Luxury and Indulgence in the Roman World*. Routledge, London.
Dasen, V., Späth, T., 2010. *Children, Memory, and Family Identity in Roman Culture*. Oxford University Press, Oxford.
Davies, D., 1988. The evocative symbolism of trees, in: Cosgrove, D., Daniels, S. (eds), *The Iconography of Landscape: Essays on the Symbolic Representation, Design and Use of Past Environments*. Cambridge University Press, Cambridge, pp. 32–42.
Davies, P. J. E., 1997. The Politics of Perpetuation: Trajan's Column and the Art of Commemoration. *AJA* 101, 41–65.
Davies, P. J. E., 2012. Pollution, Propriety and Urbanism in Republican Rome, in: Bradley, M. (ed.), *Rome, Pollution and Propriety: Dirt, Disease and Hygiene in the Eternal City from Antiquity to Modernity*. Cambridge University Press, Cambridge, pp. 67–80.
Davies, P. J. E., 2017. *Architecture and Politics in Republican Rome*. Cambridge University Press, Cambridge.
De Oliveira, F., 1992. *Les idées politiques et morales de Pline l'Ancien*. Instituto Nacional de Investigação Científica, Coimbra.
Dietrich, N., 2010. *Figur ohne Raum? Bäume und Felsen in der attischen Vasenmalerei des 6. und 5. Jahrhunderts v.Chr.* De Gruyter, Berlin.
Dinsmoor, W., 1950 3rd edn. *The Architecture of Ancient Greece: An Account of its Historic Development*. B.T. Batsford Ltd, London.
Doody, A., 2007. Virgil the Farmer? Critiques of the *Georgics* in Columella and Pliny. *CPh* 102, 180–97.
Dowden, K., 2000. *European Paganism: The Realities of Cult from Antiquity to the Middle Ages*. Routledge, London.
Draycott, J., 2015. Smelling Trees, Flowers and Herbs in the Ancient World, in: Bradley, M. (ed.), *Smell and the Ancient Senses*. Routledge, London, pp. 60–73.
Dumézil, G., 1975. *Fêtes Romaines d'Été et d'Automne Suivi de Dix Questions Romaines*. Gallimard, Paris.
Dupont, F., 1989. *Daily Life in Ancient Rome*. Blackwells, Oxford.

Dupont, J. C., 2008. Columella and Vergil. *Vergilius* 54, 49–58.
Dyson, J. T., 2001. *King of the Wood: The Sacrificial Victor in Virgil's Aeneid*. University of Oklahoma Press, Norman.
Edwards, C., 1996. *Writing Rome: Textual Approaches to the Ancient City*. Cambridge University Press, Cambridge.
Edwards, C., 2003. Incorporating the Alien: The Art of Conquest, in: Edwards, C., Woolf, G. (eds), *Rome the Cosmopolis*. Cambridge University Press, Cambridge, pp. 44–70.
Elliott, P., Watkins, C., Daniels, S., 2011. *The British Arboretum: Science, Trees and Culture in the Nineteenth Century*. Pickering and Chatto, London.
Erdkamp, P., Verboven, K., Zuiderhoek, A. (eds), 2015. *Ownership and Exploitation of Land and Natural Resources in the Roman World*. Oxford University Press: Oxford.
Evans, J. DeR., 1991. The Sacred Figs of Rome. *Latomus* 50(4), 798–808.
Fabrizi, V., 2016. Space, Vision and the Friendly Sea: Scipio's Crossing to Africa in Livy's Book 29, in: Baltrusch, E., Kopp, H., Wendt, C. (eds), *Seemacht, Seeherrschaft Und Die Antike*. Franz Steiner Verlag, Stuttgart, pp. 279–90.
Fantham, E., 2012. Purification in Ancient Rome, in: Bradley, M. (ed.), *Rome, Pollution, and Propriety: Dirt, Disease, and Hygiene in the Eternal City*. Cambridge University Press, Cambridge, pp. 59–66.
Fear, A., 2011. The Roman's Burden, in: Gibson, R., Morello, R. (eds), *Pliny the Elder: Themes and Contexts*. Brill, Leiden, pp. 21–34.
Fedeli, P., 1985. *Properzio: Il libro terzo delle Elegie*. Adriatica Editrice, Bari.
Fedeli, P., Dimundo, R., Ciccarelli, I., 2015. *Properzio: Elegie libro IV*. Verlag T. Bautz GmbH, Nordhausen.
Ferguson, J., 1970. *The Religions of the Roman Empire*. Thames and Hudson, London.
Ferris, I., 2000. *Enemies of Rome: Barbarians through Roman Eyes*. The History Press, Stroud.
Flory, M. B., 1995. The Symbolism of Laurel in Cameo Portraits of Livia. *MAAR* 40, 43–68.
Flower, H. I., 2000. The Tradition of the Spolia Opima: M. Claudius Marcellus and Augustus. *ClAnt* 19, 34–64.
Fox, A., 2018. *Roman Trees Database*. https://www.nottingham.ac.uk/Roman_Trees [accessed 21 June 2022].
Fox, A., 2019. Trajanic Trees: The Dacian Forest on Trajan's Column. *PBSR* 87, 47–69.
Fox, A., 2021. Mitigating Pollution in Ancient Rome's Green Spaces. *New Classicists* 4, 3–12.
Fox, A., (forthcoming). (Mis)Management of Roman Groves: Defining Space in the Wild.

Fratantuono, L., 2009. *A Commentary on Virgil, Aeneid XI*. Latomus, Brussels.
Freud, S., 1985. *Civilisation, Society, and Religion*. Penguin, London.
Friedländer, L. (ed.), 1886. *M. Valerii Martialis Epigrammaton libri*. Teubner, Leipzig.
Gale, M., 2000. *Virgil on the Nature of Things: The* Georgics, *Lucretius and the Didactic Tradition*. Cambridge University Press, Cambridge.
Gauer, W., 1977. *Untersuchungen zur Trajanssäule*. Gebr. Mann Verlag, Berlin.
Gianfrotta, P. A., Mazzucato, O., Polia, M., 1968–9. Scavo nell'area del Teatro Argentina, 1968–9. *Bollettino della Commissione Archeologia Communale di Roma* 81, 25–36.
Gibbon, E., 1781. *The History of the Decline and Fall of the Roman Empire*. Methuen, London.
Giesecke, A., Siede, M., 2022. Plants in Culture: Botanical Symbolism in Daily Life and Literature in: Giesecke, A. (ed.), *A Cultural History of Plants*. Bloomsbury, London, pp. 131–54.
Gleason, K., 1994. *Porticus Pompeiana*: A new perspective on the first public park of ancient Rome. *The Journal of Garden History* 14, 13–27.
Gleason, K., 2016. Design, in: Gleason, K. (ed.), *A Cultural History of Gardens in Antiquity*. Bloomsbury, London, pp.15–40.
Gleason, K., Palmer, M., 2018. Constructing the Ancient Roman Garden, in: Jashemski, W. F., Gleason, K., Hartswick, K., Malek, A-A. (eds), *Gardens of the Roman Empire*. Cambridge University Press, Cambridge, pp.369–401.
Goodyear, F. R. D., 1982. Technical Writing, in: Kenney, E. J., Clausen, W. V. (eds), *The Cambridge History of Classical Literature: Latin Literature*. Cambridge University Press, Cambridge, pp. 667–74.
Gowers, E., 2011. Trees and Family Trees in the Aeneid. *ClAnt* 30, 87–118.
Granger, F. S., 1895. *The Worship of the Romans*. Methuen, London.
Greenhalgh, P., 1980. *Pompey: The Roman Alexander*. University of Missouri Press, Columbia.
Grescoe, T., 2022. This miracle plant was eaten into extinction 2,000 years ago—or was it?. *National Geographic*. https://www.nationalgeographic.com/history/article/miracle-plant-eaten-extinction-2000-years-ago-silphion [accessed 31 October 2022].
Gruen, E., 1992. *Culture and National Identity in Republican Rome*. Cornell University Press, Ithaca.
Hardie, A., 1998. Juvenal, the Phaedrus, and the Truth about Rome. *CQ* 48, 234–51.
Hassel, F. J., 1966. *Der Trajansbogen in Benevent: EinBauwerk des römischen Senates*. Philipp von Zbern, Mainz.
Healy, J., 1999. *Pliny the Elder on Science and Technology*. Oxford University Press, Oxford.

Heller, A., 2001. Cultural Memory, Identity and Civil Society. *Internationale Politik und Geschellschaft* 2, 139–43.

Henderson, J., 2004. *Morals and Villas in Seneca's Letters: Places to Dwell*. Cambridge University Press, Cambridge.

Heyworth, S. J., Morwood, J. H. W., 2011. *A Commentary on Propertius Book 3*. Oxford University Press, Oxford.

Horsfall, N., 2003. *Virgil: Aeneid 6: A Commentary*. De Gruyter, Berlin.

Houlbrook, C., 2017. Review of Ailsa Hunt, *Reviving Roman Religion: Sacred Trees in the Roman World, Time and Mind* 10(3), 323–5.

Hughes, J. D., 2014 (2nd edn). *Environmental Problems of the Greeks and Romans: Ecology in the Ancient Mediterranean*. Johns Hopkins University Press, Baltimore.

Hughes, J. D., 1983. How the Ancients Viewed Deforestation. *JFA* 10, 435–45.

Hunt, A., 2012. Keeping the Memory Alive: The Physical Continuity of the Ficus Ruminalis, in: Bommas, M., Harrison, J., Roy, P. (eds), *Memory and Urban Religion in the Ancient World*. Bloomsbury, London, pp. 111–28.

Hunt, A., 2016. *Reviving Roman Religion: Sacred Trees in the Roman World*. Cambridge University Press, Cambridge.

Hutchinson, G. O., 2011. Politics and the Sublime in the Panegyricus, in: Roche, P. (ed.), *Pliny's Praise: The Panegyricus in the Roman World*. Cambridge University Press, Cambridge, pp. 125–41.

Jansen, G., 2018. Water and Water Technology in Roman Gardens, in: Jashemski, W. F., Gleason, K., Hartswick, K., Malek, A-A. (eds), *Gardens of the Roman Empire*. Cambridge University Press, Cambridge, pp. 402–31.

Jashemski, W. F., Meyer, F. G., 2002. *The Natural History of Pompeii*. Cambridge University Press, Cambridge.

Jennings, H., 1890. *Cultus arborum: A Descriptive Account of Phallic Tree Worship, with Illustrative Legends, Superstitions, Usages etc., Exhibiting its Origin and Development amongst the Eastern and Western Nations of the World, from the Earliest to the Modern Times; with a Bibliography of Works upon and Referring to the Phallic cultus*. London.

Jones, F., 2011. *Virgil's Garden: The Nature of Bucolic Space*. Bristol Classical Press, Bristol.

Jordan, H., 1842. Über Römische Aushängeschilder. *Archäologische Zeitung* 29, 65–79.

Keaveney, A., 1992. *Lucullus: A Life*. Routledge, London.

Kellum, B. A., 1994. The Construction of Landscape in Augustan Rome: The Garden Room at the Villa ad Gallinas. *The Art Bulletin* 76, 211–24.

Keshri, G., Bajpai, M., Lakshmi, V., Setty, B. S., Gupta, G., 2004. Role of energy metabolism in the pregnancy interceptive action of Ferula assafoetida and Melia azedarach extracts in rat. *Contraception* 70, 429–32.

Klynne, A., 2004. The Laurel Grove of the Caesars: Looking in and Looking out, in: Klynne, A., Frizell, S. (eds), *Roman Villas around the Urbs. Interaction with Landscape and Environment. Proceedings of a Conference Held at the Swedish Institute in Rome, September 17–18, 2004.* Swedish Institute in Rome, Rome, pp. 167–75.

Klynne, A., Liljenstolpe, P., 2000. Investigating the Gardens of the Villa of Livia. *JRA* 13, 223–33.

Kondratieff, E. J., 2015. Future City in the Heroic Past: Rome, Romans, and Roman Landscapes in Aeneid 6–8, in: Kemezis, A. (ed.), *Urban Dreams and Realities in Antiquity: Remains and Representations of the Ancient City*. Brill, Leiden, pp. 165–228.

Kousser, R. M., 2008. *Hellenistic and Roman Ideal Sculpture: The Allure of the Classical*. Cambridge University Press, Cambridge.

Kraan, G. van der, 2001. Juvenal I, 3, 10–20: The Location o Egeria's Abode. *Mnemosyne* 54, 472–5.

Kraft, K., 1952. Der goldene kranz Caesars und der kampf um die entlarvung des "Tyrannen." *Jahrbuch für numismatik und geldgeschichte* 3/4, 7–98.

Kuttner, A. L., 1999. Culture and History at Pompey's Museum. *TAPA* 129, 343–73.

Laehn, T., 2013. *Pliny's Defense of Empire*. Routledge, London.

Landgren, L., 2016. Plantings, in: Gleason, K. (ed.), *A Cultural History of Gardens in Antiquity*. Bloomsbury, London, pp. 75–98.

Lao, E., 2011. Luxury and the Creation of a Good Consumer, in: Gibson, R., Morello, R. (eds), *Pliny the Elder: Themes and Contexts*. Brill, Leiden, pp. 35–56.

Larmour, D. H. J., Spencer, D. (eds), 2007a. *Sites of Rome: Time, Space, Memory*. Oxford University Press, Oxford.

Larmour, D. H. J., Spencer, D., 2007b. Introduction – Roma Recepta: A Topography of the Imagination, in: Larmour, D. H. J., Spencer, D. (eds), *Sites of Rome: Time, Space, Memory*. Oxford University Press, Oxford, pp. 1–60.

Leach, E. W., 1973. Corydon Revisited: An Interpretation of the Political Eclogues of Calpurnius Siculus. *Ramus* 2, 53–97.

Leander Touati, A-M., 1987. *The Great Trajanic Frieze: The Study of a Monument and the Mechanisms of Message Transmission in Roman Art*. Lund University.

Lehman-Hartelben, K., 1926. *Die Trajanssäule: Ein römisches Kunstwerk zu Beginn der Spätantike*. De Gruyter, Berlin.

Leigh, M., 1997. *Lucan: Spectacle and Engagement*. Clarendon Press, Oxford.

Lepper, F., 1969. Review of F. J. Hassel, Der Trajansbogen in Benevent: Ein Bauwerk des Römischen Senates. *JRS* 59, 250–61.

Lepper, F., Frere, S., 1988. *Trajan's Column: A New Edition of the Cichorius Plates*. Alan Sutton, Gloucester.

Lewis, C. T., Short, C., 1897. *A Latin Dictionary. Founded on Andrews' edition of Freund's Latin dictionary. revised, enlarged, and in great part rewritten.* Clarendon Press, Oxford.

Liu, Y., 2010. Castell's Pliny: Rewriting the Past for the Present. *Eighteenth Century Studies* 43, 243–57.

Lloyd, R., 1982. Three Monumental Gardens on the Marble Plan. *AJA* 86, 91–100.

Locher, A., 1986. The Structure of Pliny the Elder's Natural History, in: French, R., Greenaway, F. (eds), *Science in the Early Roman Empire: Pliny the Elder, His Sources and Influence*. Croom Helm, London, pp. 20–30.

Lott, J. B., 2004. *The Neighborhoods of Augustan Rome*. Cambridge University Press, Cambridge.

Lowe, D., 2010. The Symbolic Value of Grafting in Ancient Rome. *TAPhA* 140, 461–88.

Mabberley, D. J., 2008 (rev. edn). *Mabberley's Plant-Book: A Portable Dictionary of Plants, Their Classifications and Uses*. Cambridge University Press, Cambridge.

Macaulay, E., 2021. Mausoleum Augusti. *Gardens of the Roman Empire* [online], https://roman-gardens.github.io/province/italia/rome/regio_ix_circus_flaminius/mausoleum_augusti/ [accessed on 21 June 2022].

Macaulay-Lewis, E., 2018. The Archaeology of Gardens in the Roman Villa, in: Jashemski, W. F., Gleason, K. L., Hartswick, K. J., Malek, A-A. (eds), *Gardens of the Roman Empire*. Cambridge University Press, Cambridge, pp. 87–120.

Malissard, A., 1982. Une nouvelle approche de la colonne Trajane. *Aufsteig und Niedergang der römischen Welt* 12, 579–606.

Manolaraki, E., 2015. 'Hebraei Liquores': The Balsam of Judaea in Pliny's 'Natural History.' *AJPh* 136, 633–67.

Manolaraki, E., 2008. Political and Rhetorical Seascapes in Pliny's Panegyricus. *CPh* 103, 374–94.

Marzano, A., 2015. The Variety of Villa Production: From Agriculture to Aquaculture, in: Erdkamp, P., Verboven, K., Zuiderhoek, A. (eds), *Ownership and Exploitation of Land and Natural Resources in the Roman World*. Oxford University Press: Oxford, pp.187–207.

Marzano, A., 2022. *Plants, Politics and Empire in Ancient Rome*. Cambridge University Press, Cambridge.

McCulloch, H. Y., 1984. *Narrative Cause in the Annals of Tacitus*. Verlag Anton Hain, Königstein.

McCulloch, H. Y., 1980. Literary Augury at the End of Annals XIII. *Phoenix* 34, 237–42.

McEwan, I., 2003. *Vitruvius: Writing the Body of Architecture*. MIT Press, London.

Meiggs, R., 1960. *Roman Ostia*. Clarendon Press, Oxford.

Meiggs, R., 1972. *The Athenian Empire*. Clarendon Press, Oxford.

Meiggs, R., 1982. *Trees and Timber in the Ancient Mediterranean World*. Clarendon Press, Oxford.

Meneghini, R., 2009. *I Fori Imperiali e i Mercati di Traiano: Storia e descrizione dei monumenti alla luce degli studi e degli scavi recenti*. Istituto poligrafico e zecca dello stato, Rome.

Meneghini, R., Messa, L., Ungaro, L., 1998. L'architettura del Foro di Traiano attraverso i ritrovamenti archeologici più recenti. *RömMitt* 105, 127–48.

Meneghini, R., Messa, L., Ungaro, L., 1990. *Il Foro di Traiano*. Fratelli Palombi Editori, Rome.

Meneghini, R., Santangeli Valenziani, R., 2007. *I Fori Imperiali: Gli scavi del comune di Roma (1991-2007)*. Viviani, Rome.

Meyers, G., 2012. Introduction: The experience of monumentality in Etruscan and Early Roman Architecture, in: Thomas, M., Meyers, G. (eds), *Monumentality in Etruscan and Early Roman Architecture: Ideology and Innovation*. University of Texas Press, Austin, pp. 1–20.

Miski, M., 2021. Next Chapter in the Legend of Silphion: Preliminary Morphological, Chemical, Biological and Pharmacological Evaluations, Initial Conservation Studies, and Reassessment of the Regional Extinction Event. *Plants* 10(1), 102.

Morgan, M., 1996. Vespasian and the Omens in Tacitus Histories 2.78. *Phoenix* 50, 41–55.

Motto, A., Clark, J., 1965. *Per iter tenebricosum*: The Mythos of Juvenal 3. *TAPhA* 96, 267–76.

Murphy, T., 2004. *Pliny the Elder's Natural History: The Empire in the Encyclopaedia*. Oxford University Press, Oxford.

Murube, J., 2009. Basal, Reflex, and Psycho-Emotional Tears. *The Ocular Surface* 7, 60–6.

Naas, V., 2011. Imperialism, Mirabilia and Knowledge: Some Paradoxes in the Naturalis Historia, in: Gibson, R., Morello, R. (eds), *Pliny the Elder: Themes and Contexts*. Brill, Leiden, pp. 58–70.

Nelson, S. E., 2009. Persephone's Seeds: Abortifacients and Contraceptives in Ancient Greek Medicine and their Recent Scientific Appraisal. *Pharmacy in History* 51, 57–69.

Nisbet, R. G. M., 1988. Notes on the Text and interpretation of Juvenal. *BICS Suppl.* 51, 86–110.

Nora, P., 1989. Between Memory and History: Les Lieux de Mémoire. *Representations* 26, 7–24.

Ogden, D., 2013. *Dragons, Serpents, and Slayers in the Classical and Early Christian Worlds: A Sourcebook*. Oxford University Press, Oxford.

Oglivie, R. M., 1965. *A Commentary on Livy Books 1–5*. Clarendon Press, Oxford.

Östenberg, I., 2009. *Staging the World: Spoils, Captives, and Representations in the Roman Triumphal Procession*. Oxford University Press, Oxford.

O' Sullivan, T. M., 2015. Augustan Literary Tours: Walking and Reading the City, in: Östenberg, I., Malmberg, S., Bjørnebye, J. (eds), *The Moving City: Processions, Passages, and Promenades in Ancient Rome*. Bloomsbury, London, pp. 111–22.

O'Sullivan, T. M., 2011. *Walking in Roman Culture*. Cambridge University Press, Cambridge.

Packer, J., 1997. *Trajan's Forum: A Study of the Monuments*. University of California Press, Berkeley.

Packer, J., Sarring, K. L., Sheldon, R. M., 1983. A New Excavation in Trajan's Forum. *AJA* 87, 165–72.

Panciera, S., 2006. *Epigrafi, epigrafia, epigrafisti: Scritti vari editi e inediti (1956–2005) con note complementari e indici*. Quazar, Rome.

Pearce, T., 1992. Juvenal 3.10–20. *Mnemosyne* 45, 380–3.

Pfister, F., 1937. Numen. *RE* 17, 1273–91.

Phillips, O. C., 1968. Lucan's grove. *CPh* 63, 296–300.

Philpot, J. H., 1897. *The Sacred Tree*. Macmillan and Co., London.

Pinto-Guillaume, E. M., 2002. Mollusks from the Villa of Livia at Prima Porta, Rome: The Swedish Garden Archaeological Project 1996–1999. *AJA* 106, 37–58.

Pollard, E. A., 2009. Pliny's Natural History and the Flavian Templum Pacis: Botanical Imperialism in First-Century CE Rome. *Journal of World History* 20, 309–38.

Prior, R. E., 1996. Going around Hungry: Topography and Poetics in Martial 2.14. *AJPh* 117, 121–41.

Purcell, N., 1987. Town in country and country in town, in Macdougall E. B. (ed.), *Ancient Roman Villa Gardens*. Dumbarton Oaks Trustees for Harvard University, Washington DC, pp. 185–204.

Radice, B., 1968. Pliny and the Panegyricus. *G&R* 15, 166–72.

Reckford, K., 1974. Some Trees in Virgil and Tolkien, in: Galinsky, G. K. (ed.), *Perspectives of Roman Poetry: A Classics Symposium*. The University of Texas Press, Austin, pp. 57–91.

Reeder, J. C., 2001. *The Villa of Livia ad Gallinas Albas: A Study in the Augustan Villa and Garden*. Center for Old World Archaeology and Art, Providence.

Reeder, J. C., 1997a. The Statue of Augustus from Prima Porta, the Underground Complex, and the Omen of the Gallina Alba. *AJPh* 118, 89–118.

Reeder, J. C., 1997b. The Statue of Augustus from the Prima Porta and the Underground Complex, in: Deroux, C. (ed.), *Studies in Latin Literature and Roman History VIII. Collection Latomus 239*. Latomus, Brussels.

Rice, E. E., 1983. *The Grand Procession of Ptolemy Philadelphus*. Oxford University Press, Oxford.
Rich, J. W., 1999. Drusus and the Spolia Opima. *CQ* 49, 544–55.
Rich, J. W., 1996. Augustus and the Spolia Opima. *Chiron* 26, 85–127.
Richardson, L., 1992. *A New Topographical Dictionary of Ancient Rome*. The Johns Hopkins University Press, Baltimore, Maryland.
Rives, J. B., 2012. Control of the Sacred in Roman Law, in: Tellegen-Couperus, O. (ed.), *Law and Religion in the Roman Republic*. Brill, Leiden, pp. 165–80.
Rizzo, G., 2001. Le anfore del giardino del tempio, in: Villedieu, F. (ed.), *Il Giardino Dei Cesari: Dai Palazzi Antichi Alla Vigna Barberini, Sul Monte Palatino: Scavi Dell'École Française de Rome, 1985–99*. Edizioni Quasar, Rome, p. 98.
Roche, P. (ed.), 2011. *Pliny's Praise: The Panegyricus in the Roman World*. Cambridge University Press, Cambridge.
Roche, P., 2009. *Lucan: De bello civili. Book I*. Oxford University Press, Oxford.
Rockwell, P., 1983. Preliminary Study of the Carving Techniques on the Column of Trajan. *Studi Miscellanei* 26, 101–11.
Rodrìguez Almeida, E., 2003. *Terrarum dea gentium: Marziale e Roma: un poeta e la sua città*. Unione Internazionale degli Istituti di Archeologia Storia e Storia dell'Arte in Roma, Rome.
Rose, H. J., 1935. Numen inest: 'Animism' in Greek and Roman Religion. *HTR* 28, 237–57.
Rose, H. J., 1948. *Ancient Roman Religion*. Hutchinson's University Library, London.
Rosner-Siegel, J., 1983. The Oak and the Lightning: Lucan, Bellum Civile 1.135–57. *Athenaeum* 61, 165–77.
Rossi, L., 1972. A Historiographic Reassessment of the Metopes of the Tropaeum Traiani at Adamklissi. *Archaeological Journal* 129, 56–68.
Rotili, M., 1972. *L'Arco di Traiano a Benevento*. Istituto poligrafico dello stato, Rome.
Rüpke, J., 2012. *Religion in Republican Rome: Rationalization and Religious Change*. University of Pennsylvania Press, Philadelphia.
Russell, A., 2016. *The Politics of Public Space in Republican Rome*. Cambridge University Press, Cambridge.
Rutledge, S. H., 2012. *Ancient Rome as a Museum: Power, Identity, and the Culture of Collecting*. Oxford University Press, Oxford.
Ryberg, I. Z., 1955. Rites of the State Religion in Roman Art. *MAAR* 22.
Sandys, J. E., 1927 (rev. edn). *Latin Epigraphy: An Introduction to the Study of Latin Inscriptions*. Cambridge University Press, Cambridge.
Schama, S., 1995. *Landscape and Memory*. Alfred A. Knopf, New York.
Seager, R., 2002 (rev. edn). *Pompey: A Political Biography*. Blackwells, Oxford.

Segal, C., 1973. Tacitus and Poetic History: The End of Annals XIII. *Ramus* 2(2), 107–26.

Settis, S., La Regina, A., Agosti, G., Farinella, V., 1988. *La Colonna Traiana*. Giulio Einaudi, Torino.

Spencer, D., 2005. Lucan's Follies: Memory and Ruin in a Civil-War Landscape. *G&R* 52, 46–69.

Spencer, D., 2019. *Language and Authority in* De Lingua Latina: *Varro's Guide to Being Roman*. The University of Wisconsin Press, Madison, Wisconsin.

Spencer, D., 2010. *Roman Landscape: Culture and Identity*. Cambridge University Press, Cambridge.

Spisak, A. L., 2007. *Martial: A Social Guide*. Duckworth, London.

Stackelberg, K. T. von, 2009. *The Roman Garden: Space, Sense, and Society*. Routledge, London.

Stearn, W., 1966. *Botanical Latin: History, Gramar, Syntax, Terminology and Vocabulary*. Nelson, London.

Stoiculescu, C. D., 1985. Trajan's Column Documentary Value from a Forestry Viewpoint (Part 1). *Dacia* 29, 81–98.

Strack, P. L., 1931. *Untersuchungen zur römischen Reichsprägung des zweiten Jahrhunderts*. W. Kohlhammer, Stuttgart.

Sturtevant, E. H., 1911. Notes on Juvenal. *AJPh* 32, 322–7.

Syme, R., 1958. *Tacitus*. Clarendon Press, Oxford.

Thiselton-Dyer, T. F., 1889. *The Folk-Lore of Plants*. Chatto and Windus, London.

Thomas, E., 2007. *Monumentality and the Roman Empire: Architecture in the Antonine Age*. Oxford University Press, Oxford.

Thomas, R. F., 1988. Tree Violation and Ambivalence in Virgil. *TAPhA* 118, 261–73.

Tomei, M. A., 1992. Nota sui giardini antichi del Palatino. *MÉFRA* 104, 917–51.

Totelin, L., 2012. Botanizing Rulers and their Herbal Subjects: Plants and Political Power in Greek and Roman Literature. *Phoenix* 66, 122–44.

Totelin, L., 2022. Trade and Exploration, in: Giesecke, A. (ed.), *A Cultural History of Plants*. Bloomsbury, London, pp. 67–84.

Toynbee, J. M. C., 1934. *The Hadrianic School*. Cambridge University Press, Cambridge.

Turcan, R., 2000. *The Gods of Ancient Rome: Religion in Everyday Life from Archaic to Imperial Times* (trans. by Nevill, A.). Edinburgh University Press, Edinburgh.

Tylor, E. B., 1871. *Primitive Culture: Researches into the Development of Mythology, Philosophy, Religion, Art, and Custom*. Vol. II. John Murray, London.

Ulrich, R. B., 2007. *Roman Woodworking*. Yale University Press, New Haven.

Versnel, H. S., 1970. *Triumphus: An Inquiry into the Origin, Development and Meaning of the Roman Triumph*. Brill, Leiden.

Veyne, P., 1960. Une hypothèse sur l'arc de Bénévent. *MEFRA* 72, 191–219.
Vigourt, A., 2001. *Les présages impériaux d'Auguste à Domitien*. Editions de Boccard, Paris.
Villedieu, F., 2001. I giardini del tempio, in: Villedieu, F. (ed.), *Il Giardino Dei Cesari: Dai Palazzi Antichi Alla Vigna Barberini, Sul Monte Palatino: Scavi Dell'École Française de Rome, 1985–99*. Edizioni Quasar, Rome.
Villedieu, F., 1992. Le Palatin (Vigna Barberini). *MEFRA* 104, 465–79.
Vons, J., 2000. *L'image de la femme dans l'oeuvre de Pline l'Ancien*. Latomus, Brussels.
Wagenvoort, H., 1947. *Roman Dynamism*. Blackwell, Oxford.
Wallace-Hadrill, A., 1990. Pliny the Elder and Man's Unnatural History. *G&R* 37, 80–96.
Warde-Fowler, W., 1911. *The Religious Experience of the Roman People*. Macmillan and Co., London.
Wardle, D., 2012. Suetonius on Vespasianus Religiosus in AD 69–70: Signs and Times. *Hermes* 140, 184–201.
Watkins, C., 2014. *Trees, Woods and Forests*. Reaktion Books, London.
Watkins, C., 2018. *Trees in Art*. Reaktion Books, London.
Watson, L., Watson, P., 2003. *Martial: Select Epigrams*. Cambridge University Press, Cambridge
Whyte, N., 2013. An Archaeology of Natural Places: Trees in the Early Modern Landscape. *Huntington Library Quarterly* 76(4), 499–517.
Wilson, A., 2012. Raw Materials and Energy, in: W. Scheidel (ed.), *The Cambridge Companion to the Roman Economy*. Cambridge University Press, Cambridge, pp. 133–55.
Wootton, W., Bradley, J., Russell, B., Pasin, M., 2013. *Art of Making* [online]. https://www.artofmaking.ac.uk [accessed on 21 June 2022].
Wootton, W., Russell, B., 2013. Carving Imperial Reliefs at Rome (version 1.0). *The Art of Making in Antiquity: Stoneworking in the Roman World* [online]. http://www.artofmaking.ac.uk/content/essays/4-carving-imperial-reliefs-at-rome-w-wootton-b-russell/ [accessed on 21 June 2022].
Zachos, K. L., 2003. The tropaeum of the Sea-Battle of Actium at Nikopolis: Interim Report. *JRA* 16, 64–92.
Zanker, P., 1997. In Search of the Roman Viewer, in: Buitron-Oliver, D. (ed.), *The Interpretations of Architectural Sculpture in Greece and Rome*. National Gallery of Art, Washington, pp. 187–91.

Index of Trees

ash 11, 57, 63

balsam 18, 74–6, 77, 79
beech 24, 27, 36, 80, 82, 83
box 6, 115–16

Capillata 28, 40, 44, 130
cedar 57, 61
cherry 73, 79, 80, 111
cherry laurel, *Prunus laurocerasus*, 26
Christmas 11
citron 66–7, 77
citrus 53, 57–61
cornel cherry 33, 36
cypress 25, 40, 44–5, 51, 80, 121, 124–5

ebony 66–7, 72–4, 77, 79
elm 8, 20

fig
    fig, olive and vine 3, 39–40
    Navia 4–5
    Ruminal 1–5, 12–14, 37, 45, 82, 100, 123
    Silvanus 3, 4
fir 6, 27, 113

larch 61
laurel 12, 13, 26, 36, 45–8, 51, 94–5, 97–101, 113, 115, 123, 125–6
lotus 40, 44

mistletoe 11
myrtle 12, 37, 40, 42, 98–9

oak 6, 11, 12, 13, 24, 65, 80, 82–3, 85, 103–8, 126
    aesculus 25, 27, 36, 38, 91, 92, 94
    ilex 27, 91
    quercus 27, 28, 36, 48, 91, 92, 94
    robur 27
olive 12, 40, 42–3, 45
    see also fig, olive and vine

pear 37–8, 123
pine 10, 27
pitch pine 27
plane 53, 62–3, 74, 121–3, 126
poplar 12, 25, 121, 125

service tree 80, 83
silphium 25
sycamore/maple 27, 80

vine 55–6, 59
    see also fig, olive and vine

willow 37

Index

Aeneas 6, 34, 40, 102–4
agriculture 56
Ara Pacis 26, 94, 100, 126
Augustus 45–8, 90, 92, 94, 100, 115–16, 126

Camenae 39–40, 49–51, 121, 123
Claudius 62, 66
control 17, 47–8, 63–7, 84–6, 89–90, 123
crowns
    corona civica 91–4
    corona graminea/obsidionalis 70–1, 89–90
    corona triumphalis 94–101

deforestation 9–10, 58, 84–5, 87

Evander's Rome 34–6

Festus, Sextus Pompeius 5, 48–9, 58, 98
forest 34–6, 46–7, 65, 67, 86–7, 126
ficus Navia 4–5
ficus Ruminalis, *see* Ruminal fig

grove 6–8, 18–19, 45–8, 48–51

Horti 14, 17, 71–2, 73, 112
hortus 14, 16, 17, 46, 69–70
Hunt, Ailsa 4–5, 13–14

imperialism 65–7, 83–5
imports 53, 55, 57–61, 62, 66–7, 71–8, 124

Judaea 76, 88

landscape 14–16, 86–7, 90
Livia, villa of 45–8, 123
Lucullus 71–2, 77
luxury 42, 53, 54–63

Marble Plan 74–5, 88–9, 114, 116–17, 119–20

Massilia 18–19
Mauretania 10, 53, 58–9
Meiggs, Russell 9–11
memory 15, 38–40, 43–4

natural monument 20–3
neighbourhoods 36–7, 38, 123
Nero 3–4, 25, 44–5

omen 3, 44–5, 47–8

planting 46, 75, 114, 125, 130
Pliny the Elder 40–5, 53–68, 89–90, 91
Pliny the Younger 86, 89, 116
Pompeii 77
Pompey
    porticus 15–16, 74, 108, 112, 121, 126
    triumphal import 71–4
produce
    fruit 55, 55–6, 92–4
    medicine 62
    oil 61, 62
    papyrus 65
    perfume 65
    timber 8, 55, 57–61, 75

Rome
    Aesculetum 30, 36–40, 123
    Argiletum 34–5
    Arval grove 6–7, 30
    Aventine 12, 33, 36–7
    Caelian Hill (Mons Querquetulanus) 28, 36–7, 123
    Capitoline 13, 28, 34–6, 39, 105–7
    Comitium 1–5, 30, 124–7
    Horti Luculliani 71–2, 73
    Lacus Curtius 3–4, 30, 39–40, 124, 130
    Lupercal 1–5, 30, 34, 124
    Mausoleum of Augustus 100, 111, 124–6
    Palatine 1–6, 13, 20, 28, 30, 33, 115, 118

Piazza della Bocca della Verità 92–5
Porta Capena 39–40, 49–51, 121
Porticus of Livia 113, 118–19
Porticus Philippi 119–22, 123, 127
Porticus of Pompey, *see* Pompey: porticus
Porticus Vipsania/Europae 115–16, 122, 127
Shrine of Venus Cloacina 98–100
Tarpeian Rock 30, 34–5
Ustrinum 125, 126
Volcanal 30, 41, 44–5
Romulus 1–5, 15, 19, 33, 34–5, 37, 105–7
Ruminal fig 1–5, 12–14, 30, 37, 45, 82, 100, 123

sacred trees 13–14, 105–8
Scipio Africanus 42–3, 45, 47
shade 55, 62–3, 113, 118–19
social utility 54–5
spolia opima 13, 105–8
Statius 16–19, 70, 103–4

tables 57–61
temples
    Adonaea 116–19, 122, 127, 130
    Apollo at Nikopolis 47
    Apollo Sosianus 77
    Divus Julius 30, 130
    Hercules Musarum 119–22
    Honos and Virtus 121
    Jupiter Fagutal 36, 37
    Jupiter Feretrius 13, 30, 105–7
    Mars Ultor 106
    Pan Lycaeum 2
    Saturn 3, 30
    Templum Pacis 75–6
Tiberius 59, 61
Titus 54, 64, 74–6
    Arch 95–6
trade 59–61, 76
Trajan
    Arch 78–9, 81, 82, 85, 87–8
    Column 78, 79–82, 84–8, 101
    Forum 88–9
    Frieze 78–9, 81, 82, 85
    Tropaeum 78, 82, 101
triumph
    import 71–8
    procession 46, 76–8, 95, 99
    spoils 58, 78, 99
Trojan horse 27

utility 53, 54–63

Vergil 6, 33, 34–6, 99, 102–4
Vespasian 44, 48, 74–6
violation 7, 48–9, 84–5
Vitruvius 17, 112–14

wine 65
woods, *see* forest

www.ingramcontent.com/pod-product-compliance
Lightning Source LLC
Chambersburg PA
CBHW052119300426

44116CB00010B/1726